Brazil

To my wife, Mar, and our children, Diana and David

Brazil

Reversal of Fortune

ALFRED P. MONTERO

polity

First published in 2014 by Polity Press

Polity Press
65 Bridge Street
Cambridge CB2 1UR, UK

Polity Press
350 Main Street
Malden, MA 02148, USA

ISBN-13: 978-0-7456-6164-3
ISBN-13: 978-0-7456-6165-0 (pb)

A catalogue record for this book is available from the British Library.

Typeset in 9.5 on 12 pt Swift Light
by Toppan Best-set Premedia Limited
Printed and bound in Great Britain by Clays Ltd, St Ives PLC

The publisher has used its best endeavours to ensure that the URLs for external websites referred to in this book are correct and active at the time of going to press. However, the publisher has no responsibility for the websites and can make no guarantee that a site will remain live or that the content is or will remain appropriate.

Every effort has been made to trace all copyright holders, but if any have been inadvertently overlooked the publisher will be pleased to include any necessary credits in any subsequent reprint or edition.

For further information on Polity, visit our website: www.politybooks.com

Fig. 3.1 first appeared as "Shifting Ideological Positions, 1990–2009" in "Elite Preferences in a Consolidating Democracy: The Brazilian Legislative Surveys, 1990–2009," by Timothy J. Power and Cesar Zucco, Jr. Latin American Politics and Society 54:4 (Winter 2012): 1–27. Used with permission.

Contents

Tables and Figures

Tables

Figures

Abbreviations

ADIn	*Ação Direta de Inconstitucionalidade*
ANC	*Assembléia Nacional Constituente*
ARENA	*Aliança Nacional Renovadora*
BNDES	*Banco Nacional de Desenvolvimento Econômico e Social*
CCT	conditional cash transfer
CPI	*Comisão Parlamentar de Inquérito*
CSO	civil society organization
DEM	*Democratas* (former PFL)
FDI	foreign direct investment
FUNDEF	*Fundo de Manutenção e Desenvolvimento do Ensino Fundamental e de Valorização do Magistério*
GFCF	gross fixed capital formation
Ideb	*Índice de Desenvolvimento da Educação Básica*
IMF	International Monetary Fund
ISI	import-substitution industrialization
MDB	*Movimento Democrático Brasileiro*
MP	*Ministério Público*
NGO	non-governmental organization
OECD	Organization for Economic Cooperation and Development
OL-PR	open-list proportional representation
PAC	*Programa de Aceleração do Crescimento*
PBF	*Programa Bolsa Família*
PCdoB	*Partido Comunista do Brasil*
PDP	*Política de Desenvolvimento Produtivo*
PDS	*Partido Democrático Social*
PDT	*Partido Democrático Trabalhista*
PFL	*Partido da Frente Liberal*
PITCE	*Política Industrial, Tecnológica e de Comércio Exterior*
PL	*Partido Liberal*
PMDB	*Partido do Movimento Democrático Brasileiro*
PND	*Programa Nacional de Desestatização*
PP	*Partido Progressista*
PPS	*Partido Popular Socialista*
PR	*Partido da República*

PRN	*Partido da Reconstrução Nacional*
PROUNI	*Programa Universidade para Todos*
PSB	*Partido Socialista Brasileiro*
PSDB	*Partido da Social Democracia Brasileira*
PSOL	*Partido Socialismo e Liberdade*
PT	*Partido dos Trabalhadores*
PTB	*Partido Trabalhista Brasileiro*
PV	*Partido Verde*
R&D	research and development
STF	*Supremo Tribunal Federal*
STJ	*Superior Tribunal de Justiça*
WTO	World Trade Organization

CHAPTER ONE

A Reversal of Fortune?

Brazil has always been a study in contrasts – a puzzle of contradictions that lends truth to legendary composer Tom Jobim's famous line "Brazil is not for beginners." As the world's sixth largest economy (just ahead of the United Kingdom) and the fourth largest democracy by population, Brazil is a country of continental size with world-class ambitions. At the same time, its economic and political development is fraught with difficulties that have on occasion made observers wonder if the country would ever meet its own expectations. Any visitor to Brazil, especially to the major cities of São Paulo and Rio de Janeiro, will notice the country's most obvious problems: inequality and poverty. Despite its modern cityscapes and advanced technology, as well as the sophistication of its educated middle and upper classes, as many as 60 percent of the country's citizens are poor. The distribution of wealth is tremendously unequal, even though the country has remained a democracy since 1985. To use one traditional indicator of inequality – the ownership of arable land – 1.6 percent of farms control 43.8 percent of all land for agriculture.[1] Such statistics underscore that Brazil is a country of sharp contrasts, a democracy with uneven distribution of wealth and income, and a developing, industrial economy of immense potential, but burdened by equally immense social obligations to its poorest citizens.

After enduring twenty-one years of military-led, authoritarian rule from 1964 until 1985, Brazil enjoyed a transition to democracy that raised hopes that fundamental political and socio-economic changes were around the corner. Yet, during the first ten years of this new democracy, the country seemed to veer off course. The first democratic government, known as the "New Republic," came to be headed by José Sarney, a friend of the outgoing military governments. Sarney's rise was a result of a series of unfortunate events – notably, the failure of democratic forces to install direct elections for the first president and then the death of the indirectly elected Tancredo Neves on the eve of his inauguration. Sarney's coming to power reflected a transition to democracy that was designed to produce less than fundamental change. To the disappointment of Brazilians who thirsted for a return to democracy, the new president was to be elected through an electoral college, specifically the national congress elected in 1986. The new political class of the early democratic period did not differ much from the figures that

1

participated in the semi-open congress sanctioned by the armed forces between 1965 and 1985. The economy of the New Republic would prove even more disappointing. Shortly after Sarney's government had tempered inflation during its first year in office, price instability returned, generating inflationary and, periodically, hyperinflationary spirals reaching more than 50 percent per month during the next nine years. Sarney's successor, Fernando Collor (1990–2), proved spectacularly even less successful. Not only did his efforts to curb inflation fail, but he was found to have engaged in corruption and was impeached before he could serve out his term.

The travails of the first ten years of democracy in Brazil generated sustained and unflinching criticism from observers of the country's political system and economic policies. Scholars such as Scott Mainwaring described its democratic institutions as "feckless," while others went so far as to call them "pathological."[2] Economic policy fared no better with critics. During the early 1990s, Rudiger Dornbusch, a well-known macro-economist from the International Monetary Fund (IMF), called the Brazilian economy "drunk" and likely to suffer a "putsch," which was rumored during the summer of 1993 to be in the planning stages (Amaral, Kingstone, and Krieckhaus 2008: 140).[3] The hyperinflationary context inspired some observers to compare the "New Republic" to the fragile democracy of Weimar Germany (cf. Fritsch and Franco 1993: 10–11). If Dornbusch's comment about a coming putsch did not carry so much resonance in 1993, the comparison would have seemed ridiculous. Yet, after two unsuccessful presidencies and as many as seven failed anti-inflation plans, Brazilian political-economic institutions appeared incorrigibly dysfunctional. The developmental state, which had forged an impressive period of industrialization during the 1940s through the 1970s, was described by neoliberal observers as obsolete and exhausted, while more sympathetic voices opined that it had become overly fragmented and internally incoherent, making a return to the halcyon days of high growth with statism a fantasy (Weyland 1998). Even public security seemed to be eroding rapidly, a sense that was underscored by the slaughter of eight street children in front of the Candelária Cathedral in Rio de Janeiro by off-duty police and hired gunmen on July 23, 1993.

This author visited Brazil during the North American summer/Brazilian winter of 1993, and, at the time, it was easy to feel that rumors of a coup against the government of Itamar Franco and the massacre at the Candelária Cathedral represented the moment that democratic Brazil was touching bottom. But, just ten years after observers such as Mainwaring and Dornbusch issued their pessimistic assessments of Brazil, the country seemed to have engineered a rather stunning turnaround. Fueled by a commodity boom and a growing domestic market, economic growth picked up, averaging 4.5 percent between 2004 and 2010 with relatively low inflation. Brazil's economic success in the past decade has been so acute that the country has become a capital exporter. By 2009, it was on the US Treasury Department's list of the largest foreign government holders of American sovereign debt. As of January 2013, Brazil is number four on the list, with US$253 billion, just behind all oil exporters, Japan, and China.[4] The social implications of this new economic status were evident by the middle of the decade, when observers began to note that Brazil was enjoying falling poverty rates and improving measures of income equality.

These tendencies, albeit slowed due to declining growth throughout much of the world after 2009, continued through the writing of this book, so one might say with some degree of confidence that Brazil has turned an important corner. Despite its fragmentation, with numerous major parties and the dominance of personalistic rather than programmatic organizations, Brazil's political system has become more governable since the "feckless" label was first applied. Indeed, at no other time in its history has the country been able to enjoy for so long growth, lower inequality, lower poverty, and stable, democratic government. Brazil's success in recent years can even be compared with China's and in terms that place it ahead of that country. For example, Marcelo Neri (2009: 229) has made this argument with reference not only to high levels of growth but also to declining inequality and a strengthening democracy in Brazil, whereas China's growth has coincided with increasing inequality and the continuation of authoritarianism. Properly understanding the dimensions and the causes of this stunning reversal of fortune – which I refer to as "the Brazilian turnaround" – is the subject of this book.

Brazil's success in recent years continues to have its detractors. Concerning the country's economic performance, the chief criticism is that aggregate growth is too dependent upon sustainable increases in demand for commodities and higher prices for these exports. Not only is this dependency not sustainable, since commodity booms by definition end with busts, but the overall pattern of development based on such exports is itself a kind of regressive specialization that can only take resources and policy attention away from industry. So some scholars have seen the commodity export economy as a symptom of a larger "de-industrialization" of Brazil (Santana 2012: 217).

Although concerns about the sustainability of commodity booms are warranted, Brazil's turnaround is hardly due exclusively to economic factors, nor is its improved economic performance completely dependent on a commodity boom. Most of its economic expansion since 2002 has been the result of growth in aggregate demand in the *domestic* market, not in international demand for soy, iron ore, and other resource-based commodity exports, and that owes much to income-enhancing social programs that have boosted the expansion of household consumption (Santana 2012; Singer 2012: 179–80). Export growth has itself been driven by non-commodity exports, including consumer durables and manufactured inputs that have composed a growing share of the export bundle since 1998 (Suzigan, Negri, and Silva 2007; Almeida 2011). A central finding of this book is that social and economic policies have created the conditions for the turnaround even when economic fundamentals did not privilege a positive outcome.

A more compelling and justified concern about the turnaround is that it has done less for the quality of Brazil's democracy than it has for social and economic development. Even after enjoying democratic freedoms for twenty-seven years, surpassing the time of military rule, Brazilian citizens in various surveys continue to report, and in shockingly large proportions, a disappointment with democracy. Just about half of all respondents to the annual Latinobarómetro surveys report an appreciable level of dissatisfaction with the way democracy works in Brazil, and a fifth of those polled entertain the idea that an authoritarian regime might be preferable.[5] Brazilians express regularly their opinions between elections, engaging in protests such as those that stunned the political class in June 2013. Hundreds of thousands of protesters in several cities manifested against a litany of concerns: high transport costs, corruption, not enough spending on schools and hospitals, and too much spending on soccer stadiums in preparation for the 2014 World Cup and the 2016 Summer Olympic Games. These attitudes reflect what much scholarship on Brazil sees as the persisting contradictions between the existence of liberal democratic institutions and the continuation of clientelistic and oligarchical forms of doing politics (Ames 1994; Hagopian 1996; Bezerra 1999). Even as formal institutions governing the accountability of elites have hardened, clientelism and patronage politics continue to be the lifeblood of how politics are practiced and how policy is shaped. And, despite periodic corruption scandals, fundamental and lasting institutional reforms are too infrequently pursued and are inadequate even when they are implemented. So regular Brazilians tend to be realists in seeing politics as a game for insiders and democracy as something that benefits those who are already on the inside. Ironically, as the economy and social welfare have improved during the last decade and a half, citizens have raised more and more concerns about democracy and the political class.

These concerns have merit, but they do not diminish the overall impression that the Brazil of today is very different from the one that was mired in political and economic crisis for ten years following the transition to democracy. The turnaround is more than a commodity boom, and, despite the problems of popular disaffection with democracy, democratic institutions work better today than they did even a few years after the transition. Of course, no turnaround of the scale engineered by Brazil is possible without some shortcomings. And the shortcomings do beg the question of how profound and sustainable the changes have been. Are the improvements to governability, patterns of economic growth, social inequality, and poverty simply ephemeral and skin-deep, or are they everlasting and substantial? Scholars embracing optimistic and pessimistic lenses on Brazil have debated back and forth throughout the democratic period. While the pessimists had the upper hand during the first ten years, the last fifteen have witnessed a stunning reversal in favor of more optimistic views. This author prefers a more cautiously optimistic perspective and a careful analytical approach that takes into account the insights produced by contending views of Brazilian democracy and economic and social development.

The Purpose of the Book

This book is focused on explaining Brazil's turnaround on three dimensions: governability, good policy (also known as *good policy governance*), and the quality of democracy. These are large, multilevel concepts that require a look at an array of indicators. But each can be understood as hinging on certain core questions. Governability asks to what extent the policy-making process works efficiently and effectively to generate legislative change. The key word is "process," as this concept is less concerned with the effects of policy or the quality of voting and elite accountability. Governability asks how political leaders and their organizations cooperate (or not) to make policy. The main venues for the governability of the political system are the presidency and the legislature, but also relations between the federal government and the states and cities. Major scholars of Brazilian political institutions such as Scott Mainwaring (1999), David Samuels (2003b), and Barry Ames (2001) have produced excellent work on the inability of political parties, the executive and the legislature, and the federal system to govern the policy-making process effectively. Their central claims are that political organizations in Brazil are typically vacuous, driven by personalist leaders focused on the distribution of material rewards for themselves and for their associates, with little devotion to programmatic government or even consistent ideology. The opposite view has gained more traction since the mid-1990s given improved conditions since the presidency of Fernando Henrique Cardoso. More scholars of Brazilian political institutions have come forth to contest the pervasive view of the party system as "feckless" and the legislative process as mired in personalism and clientelism (e.g., Figueiredo and Limongi 1999; Lyne 2005; Hagopian, Gervasoni, and Morães 2009). This debate has coincided with more empirical evidence showing that the capacity of major political actors to forge compromise has improved, making this the first dimension of the turnaround.

Improved governability has made possible the diffusion of new policy ideas that address major goals of socio-economic and institutional change. A centerpiece of the turnaround has been the capacity of major political actors to develop and implement economic and social policies, many of them innovative, which have, over time, changed fundamentally the development of Brazil's democracy. I refer to this dimension of the turnaround as good policy governance, or simply good policy, to differentiate it more neatly from governability. New industrial policies associated with the National Development Bank (*Banco Nacional de Desenvolvimento Econômico e Social*, BNDES) and poverty-alleviating conditional cash transfers are among the most notable in recent years. But even more fundamental has been Brazil's commitment to price stability under Cardoso's Real Plan (*Plano Real*), which ended bouts of hyperinflation in 1994, and numerous efforts to stave off a fiscal crisis through stopgap legislation during the 1990s that limited subnational debt and capped spending on the civil service. Most notably, the commitment to macro-economic orthodoxy has not contradicted efforts to improve social distribution. Of course, these policy achievements have not been perfect, but they have gone far enough to reinforce and even take advantage of the improvements in governability noted by scholars of political institutions. The subsequent chapters focus on the most prominent of these, noting how they have generated substantial changes in social and economic development in contemporary Brazil. As a whole, the impression one has is that the Brazilian political system has generated meaningful policy changes during the democratic period, although much is left to do in key areas.

The final dimension of the turnaround is the quality of democracy. One of the indicators of improvements in governability and policy-making is that scholars have moved away from more fundamental questions on whether the Brazilian political system could function democratically to the issue of the quality of its democracy. The quality of democracy focuses on the accountability of elites to one another and to the electorate, the effectiveness of the vote in exercising oversight on the political class, and the responsiveness of government to the will of the people (Levine and Molina 2011; Diamond and Morlino 2004). Of these aspects, the accountability of elites to citizens, defined as the answerability of these representatives to the public for institutionally inappropriate or illegal actions, is the core of democratic quality. Elite accountability also reflects the responsiveness of governments to popular preferences and the participation of citizens in the political process. Like governability, the quality of democracy is concerned with process, but it addresses arenas that move well beyond the realm of political society (i.e., the relations between the presidency and the congress, and the behavior of political parties) to encompass the judiciary, elections and campaigns, popular participation by groups and non-governmental organizations, and official institutions that are responsible for the oversight of the political class and the bureaucracy. It is regarding the quality of democracy that the Brazilian turnaround has produced its most ambiguous results. Since this is a multi-dimensional concept, it is possible to break it down in subsequent chapters and analyze the areas in which democracy has advanced notably and areas that have seen much less improvement.

The three dimensions of governability, good policy, and the quality of democracy are the objects of study in this book. In that sense they are treated as "dependent variables" in the chapters that follow. How have these dimensions changed in Brazil to produce the turnaround? This question implies that the three dimensions have correlated with larger improvements in economic performance and social development, making them "independent variables" as well. Ultimately, in trying to explain changes of such broad scale, causes and consequences can mix, but understanding causal sequences requires that we unpack these relationships carefully. It also requires that the takeaway lessons from the analysis be highlighted clearly.

I make several recurring claims that are supported in the chapters that follow. Each of these claims elaborates further on the causal description of improved governability, good policy, and enhanced democratic quality to identify specific factors and conditions that animated these dimensions of the turnaround and made them possible, including how change on one dimension affected the others.

My first claim is that the direction of change on governability, good policy, and democratic quality has been towards improvement since 1993–4, but it has been uneven and contradictory in certain areas. The political system is far more predictable and routinized than it was during the first decade of democracy. But the reasons for improved governability are in tension with other aspects of the political system that are intended to strengthen the quality of democracy, especially elite accountability, the responsiveness of government, and the quality of the vote. Regarding good policy, improvements in areas of economic and social policy are genuine, especially since the advent of inflation control under the Real Plan. Yet while innovative policy-making in areas such as economic and social reform may make governments popular, they also deflect responsibility for not addressing other nagging problems, such as the need to make the economy more efficient or the need to reform the political system to reduce the use of patronage in the creation of legislative alliances. Another caveat of the turnaround, referred to above, is that the improvements to the quality of democracy have been the most difficult to engineer and maintain. Despite stronger forms of oversight of elites, voters and civil society as a whole remain too disconnected from the political class to exert the kinds of consistent pressure a more vibrant democracy requires. This partly explains periodic and unexpected outbursts of protests such as those that captured the attention of the world in 2013. The persistence of clientelism, pro-incumbent bias, and the occasional corruption scandal are some of the indicators that suggest that the turnaround has proven weakest on the dimension of Brazilian democracy's overall quality.

My second claim is that political governability and policy-making have improved in particular due to the fact that the ideological polarization of the past has largely faded from the scene. After 1994, Brazil's democracy matured in ways that reduced the differences between right and left that once ended what the historian Thomas Skidmore called the country's "experiment with democracy" in the period 1945–64 (Skidmore 1967). The ideological convergence of right and left has been the foundation for moderate approaches to economic and social policy-making under the presidencies of the post-1993 period. These presidents – Fernando Henrique Cardoso (1994–2003), Luiz Inácio Lula da Silva (2003–10), and Dilma Rousseff (2010–present) – are key protagonists in the narrative of the Brazilian turnaround. Cardoso and Lula, both prominent representatives of different currents of the opposition to military rule during the transition to democracy, are the most important leaders of two major parties, the Brazilian Social Democratic Party (*Partido da Social Democracia Brasileira*, PSDB) and the Workers' Party (*Partido dos Trabalhadores*, PT), respectively, whose rivalry has come to shape the Brazilian political system for the last twenty years. Yet, despite hard-fought and often viscerally negative campaigns during electoral cycles, Brazil has enjoyed a tremendous amount of continuity in the framing of macro-economic, industrial, and social policy across these governments. This continuity has undergirded both sustained governability and good policy, making further improvements possible. Notably, both Cardoso's and Lula's commitment to macro-economic orthodoxy has *coincided sustainably* with the pursuit of an increasingly more robust distributionist social policy. Once again, this should not be taken to mean that Brazil's problems will all be solved inevitably, but it is clear that a foundation was created by the resolution of governability problems, especially after 1994, that allowed some policy solutions and institutional changes to occur that have proven sufficient for generating substantial improvements to the country's social and economic development.

In virtually all of the dimensions on which the turnaround may be judged, institutional changes have created the conditions for further adaptation and innovation. Scholars of institutional change refer to this process as one of "layering" (Mahoney and Thelen 2010). Layering refers to the development of incremental changes in formal and informal rules, norms, and practices that in the aggregate set the stage for larger, transformative shifts. At times changes have been "punctuated" due to the advent of a corruption scandal, an economic crisis, or a sudden turn in an election. But more frequently, in the causal narrative told in this book, change has happened slowly and through gradual, but progressive, alterations in policy and political strategies. The result has been improvements in governability, policy outcomes, and democratic quality. But a central finding of this study is that these changes have occurred within the parameters of a great deal of continuity concerning the frameworks of policy-making. Despite the rivalry of the PSDB and the PT, the Brazilian political class has not been riven by ideological conflicts over the fundamentals of the political economy or the extent to which social welfare distribution should be taken. It is crucially in this context that institutional layering has produced a pattern of change that is best described as *progressive policy continuity*, where policy innovations and improvements have followed on earlier iterations of reform.

A third claim I make in this book concerns how judgments about Brazilian politics have changed due to shifting contexts over time. As I note above, many of the more pessimistic, initial views of the country have been proven wrong, compelling observers to ask why these analyses were off target. Of course, not all of the analytical assumptions and findings of these pessimistic views were wrong and not all of the more optimistic rejoinders have been right or unproblematic. Some of the negative assessments remain relevant for understanding the limitations of inter-branch relations, the party system, and the web of accountability. The third claim is that both approaches have proven to have merit, but that has been clear only when sufficient time has passed to assess their explanatory power. All too often, scholars of Brazil have produced focused and well-supported propositions about political institutions and socio-economic change that have seemed plausible at one point, only to find that their relevance for understanding change has become obsolete with the passage of time. Brazil is, as Timothy Power has put it, "a late bloomer" (2010b). This book attempts to evaluate which propositions have stood the test of time but also which have been able to travel between different arenas of the Brazilian polity, to explain change in multiple domains of policy-making and politics. The next sections explain the methodological orientations of the study.

Explaining Change in a Multidimensional/ Multi-Arena Polity

Demonstrating the substantive claims I discuss above requires that this study set out a number of methodological principles. The most important defining the present study is the adoption of a holistic approach, one that takes into account the multidimensional and multi-arena aspects of democratic Brazil's political-economic system.[6] The working assumption is that a focused analysis on any one area – congress, the presidency, the bureaucracy, or civil society – cannot render a sufficient explanation for the turnaround on the three dimensions of governability, policy governance, and the quality of democracy. Only explanations that employ what Ragin (1987) calls "multiple conjunctural causation" may provide a realistic account for these aspects. For example, the enhanced governability of the political system after 1994 involves an understanding of not only presidential-legislative relations but elements of democratic quality, such as the strengthening of auditing institutions, prosecutorial agencies, and the courts, not to mention the broader context in favor of governability created by a sequence of political-economic reforms. A related methodological concern is that causal relations in a multidimensional and multi-arena setting are not always positive or linear. One of the insights of this study is that the three dependent variables do not rely on the very same causes. What is good for policy governance may not work to help democratic quality. What is good for governability may limit more effective and innovative policy-making as well as democratic quality. The advent of democracy in 1985 did not resolve these tensions; indeed, it made them more apparent. These processes all have non-linear relationships, with not all good things going together. Seeing the whole requires multilevel and longitudinal analysis, what Pierson (2004) calls a perspective on the "meso-institutional." A meso-institutional approach emphasizes the interactions that occur between institutions – how changes in one can elicit changes in others.

All of this stands as an important corrective to much of the current scholarship on Brazilian politics. Institutional arguments in particular have been most prone to indulging in a laser-like focus on how particular rules create incentives for certain forms of behavior. An example explored in chapter 3 is the view that the rules of the electoral system shape the relative strength of the party system and the choices made by members of the political class in the congress and the presidency. Although such arguments based on clearly defined and operationalized variables offer straightforward and testable propositions, the payoff from such a focus has rarely proven sufficient for understanding the non-linear and meso-institutional ways in which a change in the rules affect the polity. One example is how improved governability between the presidency and the legislature has weakened other accountability mechanisms such as congressional committees of public inquiry, which are now less likely to investigate cases of malfeasance if they must target politicians in the pro-government coalition. Only by taking several steps back and understanding how multiple dimensions of democratic behaviors and institutions interrelate can one appreciate the aggregate effects on democratic quality.

Another important aspect of adopting a broader analytical perspective is that we can understand how different dimensions of the economy and the polity affect one another. Taking a "political-economic" approach allows us to understand causes that are infrequently isolated to political institutions or to economic changes but that rely on the interaction between these two major spheres. Too often, Brazil has been analyzed from the standpoint of trying to understand governability, with little reference to political-economic conditions. Sometimes economic reforms have been the focus, but market conditions and international factors have been ignored, while seemingly more proximate institutional causes such as the organization of the party system have received pride of place. Such analysis is vulnerable to several methodological problems, most obviously errors of spuriousness and omitted variable bias. In virtually all of the areas in which governability, good policy, and democratic quality have changed, the political-economic context has been an important source of this change. For example, it is difficult to imagine how the Brazilian state could have adapted to the need for market-sustaining policies along with developmentalist interventions without the macro-economic reforms that eliminated hyperinflation during the mid-1990s. Nor would have political governability or elite accountability, and particularly fiscal accountability, improved as they did without the end of runaway inflation.

A holistic approach also makes clear that the relevant causes are not just the proximate ones, especially when the level of analysis deals with macro-political and macro-economic changes. Structural and historical causes matter, even if they do not determine outcomes directly. Therefore, a holistic approach requires the analysis of both *distal* and *proximal* causes. One example explored in this book of the attention to structural causes is the evolution of Brazil's developmentalist economy. Despite the advent of macro-economic instability during the first decade of democracy, Brazil's leaders eschewed the pursuit of the same orthodox stabilization and structural adjustment policies practiced in Mexico and Argentina during the 1980s and 1990s and in Chile during the 1970s. Such policies would have downsized the state by privatizing and liquidating many of the public firms and agencies that played key roles in the statist period. Instead, the Brazilian economy became liberalized slowly by the reduction of tariffs and selective privatization. This process preserved many of the institutions and policies associated with the developmentalist period. Presently, these agencies, and especially the national development bank, public utilities, and state-controlled firms, play a proximate role in generating higher levels of private investment and growth.

We need to approach these effects with a careful eye to the incremental nature of change but also to the *sequencing* of institutional layering. Brazilian democracy has rarely produced radical change in a short period of time – say, in the context of a single presidential administration. Instead, the pattern has been incremental, with each government achieving a handful of significant reforms but failing to enact broad-based changes in the form of one bill or a series of bills. So, while the Collor administration was a prime example of legislative failure and poor relations between the presidency and the congress, his government consolidated the liberalizing and privatizing reforms initiated under his predecessor, Sarney. More important, such actions, while seemingly limited at the time, had a tremendous impact on subsequent reforms and institutional changes. Cardoso's Real Plan represented a marked change from the past failures of inflation control, but less heralded policies on land reform and social welfare provided a foundation for future innovation and qualitative improvements. Lula's presidency benefited fundamentally from the macro-economic, fiscal, and social policies established by Cardoso's eight years in power. Based on this, Lula was able to engage in expansive policies in industrial promotion, infrastructure, and the welfare state. The Brazilian political class changed fundamentally during the almost thirty years of democracy, moderating many of the erstwhile cleavages between right and left and statist and anti-statist that bedeviled the governments of the first decade of democracy. Without this ideological convergence, it would have been difficult to envision the rise to the presidency of the formerly avowed socialist Lula da Silva or his succession by a former guerrilla who was tortured by the military, Dilma Rousseff.

Many of the weaknesses of prominent approaches to Brazilian politics arrived at conclusions about the country's democracy based on a relatively short period of observation. When broader historical contexts are considered, or just when sufficient amounts of time have passed, the misconceptions and limitations of these analyses become more apparent. One prominent example is what happened to the largely pessimistic views of democratic institutions in the period 1985–94. Both comparisons between the earlier democratic period of 1945 to 1964 and the improved governability of presidential–legislative relations after 1994 revealed that many of these pessimistic interpretations had overclaimed the dangers by relying too heavily on theoretical intuitions about democratic institutions inspired by insights taken from studies of American politics. The chief lesson for the analysis in this book is that attention to more particular historical and multidimensional contexts produces more reliable analyses when trying to understand a complicated country such as Brazil. Therefore, the current study will emphasize, whenever relevant, the meso-institutional context, the ties between the political and the economic, the distinct contributions of distal and proximal causes, and historical sequencing.

This analysis does not embrace complexity for its own sake, nor does it abandon the attempt to be parsimonious. The complexity can be managed if the holistic approach is firmly grounded in a careful periodization, which is provided in chapter 2. The delimited focus of the current project is also simplifying. This study is intended primarily to describe and explain the dimensions of the turnaround in Brazil, not to outline and test a particular explanatory theory. I appreciate and justify the analytical apparatus of the holistic approach for its use value. Applying the analytical framework in a broader comparative perspective to ascertain its utility to other countries is beyond the scope of the current project. This study seeks to make a contribution to the understanding of Brazil, with the comparative scope limited to how the country has changed since the transition to democracy in 1985.

Persisting Tendencies in Brazilian Democracy

No experienced observer of Brazilian democracy can make substantive claims without caveats. Those made above concerning the overall positive nature of the turnaround on governability, policy, and the quality of democracy are tempered by partial contradictions and limitations, most of which will be noted specifically in the chapters that follow. But it is also important to draw more general caveats regarding dimensions of Brazilian politics that have changed less quickly or have not changed at all despite the turnaround. Brazil never experienced a social revolution, so it is not surprising that many of the erstwhile tendencies of its past continued into the democratic period. Most fundamentally, Brazil remains a highly unequal society. The powerful maintain, as they have since the country's independence from Portugal in 1822, privileged access to authority and economic resources. This was manifested not only in formal institutions but in social structures and understandings that are most consequentially reflected in the way that the political class controls and uses the formal apparatus of the state.

If there is a meta-framework for understanding Brazilian political history it is the centrality of the state. The federal and subnational bureaucracy composes a multidimensional arena for political actors to acquire and dispense public resources and favors to cultivate allies and gain greater authority and even personal wealth. Patronage, defined as the dispensing of jobs, public contracts, access to public services, and fiscal and regulatory protections, has been long understood by classic thinkers of Brazilian politics such as Raymundo Faoro, in his *Os donos do poder* (1958), and, more recently, Marcos Otávio Bezerra, in his *Em nome das "bases"* (1999), as the currency of politics. Yet this currency is only useful if there are "markets" in which its value is respected. Such markets exist as networks among members of the political class and business who exchange favors (*troca de favores*) to maintain or gain power. The structure of the state facilitates these exchanges by remaining fragmented and penetrable by societal interests (Weyland 1996).

These networks also connect subaltern classes, the members of which are well understood as "clients" to powerful "patrons." The traditional depiction of these unequal and hierarchical relations of patron–client ties was done best by Victor Nunes Leal (1976), who describes repressive social and political relations in the countryside in which landed elites, known as "colonels" (*coronéis*), employ poor peasants to work the land and use their dependency to manage their political choices at the ballot box or keep them from voting in the first place. Generations of scholars of Brazil have extended and modernized this logic of *coronelismo* to understand clientele networks that have long since moved from their rural and parochial foundations to extend into the urban and modern system of political-economic domination (Hagopian 1996; Bezerra 1999; Weyland 1996; Vilaça and Albuquerque 1988). In this way, urban workers and the poor become dependent on the material incentives incumbent politicians may dispense to "buy" their votes. In a similar way, political bosses control the behavior of lesser politicians, who depend on the largesse of governments controlled by these patrons so that they might garner the patronage they need to buy support for themselves.

The strategic use of patronage within and between clientele networks forms the basis for what Faoro saw as the historical legacy of Portuguese colonialism: the patrimonial state. Patrimonial politics exists where members of the political class view the state as their own personal property – where they dispense it legally or quasi-legally in the form of "pork-barrel politics" by appropriating funds for constituents and bailiwicks or illegally through corruption. The patrimonial state extends the oligarchical tendencies of Brazilian politics even into the democratic period by causing the state not to act in the public's interest but to provide an arena and an apparatus for protecting the interests of elites over those of the citizenry.

Democracy would seem to provide an antidote for this historical tendency in Brazilian politics, but clientelism has survived because of the weakness of electoral and legal forms of elite accountability coupled with persisting social and economic inequalities. Even as scholars now consider the possibilities that Brazil has staged a reversal of its political and economic fortune, observers are divided on how deep these changes go. For example, despite the expansion of opportunities for citizens to participate in politics and the emergence of greater oversight by official institutions, vote-buying is a pervasive weakness of Brazilian democracy. Political bosses, usually at a local level, are able to extract promises from voters that they will support their candidates and, in what has become a typical low-intensity tactic, require that voters publicly declare their allegiance by wearing or showing candidate and party propaganda in their neighborhoods. Such forms of "declared choice" exert an *ex ante* guarantee that some voters have committed to a candidate with the promise of a reward following the election (Nichter 2009). These tendencies, if they persist and remain significant, undermine the competitiveness and quality of elections, strengthening incumbency bias that is well known in Brazilian politics as *governismo*.

Patronage is more valuable and immediately implementable for some politicians more than others. In Brazilian politics, *political executives* (i.e., presidents, governors, and mayors) are particularly privileged because they dispense patronage and are more likely to receive the credit for its distribution or use. Federal, state, and municipal legislators broker patronage from executives and employ it to attract support from constituents but more often from the private sector that largely bankrolls political campaigns (Samuels 2002). The electoral system is one determinant of these inequalities. Executives are easily identifiable by voters, who must select one winner in either a first-round or a run-off contest. The positions that the winners take are offices with direct power over the implementation of budget items. Federal and state legislators, on the other hand, struggle to differentiate themselves from the pack, as they run in multi-member districts in which votes are pooled across the entire state. And they assume offices that do not offer them the opportunity to claim credit for all of the "pork" that they bring back, since other incumbents claim the benefits as well. Comparatively, this makes presidents, governors, and mayors the hubs of Brazilian politics while legislators are the spokes.

These orientations in favor of patronage politics, clientelism, and executive bias are persisting elements of Brazilian politics that have by no means been removed from the country's democracy during the turnaround. Such tendencies have been and continue to be the foundation for pessimistic assessments of Brazilian politics. But what separates the most pessimistic views from more cautiously optimistic ones is the degree to which these persisting tendencies are seen as immovable and noxious for democracy. One of the lessons taken from the present study is that overly pessimistic analyses of Brazilian politics and economy have often proceeded from premises that did not fit Brazil. This is, in fact, an old debate, encompassing not only the disciplines of political science and economics but also literature and culture. The literary critic Roberto Schwarz famously argued that liberal democratic standards applied in their schematic form to Brazil were "misplaced ideas" (Schwarz 1992). He posited that, in Brazilian history, the main elements of democratic politics – elite accountability, competitive elections, the quality of the vote – have always been enmeshed in ambiguity, compromise, and informal, sometimes highly personalized understandings that discomfit some scholars of democracy. In Schwarz's formulation, it is not the norms of clientelism, *governismo*, and the informal, temporary suspension of rules known as the *jeito brasileiro* (the "Brazilian way") that must be swept away and displaced by (imported) democratic norms, but the latter that must develop in the context of a political and civil society that has long operated according to these erstwhile logics. The present study embraces this point of view by underscoring the problematic nature of these persisting tendencies but without ignoring how democratic and advanced capitalist forms are still possible in their presence. Indeed, the implicit argument here is that the scholarship on the post-1985 democracy must understand how these persisting elements of Brazilian politics and society have coexisted and evolved with the improvements of governability, policy governance, and democratic quality reflected in the turnaround since 1994. Perhaps the most inconvenient fact for studies of democracy and good government in Brazil is the reality of improved performance in a context in which many of the old ways of doing politics have remained firmly rooted. It is in this way that we can claim improvements to governability and policy governance that may come at a cost to democratic quality.

The Plan of the Book

The effort of the current project to analyze the turnaround by understanding change in the multidimensional Brazilian polity is organized with thematic areas. Implicit in all of the work in subsequent chapters is the premise that Brazilian democracy has experienced change imbedded in a particular periodization. Indeed, this is the organizing principle of the turnaround idea: that the first decade fed pessimistic claims about the new democracy while subsequent years reversed these conclusions and suggested that more positive change was possible. The main causal mechanisms of this study show how ideological moderation, improved governability – despite the continuation of clientelism and patronage politics – and the progressive continuity of policy fed the prospects for a turnaround and made it possible. These processes were temporally sequenced. Understanding the sequence and how it favored the turnaround is a primary analytical frame. So chapter 2 outlines the periodization and the main political actors, institutions, and processes that are analyzed in the subsequent chapters. It demonstrates that the periodization of the Brazilian turnaround relies heavily on the strategic choices of two presidents in particular – Cardoso and Lula. Both made use of favorable political and macro-economic conditions, and most importantly, when conditions were not so favorable, both opted for pragmatic choices that embraced ideological moderation and the progressive continuity of policy.

Chapter 3 addresses why governability improved during the democratic period despite early, highly pessimistic views of the prospects for Brazil's new democracy. It profiles the transition from overly pessimistic to more optimistic views among scholars and then to the consolidation of a meta-frame for the evolution of macro-political institutions – the advent of "coalitional presidentialism" (*presidencialismo de coalizão*). Premised on the sharing of power between the presidency and the legislature, coalitional presidential scholars believe that they have developed the best understanding for the improved governability of Brazilian policy-making. But a number of underexplored and contradictory tendencies bedevil coalitional presidentialism, including the reliance on patronage politics and the weakness of programmatic parties. The scholarship is divided by seemingly intractable differences in interpretation of the same evidence. The chapter unpacks these deficiencies and provides a balance of perspectives to appreciate what we have learned about Brazil's improved governability. It addresses the need for further work across arenas of the Brazilian polity, linking this chapter to the subsequent ones on democratic quality, renewed developmentalism, and social welfare policy-making. Finally, it explores some underanalyzed aspects of political parties and the ideological convergence of the political class. These areas, I argue, provide a basis for understanding how the groundwork was laid not only for improved governability but also for advances in democratic quality and good governance. Yet, for all of the attention that the macro-political has received in the scholarship of Brazil, it has proven insufficient for understanding the turnaround.

Chapter 4 moves beyond the governability of Brazilian democracy to address its quality, and specifically along the lines of elite accountability, government responsiveness, voting and the electorate, and participation. I find that these dimensions have not all improved together, though there has been enough change to suggest that Brazilian democracy today is of greater quality than that which inspired pessimistic critiques during the first ten years after the transition. The chapter makes a related claim that the evolution of democratic quality along these four dimensions continues to suffer from contradictions. The emergence of stronger checks and balances, for example, has been undermined by the continuation of the *troca de favores* system, whch underwrites coalitional presidentialism and also determines how responsive government is to the electorate and how much popular participation can affect the decisions made by elites. The ineffectuality of partisanship and ideological orientations among the electorate weakens ties that would otherwise bind political representatives to their constituencies and force them to adhere to their policy preferences rather than those of influential campaign benefactors and entrenched policy interests. And yet, Brazil enjoys today a more robust "web of accountability" linking auditing, investigatory, prosecutorial, and policing institutions along with a more vibrant array of civil society organizations exerting oversight than it did in 1985. Follow-through remains weak, but there is sufficient evidence of progressive continuity through reforms across governments to conclude that there will be opportunities for further enhancement of democratic quality and political citizenship.

Chapter 5 unpacks the role that developmentalist policy-making played in the economic growth trajectory of the 2000s. Beginning with the transition to democracy, I argue that Brazil never pursued a bona fide "neoliberal" adjustment process but embraced a progressive continuity of developmentalism during the 1990s and 2000s. Where market-oriented reforms were implemented, such as tariff reductions, deregulation, and privatization, these policies were shaped by strategic concerns for improving the competitiveness of domestic industries by enhancing their internationalization and technological adaptability. Far from rolling the state back, the Brazilians made state intervention in the market a fulcrum of the new development policy, utilizing erstwhile statist organizations such as the National Development Bank (BNDES) to channel long-term finance and strategic investments in infrastructure and energy to underwrite and make the most of the expansion of the 2000s. The chapter not only challenges pessimistic views of the Brazilian state's capacity for continuing a developmentalist policy, it also explains why the economic turnaround is more than the "commodity boom" of the 2000s. Once again, progressive policy and institutional changes sustained pragmatic responses that were neither wholly statist nor neoliberal, but that supported a pro-business strategy balanced on both the advantages of Brazil's large domestic market and its new opportunities for exploiting its global reach.

Chapter 6 examines the innovation and impressive scope of new social policies, especially since 1994, as key factors in the reduction of poverty and inequality in Brazil. But, as with the quality of democracy, different dimensions contradict one another, undermining the potential to see more fundamental and widespread improvements. I argue in this chapter that, while the turnaround has been very real in welfare policy-making, especially as it regards non-contributory cash transfers to the poor and other income-supporting policies that have reduced inequality as well as poverty, Brazilian social welfare still maintains pension, health, and education policies that favor the more privileged. The presidents of the turnaround have not sought more transformational social policies that distribute income and land ownership on a scale that would address these structural inequalities. Rather, the social welfare agenda follows a trajectory of progressive but marginal changes that will help the very poor while addressing some issues of access and quality of education and healthcare for most Brazilians, all the while preserving the resources and privileged access of the more well-to-do.

It is in the area of foreign policy, the subject of chapter 7, that the turnaround has experienced its most ambiguous effects. In large part, Brazil's foreign policy remains a work in progress, still not guided by a clear understanding of the country's emerging economic and political importance in the world, but not entirely unaware that the conditions exist for a more assertive and even nationalist diplomacy in economic and security affairs. As the importance of Brazil's trade with other emerging large economies such as China and India place it in that company and simultaneously make it a determinant of these countries' influence in the world, policy elites and scholars struggle for ways of understanding the trajectory of Brazilian foreign policy. The chapter argues that several trends are evident, among them the increasing role of the presidency rather than the Foreign Ministry in foreign policy-making and the continued embrace of reciprocal multilateralism tempered by an emerging, aggrandizing self-image of the country's potential that has at times placed it against the United States and incited the ire of its neighbors. Foreign policy is the last area in which the turnaround is being registered, as policy-makers continue to make sense of the changes Brazil has experienced since the mid-1990s but without signs that they are reaching a consensus in the foreign policy community. The lack of such a consensus means that, for the short to medium term, Brazilian foreign policy will remain reactive. Yet, over the long haul, it will need to become a factor in consolidating the positive aspects of the turnaround by engineering more strategic relations with like-minded democracies in the developed and developing worlds.

Given that this book is dedicated to the study of Brazil in great depth, there is little space to explore the comparative aspects of the turnaround. What does Brazil's turnaround, albeit with its attendant contradictions and inconsistencies, mean for the study of political, economic, and social change among countries of the developing world? How are the lessons of Brazil's mature and consolidated, though still flawed, democracy applicable to other countries? How are the experiences of new democracies elsewhere applicable to it? Chapter 8 provides some answers based on understanding the turnaround in a comparative perspective. One of the distinct advantages of a holistic approach is that it lays bare the contradictions among improved governability, policy governance, and democratic quality, especially when these are analyzed in a periodization. The narrative of Brazil's reversal of fortunes challenges the conventional wisdom that economic and social development should sustain and even enhance democratization. Despite a first decade and a half of economic crisis and social dislocation, democracy survived and even improved in key areas such as governability and policy governance. The Brazilian turnaround is characterized by non-linear relationships that belie the notion of a positive correlation between socio-economic change and democratization. As I will show, democratic quality has improved in some areas, only to take a step back in others even as the country experienced economic growth with greater equity and less poverty. "All good things do not go together" is an appropriate mantra for understanding the Brazilian turnaround.

CHAPTER TWO

Democracy and Economy from Bust to Boom

Brazilian democracy after 1985 progressed through distinct phases. Each of these saw advances and continued challenges to governability, policy-making, and the quality of democracy. The transition to democracy produced a regime that was flawed from the beginning, requiring adjustments and reform in subsequent years. Indeed, the reform process became the center-piece of the democratic period, and it remains the focus of much thinking concerning the pathways of Brazilian politics. Governability, good policy, and democratic quality are each a function in one way or another of how the reform process has proceeded and what there is still left for the political class to do.

The political history of the reform process is organized in this chapter based on three periods.[1] The first encompasses the first decade of democracy, 1985–94, a period that saw the regime transition, the drafting of the 1988 Constitution, and the first democratic governments of José Sarney (1985–90), Fernando Collor de Mello (1990–2), and Itamar Franco (1992–4). The denouement of the first phase was the Real Plan, which ended the spiraling inflation and economic malaise that had besieged Brazilian governments and society and inspired the most pessimistic analyses of the country's prospects by foreign and domestic observers. During this period, the key challenge for the political class was establishing governability of the policy-making process, including improved relations between the presidency and the congress, enhanced capacity of the federal and subnational bureaucracy to implement policy, and the ability of politicians to organize themselves into coherent parties to contest elections yet still compromise on legislation. Most of these goals were left unfulfilled. But, since much of the groundwork for later improving governability was laid during this time, it would be inaccurate to label this period as one of governability crisis. I prefer more neutral terms: the first decade of the democratic period.

The advent of the Real Plan and, soon after it, Fernando Henrique Cardoso's first term as president initiated a period focused on reform in the absence of spiraling inflation. The sequencing and progress of economic, fiscal, social, and political reform were highly dependent on the careful dance of alliances between the president and the congress, the governors, and powerful groups of business, labor, and civil society organizations. Although it seemed that

Brazil had avoided a governability crisis during this period, there was much in the reform process to frustrate observers eager to see progress in major areas of the economy and the polity that had not been corrected (or were made even worse) during democracy's first decade. With inflation tamed, renewed energy and attention could be applied to issues of policy governance. Reforms held out the promise to make the economy more efficient and competitive, restore economic growth, and address long-neglected and worsening problems of poverty and inequality. Yet the limitations on what was politically feasible and within the capacity of the state, which was still hampered by a fiscal crisis, created a long-drawn-out and somewhat contradictory course. This long reform process had fits and starts, periodic crises and setbacks, but the overall momentum was positive for consolidating improvements to governability and introducing improved policy governance in key areas of economic and social policy.

The third period analyzed below began with the election of Lula da Silva in 2002. The mere prospect of his rise to the presidency was seen at first by international observers, and especially those in the financial markets, as a disjuncture with the past. The darkest scenarios pictured a return to ideological fragmentation, conflict, and unstable macro-economic strategies. Lula disappointed these expectations by continuing Cardoso's commitments to economic and political governability and innovation in social policy. Lula's two terms (2003–10) and the election of his chosen successor, Dilma Rousseff, created a period of sustained dedication by the Workers' Party (PT) presidencies to improved social and economic development. Supported by the gains made during the Cardoso administration and favorable international economic conditions, the PT presidencies were able to pursue a greatly expanded policy agenda, including developmentalist industrial policy that contributed to economic growth; social policy innovations that accelerated the fall in poverty rates and increased income equality; and institutional reforms that enhanced policy and elite oversight and the prosecutorial powers of government agencies. But corruption scandals and their aftermath threatened to undermine the limited progress that was made to improve the quality of Brazilian democracy.

Democracy's First Decade

The transition to democracy in 1985 was a study in contrasts. The military government that had ruled Brazil since a coup in March 1964 against João Goulart had initiated a gradual political liberalization of the regime in 1973–4, a process known as "depressurization" (*distensão*). President Ernesto Geisel allowed political speech, albeit limited, and opened more space for an official party of the opposition, the *Movimento Democrático Brasileiro* (the Brazilian Democratic Movement, MDB), to compete with the military's own party, the *Aliança Nacional Renovadora* (National Renovation Alliance, ARENA), in elections for the federal congress. Political liberalization from above combined with the mobilization of civil society actors. Middle-class organizations, professional associations, church-based groups, and working-class unions began to challenge the institutions of authoritarianism and rally behind the MDB and, eventually, other opposition parties that were allowed to form later during the *distensão* process (Alves 1985; Della Cava 1989; Keck 1992). The emerging crisis of the import-substitution industrialization economy galvanized business opposition to the continuation of military rule (Payne 1994). *Distensão* took on the energy of a full-blown democratic transition once the ARENA began to lose elections, beginning with the 1974 contests in São Paulo and culminating in the loss of the party's absolute majority in the federal Chamber of Deputies in 1982. In that same electoral cycle, governors were directly elected for the first time, and the opposition took ten states. The generals tried to divide their rivals by using an electoral reform in 1979 to split the MDB into numerous parties – the Party of the MDB (PMDB), the Democratic Labor Party (*Partido Democrático Trabalhista*, PDT), the Brazilian Labor Party (*Partido Trabalhista Brasileiro*, PTB), and, in 1980, the Workers' Party (PT). Yet opposition parties, and especially the catchall PMDB, took more legislative seats and even catalyzed a popular movement on behalf of direct elections for the presidency (*Diretas Já*, or "Direct Elections Now!"). Yet, despite a surging tide of opposition, the transition happened under the purview of the military regime, and it brought to power some of the regime's closest associates. The first president would be indirectly elected through an electoral college, which was also the national congress elected in 1986 but substantially influenced by the armed forces. Tancredo Neves, a venerable politician from Minas Gerais state who had served in the administrations of the democratic governments of the period 1945–64, was chosen, but he died on the eve of his inauguration. His vice president, José Sarney, affiliated with the new Liberal Front Party (*Partido da Frente Liberal*, PFL), an organization filled with ex-ARENA politicians who were eager to continue their political careers in the new democracy (Power 2000). The new democracy, which was called the "New Republic," produced a government under Sarney that was composed of many of the center-right and conservative leaders who maintained close ties to the preceding authoritarian regime. The decidedly conservative democracy had many of the elements associated with authoritarianism, such as the continuation of much formal and informal power by the armed forces over civilian areas of policy, technocratic policy-making, and the dominance of the presidency over the congress (Hagopian 1990).

One important dimension of the democratic transition involved decentralization. Brazil is a federal country composed of twenty-six states and the federal district and as many as 5,564 municipalities. Subnational politics and intergovernmental relations played a key role before, during, and after the transition to democracy. It should be recalled that the military kept congress open and allowed for mayoral elections in all but the largest cities. Elections in key states such as São Paulo gave the opposition MDB its first real electoral successes before the first direct elections for governor were held in 1982, three years before the transition and a full seven years before the first direct election of the president.

Progressive forces had another opportunity to broaden the regime by influencing the drafting of the new constitution. Social movements that had mobilized in favor of the regime transition remained at the center of politics by pressuring political representatives and staging public demonstrations in favor of social rights. Progressive politicians who had never seen the inside of the federal congress, such as Lula da Silva of the Workers' Party, would serve in congress for the first time. Of course, occurring so soon after the transition, the Constituent Assembly (*Assembléia Nacional Constituente*, ANC) of 1987–8 reflected a number of competing claims by groups that saw in the constitution drafting process a chance to put their stamp on the new democracy (Martínez-Lara 1996). Progressive forces within the PMDB gained the upper hand initially and managed to put forth a draft that proved unacceptable to Sarney, the armed forces, or conservatives in the ANC. After 100 right-wing and center-right members of the ANC, who were known as the "big center," or *Centrão*, met in October 1987 to deliver their own draft carrying the armed forces' stamp of approval, the PMDB leadership relented. The victory of the *Centrão* deepened the rift between right and left forces within the PMDB. The latter soon formed the Brazilian Social Democratic Party (PSDB), led by Mario Covas and Fernando Henrique Cardoso. But conservatives had their own divisions along geographic and pro- and anti-foreign business lines. Leftists outside of the PMDB, notably Leonel Brizola's PDT and Lula da Silva's PT, exploited these collective action weaknesses to secure human rights, social welfare, and other progressive amendments. The balance of such changes made the final draft of the constitution one that reflected more the preference of center-left and leftist forces than the conservatives and moderates who formed the *Centrão* (ibid.). Most important, in areas such as securing the rights to participate in public policy-making, the constitution was infused with deeply progressive ideas that would become more apparent only years later, as participatory politics would enter virtually every sphere of policy-making, including urban reform ("right to the city") and healthcare (Avritzer 2009).

The result was also a document rife with contradictions that the political right saw as a pro-statist and anachronistic basic law (Power 2008: 86). The most important contradiction in the constitution was the desire to restore the powers of the federal bicameral legislature vis-à-vis the executive and the preference to maintain a strong presidency for fear of returning to the governability crises that preceded the 1964 coup (Alston and Mueller 2005: 88–9; Amorim Neto and Tafner 2002: 8). On the one hand, the new constitution gave the congress a role in approving annual budgets and allowed the assembly to overrule presidential vetoes with absolute majorities rather than a two-thirds vote. On the other hand, it gave the presidency the sole right to initiate and execute annual budgets and force 45-day timeframes on congressional reviews of bills ordained as "urgent" by the president, the power to appoint a cabinet (subject to Senate approval), and, most importantly, the power to issue executive decrees (*medidas provisórias*) with the power of law, while congress had thirty days to review the measure. As chapter 3 shows, these powers and their implications for executive–legislative relations would play themselves out in a tortuous manner during the 1990s.

The Constitution of 1988 gave the states and municipalities unprecedented fiscal resources and policy authorities, making them even more influential hubs for the distribution of patronage as well as centers of innovative policy-making (Samuels and Abrúcio 2000). The latter would play a role during the late 1990s and 2000s when innovative experiments in social policy would be scaled up to the federal level (see chapter 6). Regional groups (*bancadas regionais*) within the ANC organized along geographic lines, with northeastern politicians leveraging their ties to the Sarney government to gain an upper hand over southern and southeastern representatives, who moved to block these efforts and retain their access to fiscal resources (Rodriguez 1995). Judging by the fact that tax assignments and fiscal transfers were strongly decentralized, the *bancadas regionais* proved successful in fulfilling their preferences for the devolution of resources and policy authorities. The states and cities controlled 27 and 12 percent of revenues, respectively, in 1985, but these proportions increased to 32 and 16 percent by 1990 (Montero 2000: 65). By delegating policy responsibilities as well as resources, the constitution gave subnational governments reasons to spend, a tendency that was reinforced by the removing of earmarks from most federal fiscal transfers. More than 30 percent of all earmarks were labeled as "free," since they could be applied to areas of education and healthcare based on the discretion of governors and mayors (Afonso 1995). During the 1990s, subnational governments assumed responsibility for upwards of 69 percent of all spending on education and 44 percent of all spending on healthcare (Affonso 1997). But these responsibilities came with strings attached. In healthcare, the absence of a common policy drove up service costs for municipalities and led them to accrue debt before 1998, when subsequent reforms initiated by Cardoso's most important health minister, José Serra, took effect (Arretche 2004). The years immediately following the ANC saw a rapid accumulation of debt by states and cities. These arrears became a major driver of the fiscal crisis of the state and one of the key causes of the state's perceived weakness during the 1990s (Samuels and Mainwaring 2004; Weyland 1998, 2000).

The Constitution of 1988 resolved a couple of major problems that were evident during the 1945–64 period of democracy, namely the universalization of the franchise to all aged sixteen and above, including illiterates, and the legalization of the Communist Party. But the new constitution left several issues unresolved by the regime transition. First among the persisting problems was the return of a highly fragmented party system (Abranches 1988). The *Centrão* did not consolidate around a single organization, but it did provide the basis for a center-right–conservative alliance that would become more fully formed only under the first term of Fernando Henrique Cardoso's presidency, beginning in 1994. Several of these parties became the organizations of choice for formerly pro-military members of the ARENA, who formed the right-wing Democratic Social Party (*Partido Democrático Social*, PDS) to contest elections in democratizing Brazil (Power 2000). The primary beneficiary of this exodus from the PDS was the PFL, which grew into the largest conservative party. The PMDB remained center-right and catchall in nature, while the PSDB gradually moved from its center-left origins to the center right during Cardoso's administration. These changes, along with the brewing disappointment that old members of the *Centrão* retained with the 1988 Constitution, became the basis for an alliance of the PFL, PSDB, and PMDB in favor of a long-drawn-out constitutional reform process during Cardoso's two terms (1994–2002). On the left, the PT and the PDT shared political space with numerous communist and socialist parties. Under the Collor administration, the president's own personal party, the Party of National Reconstruction (*Partido da Reconstrução Nacional*, PRN), represented the weaknesses of the party system as it had been created for Collor's run for the presidency in 1989–90 and hardly survived after his impeachment in 1992. Using the percentage of seats in the Chamber of Deputies as a measure of party size, five of the parties listed above collectively held 73 percent of the seats between 1994 and 2006: the PMDB, the PFL, the PSDB, the PT, and the PDS and its successors (Santos and Vilarouca 2008: 63).

In hindsight, the absence of institutional closure created a *de facto* open-ended and highly contingent set of conditions that would later enable the branches of government, the political class, and elements of civil society to reorient Brazilian politics and society in ways more relevant to the challenges posed by consolidating democracy and facing the challenges of globalization. The situation was most fluid, and dangerously so, during the period immediately after the Constituent Assembly. Hyperinflationary spirals plagued the final two years of the Sarney administration, worsened by several failed stabilization plans and the plummeting popularity of the president. For the first time in thirty years, the people would directly elect the president in 1989. The hard-fought contest eventually pitted, in the run-off round, Lula da Silva, as the fiery labor leader and socialist he still was, against Fernando Collor, the scion of a traditional, conservative family and leader of a political machine in the poor northeastern state of Alagoas. In the view of the business class and foreign investors, Collor's victory over Lula was seen as critical to saving Brazil from a radical turn away from democratic capitalism (Kingstone 1999). The voters' fears were stirred by broadcast media and principally the Globo Network, the largest in Brazil. The support that Collor received among the poor surprised observers the most, as the candidate's populist message resonated with those most hurt by runaway prices that were averaging 29 percent increases per month (Singer 1999).

Collor's ill-fated administration (1990–2) laid bare many of the new democracy's problems with governability. Having been elected as the anti-Lula option, and having only his own PRN to back him in the congress, Collor struggled to secure sufficient support in the legislature, so he implemented his agenda via executive decree (*medidas provisórias*). These constitutional powers had the force of law pending congressional approval, but they were reserved as emergency measures. Still, Collor employed them constantly, reissuing decrees that congress would not approve. He delivered a fierce volley of 250 decrees during his first year in office, punctuating his actions with promises of quick and transformative reform of the civil service and, in particular, his claim that he would remove highly paid but indolent public workers, whom he called *marajás* (maharajahs). Collor also proclaimed that he would "kill off inflation with a single shot." To make good on his claim, he enacted a series of harsh measures, including price and wage freezes. But these efforts became unglued within months, as his two major stabilization plans (Collor I and Collor II) failed to tame the inflationary spiral. The president's attempts to do an end run around the congress also failed, as the legislature rebuffed his decrees. His sacking of thousands of public employees under Collor II threatened the political class's supply of patronage, thereby hardening legislative opposition even among the pro-business and conservative parties who had backed him in 1989.[2]

In the midst of these failures, several events and processes broached possibilities for more fundamental changes. First among these were the corruption scandals that first plagued the Collor administration and then vexed the congress's budget committee. Not long after Collor was elected to the presidency, his campaign manager, Paulo César ("P.C.") Farias, came under intense scrutiny caused by rumors that he was implicated in a vast influence-peddling scheme that involved campaign funds. Once Collor's own brother confirmed these suspicions, a special congressional committee of inquiry was assembled to investigate. Farias was found to have diverted between $2 billion and $5 billion with the complicity of the president. The resulting investigative report was the basis to initiate impeachment proceedings against Collor in December 1992, removing the president and elevating his vice president, Itamar Franco. Within a year, accusations that members of the joint congressional budget committee were involved in kickbacks and bribes led to another special congressional committee of inquiry, which resulted in the expelling of six and the forced resignation of four members of congress. The scandals empowered (indeed, jumpstarted) the oversight mechanisms of the Brazilian accountability system, particularly public prosecutors and the congressional oversight agencies. A revamped federal budgetary process and new public disclosure policies made it more difficult for politicians to misallocate funds either for personal gain or for that of supporters.

Despite his failure in controlling inflation, Collor proved more adept at initiating and deepening a significant structural reform program. The cornerstone of his effort was the National Privatization Program (*Programa Nacional de Desestatização*, PND), which targeted for full or partial privatization the most potentially competitive industrial sectors, many of which had already adjusted to the lower tariff rates and modest deregulation enacted by the Sarney government (Cano and Silva 2010: 183). By empowering the National Development Bank (BNDES) to take the primary role in implementing the PND, Collor's government made an explicit connection between the developmentalist strategies of the past to the emerging, market-oriented approaches to be followed during and after his administration. As chapter 5 demonstrates, this was part of the continuation of developmentalist industrial policy in a neoliberal context that would allow the state to retain a key role in shaping industrialization and growth well into the democratic period. In the short term, privatization proved significant for sectors such as steel, fertilizers, and mining. In the steel sector, more than $4 billion worth of assets were auctioned off to private companies and investors as well as state agencies that kept golden shares (Montero 1998). Eventually, Cardoso would expand the privatization process further into telecommunications, placing another $22 billion in state assets up for auction (Kingstone 2003a).

In the Brazilian winter (North American summer) of 1993, in the midst of rumors of a planned military coup against the inadvertent president Itamar Franco, Brazil's new democracy seemed to be facing its darkest hour. The failure of the Collor presidency and the social costs of his anti-inflation programs, which had involved freezing bank accounts holding more than $1,200 ("the confiscation," *o confisco*), continued to reverberate throughout the country. The *confisco* had compelled organized crime to turn to other means to gather and hoard cash, setting the stage for kidnappings and mass robberies, known as *arrastões*, on the public beaches of Rio. Citizens' sense of security, both financial and personal, had been shaken to the core. This was the context that was completely changed by the Real Plan, which had simultaneously stabilized the economy and led to an increase in the real value of the cash earned by even the poorest workers. As demonstrated by figure 2.1, annual inflation rates approached an incomprehensible 3,000 percent at the end of 1990 as Collor I came apart. The failure of Collor II and the pre-Real Plan macro-economic reforms sent prices spiraling upwards again in 1993 and early 1994. With the Real Plan, annual inflation rates dropped precipitously, to 66 percent in 1995, 16 percent in 1996, and then an average of 6 percent between 1997 and 2011. Indeed, one of the most unheralded aspects of the turnaround in recent years is the sustained control of annual inflation rates, a condition that seems taken for granted by those with no memory of the hyperinflationary period of the late 1980s and early 1990s.

Even as Itamar Franco's finance minister, Cardoso had secured a reputation for effective leadership and for avoiding the errors of past economic

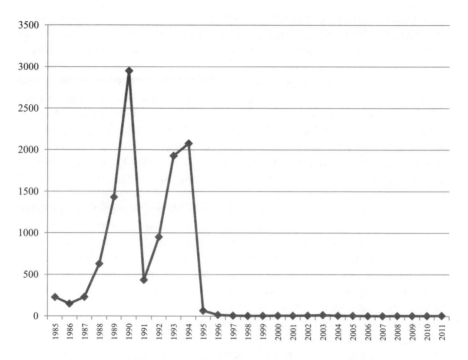

Source: World Bank, World Development Indicators Database (*http://data.worldbank.org/data-catalog/world-development-indicators*) (accessed November 28, 2012).

Figure 2.1 *Percentage annual inflation rates, 1985–2011*

reformers. In contrast to Collor, Cardoso eased the Brazilian people into a new stabilization plan that he announced in December 1993. In order to counteract the tendency of producers and consumers to engage in monetary speculation ahead of stabilization plans by anticipating changes in the value of money, Cardoso removed the onus on the currency by creating a "unit of real value" (*unidade real de valor*) pegged to the exchange rate and against which prices could be adjusted daily. Over time, as government and private contracts came to use the unit of real value, it became a *de facto* basis for the new currency, the *real*. The change was made law on July 1, 1994. Having conquered hyperinflation and instantly put value into the pockets of millions of Brazilians, Cardoso became the overwhelming favorite to win the presidency in October 1994 in the first round.

In its design, the Real Plan sought to combat "memories of inflation," the expectations by everyday consumers that prices would rise. This thinking was based on the "inertial theory" of inflation that had been the basis for previous failed stabilization attempts. This time, the Central Bank would fix the currency to the dollar using a band system, allowing the *real* to float within designated limits against the dollar. What is striking about the macroeconomic stabilization method chosen by Cardoso's Finance Ministry was that it retained a heterodox approach that departed significantly from the more orthodox neoliberal monetary policy frameworks used elsewhere in the region, and particularly by Chile, which was seen by the IMF as the model (Dornbusch 1993).[3] Under the *Plano Real*, the Central Bank would have to manage the exchange rate by periodically intervening in the currency markets rather than allowing the *real* to float freely. Sustained inflows of capital would allow the government to roll over debt, thereby keeping the fiscal as well as the monetary system stable.

The effects of the Real Plan were felt immediately, as household incomes improved with the stabilization of prices. Consumer spending increased in the months following the introduction of the *real* and poverty rates began to fall. An estimated 5 million urban poor citizens earned enough to place them above the poverty line in the first two years of the plan (Kingstone 1999: 219). The stabilization of prices removed the use of the "inflation tax" – the use of the eroding value of money to control the real impacts of spending and inflate away debt issued in the national currency. This brought much greater transparency to public accounts and private contracts and, together with the tightening of fiscal rules limiting spending, helped end unsustainable profligacy by subnational governments and public firms (Taylor 2010: 96). Significant advances in anti-trust legislation and prosecution also emerged from these changes. Politically, the Real Plan laid the groundwork for the presidency of Fernando Henrique Cardoso. The plan's positive effects on household incomes greatly attenuated the sense of social unease that had preceded Cardoso's reform and within months made him the favorite to win the presidency in 1994 in a first-round ballot against his chief rival, Lula.

The Long Reform Process

Cardoso's success in finally taming hyperinflation made possible a more ambitious reform agenda that included pension and tax reform, downsizing of the civil service, and limitations on the debts of subnational governments. These conditions enabled Cardoso to overcome the problems of governability that vexed Brazilian political institutions, particularly in the relations between the presidency and the legislature (Melo 2005). An emerging and durable division within the political class that mapped onto the conventional left–right ideological gamut also defined the pathway to reform politically. Although Sarney and Collor had embraced liberalization and privatization, the institutionalization of these policies under Cardoso was possible due to an alliance between his PSDB and the right-wing PFL. Lula's PT and other leftist parties, such as the Brazilian Socialist Party (*Partido Socialista Brasileiro*,

PSB) and the Communist Party of Brazil (*Partido Comunista do Brasil*, PCdoB), composed the opposition. These organizations advocated a more proactive public sector and, for some time, more radical approaches to land reform and income distribution. But they did not have the share of seats needed to block Cardoso's alliance in the legislature.

The reform process was arduous on account of its institutional parameters. Each major initiative required a change to the 1988 Constitution. Constitutional amendments had to be approved by *two* three-fifths votes in both houses, the Chamber of Deputies and the Senate. Discrepancies between the bills under consideration in each chamber would have to be worked out without the benefit of a conference committee to iron out a common product, as is the case in the United States Congress. But, unlike Collor, Cardoso was able to craft a large majority in both houses by doling out cabinet portfolios to allied party leaders and patronage through the annual budget (see chapter 3). His PSDB forged an alliance with the conservative parties (PFL, PTB, and several others) and the center-right PMDB, giving the president 73 percent of the seats in the Chamber of Deputies, 83 percent of the seats in the Senate, and twenty-one of twenty-seven governorships. It was also evident that by this time a more fundamental "pragmatic consensus" was possible in the congress concerning market-oriented reform. The economic liberal wing of the major parties – the PSDB, PMDB, and PFL – had already declared their support for structural adjustment during the preceding Collor and Franco governments (Melo 1997; Almeida 1996). But support for these policies increased during Cardoso's first term. In a poll of the Fiftieth Congress (1995–9), Timothy Power (1998) found that an absolute majority of deputies described themselves as economic liberals, and thereby disposed to Cardoso's reform agenda. Yet, as chapter 5 demonstrates, this commitment to liberal ideas was not so heartfelt as to prevent the design and implementation of developmentalist policies during the 1990s or afterwards.

To make matters more complicated, the economic context remained unstable due to two major liabilities produced by the Real Plan. First, the plan appreciated the currency against the dollar, which undercut the competitiveness of exports.[4] This hurt growth and put pressure on public finances, since the country began to run current-account deficits that needed to be financed with the accumulation of public debt. Financing the debt required sustained foreign capital inflows that grew ever more sensitive to default risk. Second, the plan relied on high benchmark interest rates, as high as 20 percent during much of the 1990s. These high rates helped to keep prices down and also attracted foreign portfolio capital seeking higher returns. This helped to finance the public sector and expand current-account deficits. The vicious circle was stable until foreign investors no longer believed that it could remain so. By mid-1998, the *real* had been buffeted by a series of financial crises in developing countries that scared portfolio investors away from emerging markets. Led by the Mexican "tequila crisis" in 1994–5, the Asian financial crisis in 1997, and the Russian *ruble* crisis in August 1998, foreigners began pulling their money out of Brazil, reducing the ability of the government to finance yawning current-account deficits. In the context of modest growth rates, the Real Plan would succumb to capital flight in January 1999, when the band system evaporated and the currency was forced to float. Fortunately, hyperinflation did not return largely because of an effective shift in the monetary policy framework to inflation targeting (Gómez Mera 2011). Still, the economy was plunged into a deep recession after the financial crisis in Argentina in 2001.

The success of the Real Plan hinged on the ability of the government to keep public spending under control. At the time the plan was initiated, the greatest threat to fiscal stabilization was the rising imbalances of state government accounts and the tendency of the governors to seek bailouts from the federal government. The direct election of the governors in 1982 before the transition and the subsequent decentralization of fiscal resources and policy authorities following the drafting of the 1988 Constitution made subnational executives powerful actors in the new democracy (Souza 1997; Abrúcio 1998). On the revenue side, this meant expanding states' control over the value-added tax, the Tax on the Circulation of Goods and Services (*Imposto sobre Circulação de Mercadorias e Serviços*, ICMS).[5] In electoral politics, the extensive capacity of governors to dispense public-sector jobs and other patronage gave them influence over federal deputies elected in their states (Samuels 2000, 2003b). Governors are major conduits of campaign finance from private-sector firms, and especially construction companies (*empreiteiras*), because they have direct control over public funds for large projects (Bezerra 1999; Samuels 2001a: 37). Given their power, governors and mayors were likened to "veto players," making or breaking the reform agenda of Brazil's presidents depending on their alliances. The result, for some observers, is a political system of "excessive consociationalism" (Lamounier 1992) or, simply, "robust federalism" (Mainwaring 1995; Samuels and Mainwaring 2004; Abrúcio 1998).

State and municipal governments employed their enhanced fiscal powers extensively but often without the prudence to avoid imbalances between receipts and spending. Much of this was enabled by the presence of few restrictions on spending (i.e., soft budget constraints) and politically motivated by the need to buy support through the dispensation of public-sector jobs in state and local government. Between 1985 and 1994, subnational civil-service payrolls represented an average of 80 percent of total receipts, an unsustainable level (Dillinger, Perry, and Webb 1999). Another problem was state-owned banks, several of which claimed to be development banks. With few exceptions, these banks loaned money to their own governments, which soon proved delinquent on the payments (Werlang and Fraga Neto 1995). State debts accumulated rapidly, as profligacy continued to be a problem, leading to an accumulation of subnational debt on the order of $139 billion by 1997. That represented a doubling of the total from the beginning of the decade (Samuels 2003a: 549; Haggard and Webb 2004: 262). The governors found themselves unrestrained by the federal government in accumulating these obligations. After all, these executives retained their privileged position in Brazilian politics as conduits of patronage and campaign finance (Abrúcio 1998; Samuels 2003b). They also faced few formal hard budget constraints as they had direct control of the most important tax, the ICMS, which single-handedly accounts for almost 22 percent of all government revenue. Increasingly, as the states found themselves unable to roll their arrears over, the federal government was forced to step in and assume state debts, generating severe "moral hazard" problems (Hillbrecht 1997: 60). Presidents from Sarney to Cardoso would trade debt bailouts for political support in a form of intergovernmental distributive game, even though the process undermined their efforts to stabilize prices and federal budget deficits.

Reining in the profligacy of subnational governments became a consuming dimension of the efforts of the Cardoso administration to limit public spending. Cardoso's predecessors, and actions he himself took as Itamar Franco's finance minister, helped set the stage for a re-equilibration of intergovernmental finances. The Collor government prohibited the states from rolling over their debt to the *Banco do Brasil*, effectively scaring away foreign investors from state debt paper they once believed to be secure. As Itamar Franco's finance minister in 1993 and 1994, Cardoso secured passage of the Social Emergency Fund (*Fundo Social de Emergência*), which allowed the federal government to keep 20 percent of all funds allotted to subnational governments. This served as a stopgap against the constitutional provision that required the federal government to transfer a quarter of its tax receipts to the states and cities without earmarking these funds for spending obligations. But it was the advent of price stability with the Real Plan that created new conditions in favor of re-equilibration of intergovernmental finances. The stabilization of prices squeezed the profits of the state banks. The Cardoso administration then gradually stripped away the capacity of the states and cities to spend while limiting their fiscal autonomy.

Cardoso was skillful in parlaying stopgap measures such as the Social Emergency Fund, strategic interventions in state banks, and privatization to pressure the governors to restrain spending (Montero 2004: 142–3). Federal bailouts of the states came with conditionalities that provided the president with additional leverage (Melo 2005). The end of inflation removed the option that many governors employed before 1994 of inflating away the real value of their civil service payrolls and non-dollar denominated debt owed to suppliers. Facing high benchmark rates on finance and reluctant foreign investors, the governors were cut off from interbank credit and had little choice but to negotiate their debt obligations with the Central Bank and the Ministry of Finance (Sola, Garman, and Marques 1998). The president wielded the stick of Central Bank intervention and the carrot of debt workouts to compel the governors to restructure or privatize their state banks and lower their civil-service payrolls.

The combination of stopgap measures accumulated into harder budget constraints and endgame conditions that staved off the worst effects of out-of-control subnational profligacy. One early endgame strategy involved the future of the state banks. Cardoso determined to end this source of profligacy by using the carrot of federal debt workouts to convince the governors to part with these institutions. By 1999, virtually all of the state banks had undergone intervention or been liquidated or privatized, and the remaining ones recognized the authority of the Central Bank to prohibit loans from existing state banks to their own governments. Harder budget constraints would also come gradually. In 1995, one law (the Camata Law) stipulated that the states would have to limit civil-service payrolls to no more than 60 percent of total receipts by 1999 or face suspension of constitutionally mandated fiscal transfers. As of 1998, state governments were not allowed to contract for foreign debt. These and other restrictions were made provisions of the Fiscal Responsibility Law (*Lei de Responsabilidade Fiscal*, LRF) in May 2000. The LRF prohibited the federal government from bailing out the states in any future fiscal crisis. Such hard budget constraints changed the incentive structures so that the states had no choice but to run larger primary surpluses after 2000.

Following the data presented in table 2.1, it is clear that, if the period 1985–95 was one of "radical decentralization," the years after that point saw an evident re-equilibration of intergovernmental finances that prevented the most pernicious aspects of robust federalism from undermining governability entirely (Montero 2000, 2004; Melo 2005). The table shows a notable recovery of federal revenues both as a percentage of GDP and as a percentage of total revenues between 1991 and 2005. The limitations placed on state spending and debt, the end of the moral hazard problem created by Central Bank bailouts of the states, and the recovery of federal revenues reflect a promising chapter in the rebalancing of fiscal federalism. These efforts, combined with rising tax receipts, helped to produce primary surpluses beginning in 1999 and continuing through the present government of Dilma Rousseff. Once characterized as a giant Gulliver tied down by subnational and special-interest Lilliputians (Weyland 1998), recentralization enabled the state to recover its capacity to play the more enhanced protagonist role, which is profiled in later chapters on developmentalism and social welfare policy.

Whether the LRF and other provisions marked a process of *recentralization* is a matter of some debate. Melo (2005) and Melo and Rodden (2007) see the process of re-equilibration described here as part of the federal executive reasserting programmatic control over public policy. In this sense, the LRF is the fiscal side of what in social policy was operationalized in the FUNDEF, *Bolsa Escola*, and *Bolsa Alimentação* under Cardoso (see chapter 6). Nevertheless,

Table 2.1 Revenues by level of government, 1991–2005 (US$billion, current)

Year	Federal	State	Municipal
1991			
Total in dollars	$64.4	$29.7	$4.8
As % of GDP	16.1	7.3	1.2
As % of total revenue	65.5	29.7	4.8
1997			
Total in dollars	$153.4	$60.5	$9.7
As % of GDP	19.1	7.5	1.2
As % of total revenue	68.6	27.1	4.3
2001			
Total in dollars	$120.0	$46.0	$7.8
As % of GDP	23.5	9.0	1.5
As % of total revenue	69.0	26.5	4.5
2005			
Total in dollars	$208.7	$76.8	$12.5
As % of GDP	26.2	9.6	1.6
As % of total revenue	70.0	25.8	4.2

Note: Percentages do not total to 100 on account of rounding.

Source: Receita Federal (www.receita.fazenda.gov.br/) (accessed October 5, 2012).

many aspects of robust federalism remain. The LRF did not incapacitate the governors' abilities to employ patronage, since budgeted spending can still be directed in politically useful directions. The aggregate amounts must just stay within fiscal limits. If anything, lower levels of spending elevate the political value of the governors' largesse to candidates for office since these resources became scarce overall.

Cardoso's fiscal stabilization efforts worked well as stopgap measures but fell short of the fiscal reform the country needed (cf. Samuels 2003a; Montero 2004). The growth of internal debt under his administration was an indicator of the transfer of subnational debt obligations to the federal level, but at a rate that was unsustainable. The short-term nature of most of this debt, its dollar-denominated content, and the shakiness of the *real* at this time led foreign investors to see Brazil as a default risk. The combination of high interest rates, which hurt investment, restraints on government spending due to the need to preserve primary surpluses, and the context of anemic growth created what David Samuels (2003a) has called a "fiscal straitjacket." The burdens of this straitjacket became apparent with the January 1999 crisis of the Real Plan, but these factors continued to threaten the economy throughout Cardoso's second term. A partial response was the administration's ability to engineer an increase in tax revenues. Between 1994 and 2002, the tax burden increased from 24 to 34 percent of GDP, but most of this came from social contributions paid largely through payroll taxes and a tax on financial transactions. Such receipts accounted for almost 50 percent of total tax revenues (Melo 2005, 2008; Samuels 2003a). The federal government had strong incentives to take this route, since these revenues were not shared constitutionally with subnational governments, but the dependence on social contributions could not substitute for tax reform that would centralize tax collection in a way that would give the federal government more authority over subnational spending.

The combination of high real interest rates, slow growth, and higher public expenditures led to a ballooning public debt that exceeded 50 percent of GDP by the end of Cardoso's second term, as shown in figure 2.2. The debt-to-GDP ratio descended during Lula's first term. The strong growth of commodity exports and the contribution of a recovered manufacturing sector improved the ratio during the rest of the 2000s, keeping it from producing a renewed fiscal crisis (Castro 2008). But the lesson was clear that an overly restrictive exchange-rate policy could not survive the continued globalization of finance, and its demise could have terrible effects on public debt in the absence of compensating economic growth.

Source: Central Bank of Brazil.

Figure 2.2 *Total public debt as a percentage of GDP, 1991–2012*

One of the core arguments of the current study is that the effects of institutional changes and reforms in Brazil's political economy lagged behind their implementation, setting the stage for the turnaround. This is the case with the Lula government's enhanced capacity for dealing with the growth in public debt. Moving further back in time, several structural reforms dating from the administrations of Sarney and Collor laid the groundwork for a more competitive economy. Chapter 5 details much of this, but it should be noted here that the extent of the changes was modest when they were enacted but their effects grew profound over time. Trade liberalization presents a good example. At the time of the transition, Brazil retained one of the most closed markets in the developing world. Average nominal tariffs stood at 57.5 percent in 1987 (Veiga 2009: 117). Sarney adjusted down average applied tariffs from 41 to 14 percent, with most of that decrease occurring during the final two years of his administration (Averbug 1999). The Fernando Collor (1990–2) and Itamar Franco (1992–4) administrations continued liberalization by removing non-tariff barriers and reducing tariffs further, causing average tariffs to fall to 13 percent by late 1993 (Baer 2008: 371). The effects of these adjustments would be felt over some time. Liberalization failed to curb the inflationary spiral immediately and added to the recession of the early 1990s by forcing uncompetitive firms to close their doors. But trade openness did eventually reinforce the inflation-fighting effects of the Real Plan, as imports prevented domestic producers from passing on higher prices to consumers. This helped to clean out speculative profit-taking from the market by driving buyers towards more competitive imports. The effect on industry proved eventually to be salutary. The pincer of price stability (and clarity) and increased import competition led to a deepening of industrial restructuring in a number of sectors that had initiated the process either during the Collor-era privatization policies or during the previous period of liberalization under Sarney (Coutinho and Ferraz 1994).

Liberalization presented several challenges as well. Since the open-market reforms occurred during a series of severe recessions and hyperinflation during the early to late 1980s and early 1990s, foreign investors and exporters were less interested in the Brazilian market. With the advent of price stability, which coincided with the final phase of liberalization, the increase in consumption of imported goods led to the market being flooded. This created an unprecedented level of competition for many domestic producers who had enjoyed little time to adjust (Kingstone 1999: 221). Worse still, Brazil had no executable anti-dumping law, so sectors that were particularly vulnerable to cheap foreign imports, such as toys and light consumer durables, buckled as a wave of foreign goods entered the market. Facing these pressures, the Cardoso government proved less willing to reduce tariffs even further, resisting pressures from trade partners in South America who were actively attempting to construct a customs union known as Mercosul (see chapter 7). Trade liberalization became "an unfinished agenda," as rising current-account deficits caused mostly by exchange-rate appreciation and external crises (Mexico 1995, Asia 1997, Russia 1998) placed further tariff reductions on the back-burner (Moreira 2009: 138–9).

Although slow, and never to the proportionate extent seen in other Latin American economies such as Mexico and Chile, the opening of the domestic market during the first half of the 1990s produced strong incentives for Brazilian industry to adjust by becoming more specialized and inserted into global intra-industrial production and trade (Moreira 1999). With some exceptions, such as autoparts and most textiles, the vast majority of sectors that had benefited the most from the previous period of import-substitution industrialization (ISI) survived and even prospered after liberalization, allowing Brazil more than its Latin American neighbors to retain a diverse industrial base (Castro 2008). This is one reason why the increase in imports by the middle of the 1990s was followed by an increase in exports by the end of the decade, as several of these sectors, notably automobiles, electronic parts, and telecommunications, began to export more. The BNDES promoted the internationalization of these and other sectors deemed among Brazil's most competitive. Many of the developments were clouded over by the acute readjustment of the *real* following the January 1999 crisis, the financial meltdown in Argentina in 2001, and the commodity boom after 2002. But these facts remained fundamental to the thinking of policy-makers in the economic bureaucracy who understood the nuances of how former ISI industries were able to respond to the challenges to become more competitive (see chapter 5).

Cardoso pursued privatization with greater ambition than he did liberalization of trade. His most notable achievement in this area was the privatization of the state-owned telephone company, Telebrás, in 1998 and the sale of licenses for cell-phone network development. Unlike the sectors that were targeted by the Collor government's PND, telecommunications was protected as a "strategic sector" in the 1988 Constitution, meaning that Telebrás was to remain public. Before sales could be organized, the constitution had to be amended by two three-fifths votes in both houses of the congress. As a result of his alliances in the legislature, the services of a uniquely skillful minister of communications in Sérgio Motta, and the inability of the leftist opposition to win over a public generally displeased with the quality of their telephone services, Cardoso was able to secure passage of a reform that broke Telebrás into three regional monopolies and a long-distance carrier and allowed private firms to compete fully in the sector by 2002 (Kingstone 2003a). The effects over time were astonishing. Brazilians had only 13 million landlines when the state monopoly was broken. In 2010, there were 43 million landlines and 180 million cell phones (Power 2010b: 225). The privatization of telecommunications capped off a reform process that sold $110 billion worth of public assets between 1991 and 2001. The state retained ownership of some of the key firms, including thirteen of the largest 100, with the state oil company, Petrobras, being the crown jewel (Brainard and Martinez-Diaz 2009: 6). But previous sacred cows, such as Telebrás, CVRD (Vale), the largest iron ore exporter in the world, and the airplane manufacturer Embraer, were sold, with the state retaining golden shares in the largest concerns.

Private businesses found much to like in Cardoso's reform agenda, but they were hardly quiescent about the fact that it did not go far enough. Given high interest rates, taxes, and increased foreign import competition fueled by an overvalued currency, entrepreneurs were especially worried about the costs of doing business. Tax reform was at the top of the agenda for the main business associations, whose concerns were captured by a lot of hand-wringing about the so-called Brazil cost (*o custo Brasil*). This was the differential in the cost of production in Brazil versus importing the same product from abroad. Entrepreneurs bristled at the high payroll taxes they paid along with the costs of complying with regulations mandating paid leave and vacation (Kingstone 1999: 209–10). Poor infrastructure was another target of business criticisms of the government's privatization policies, which had been slow to address the inefficiency of the ports and the antiquated energy utility sector. Firms that could not adjust had to close, causing the bankruptcy rate to increase by 40 percent in 1994–6 alone (ibid.: 220). Private-sector frustration reached a peak in May 1996, when the two largest business associations, the National Confederation of Industries and the Federation of Industries of São Paulo, staged a "March on Brasília" to protest the slow pace of the reforms.

In addition to businesses, labor unions, consumer groups, and professional associations remained displeased with the lack of reform in key areas such as the pension system, healthcare, tax, and political reform. Despite the sustained criticism, Cardoso's government did make progress on several of these, which are discussed in the relevant chapters. In the area of pensions and healthcare, Cardoso's reforms languished in congress due to many factors, but several of these initiatives were eventually taken up again by Lula and passed successfully. To be sure, international factors distracted the government during the long reform process. The Asian financial crisis of 1997 created a fundamental challenge to the Real Plan, forcing the Central Bank to intervene in the dollar market to reinforce the value of the currency and causing benchmark interest rates to double (Kingstone 1999: 231–2). In the fall of 1998, Cardoso turned to the IMF to negotiate a $35 billion standby agreement that would provide much needed liquidity to staunch the outflow of foreign capital fearful of an impending default. The devaluation crisis of the *real* came all the same in January 1999 and was succeeded by the Argentine financial meltdown and an acute recession. The crisis was punctuated by power rationing between June 2001 and March 2002 brought on by a drought that debilitated Brazil's hydroelectricity industry. Cardoso's approval ratings tumbled, and financial markets grew fearful that Lula, whom many in the sector viewed as an ardent critic of capitalism, would ride a wave of popular sentiment against Cardoso's "neoliberal" reforms all the way to the presidency.

Despite the numerous shortcomings of the reform process, it is difficult to imagine how the expanded policy agenda of the subsequent PT presidencies would have been possible without it. Marcus André Melo (2005) argues, in my view correctly, that the long reform process during the Cardoso years reconstituted the state as a central actor in implementing innovative economic and social policies.

The Expanded Policy Agenda

Lula faced a choice concerning whether to claim Cardoso's agenda for himself or to revert back to the "anti-neoliberal" campaigns of the past. In contrast to his twenty-plus years in the radical opposition, Lula presented on June 22, 2002, in the form of a "Letter to the Brazilian People" (*Carta ao Povo Brasileiro*), a statement of principles that placed him firmly in the pro-reform camp. His proclamation echoed erstwhile concerns of the PT with income distribution and poverty alleviation, but it also specified a commitment to maintain primary fiscal surpluses, property rights, and low inflation. Presented as a missive from Lula himself and not the PT, the *Carta ao Povo Brasileiro* sought to calm foreign financial markets and investors who remained wary of his commitment to market-oriented policies. It was designed to be a credible commitment, given how much it upset radicals within the PT, who were unable to veto the document since it came from the man himself and not the party (Hunter 2010: 137).

What is often forgotten in the commentary on Lula's conversion to market-based principles is that the economic conditions that Cardoso bequeathed to the country upon the conclusion of his second term created few alternatives for the PT president. First, Brazil had committed to structural adjustments, beginning with Sarney's liberalization of trade in 1987, followed by Collor's privatization program and Cardoso's continuation of the reform agenda under conditions of relative price stability. Changing course after fifteen years of market-oriented reform would have been difficult and costly for Lula. Second, a change of course along socialist principles would have been impossible given the growth of public-sector debt and the dependence of Brazil on foreign investors, particularly buyers of sovereign bonds. Since these investors prefer fiscal discipline, Brazil could have suffered another capital flight debacle to rival the 1998–9 crisis of the *real* had Lula's government gone back on the commitment to the IMF to maintain nominal fiscal surpluses (Martínez and Santiso 1993; Amaral, Kingstone, and Krieckhaus 2008). Indeed, there is much evidence to support the notion that these constraints *caused* Lula and his closest advisors within the PT to embrace a more moderate path (Campello 2013). Finally, the consolidation of Cardoso's reform agenda did not preclude the implementation of more statist economic initiatives along with more social-democratic welfare policies. Indeed, both were implemented under the PT presidencies. It can even be argued that Lula's commitment to his predecessor's macro-economic policies created a meta-frame for the expansive direction that some of the country's structural-economic and social policies took under the PT presidencies.

Once in power, Lula signaled in no uncertain terms that his presidency would continue Cardoso's macro-economic policies. First, he appointed a prominent economist, Henrique Meirelles, who was also a member of Cardoso's own party, the PSDB, as president of the Brazilian Central Bank, and Antônio Palocci, a leader of the PT but one associated with the moderate, pro-market wing of the party, as the finance minister. Second, the government committed in its macro-economic policy to two principles that were crucial to its credibility in the eyes of foreign investors: the IMF targets for the primary surplus and the continuation of inflation-targeting in the management of the money supply. The first was the easier to verify, so Lula made a point of going further than the targets that Cardoso had negotiated with the IMF. Third, Lula chose pension reform as his first major legislative initiative in 2003. This move gratified investors who remained uneasy about the PT president's commitment to structural reform, and particularly in an area such as pensions, where the labor unions, a core support group for Lula's PT, are extremely influential.

The performance of the economy rewarded Lula's macro-economic policy choices. The continuation of high interest rates (average benchmark rates of 17 to 19 percent) drew in portfolio capital focused on high returns. But, after 2003, such inflows occurred without much fear of an impending financial crisis and sovereign default. Exports, led by commodities such as iron ore and agricultural products such as soy, increased foreign-exchange reserves. Together, capital inflows strengthened the *real* against the dollar but, more important, allowed Lula to pay off the IMF, reduce the debt-to-GDP ratio that had so worried foreign investors during Cardoso's second term, and even expand Brazil's holdings of US Treasury notes. Figure 2.3 shows the secular rise in foreign currency holdings, which by 2013 gave Brazil one of the largest reserves in the world. The upsurge in reserves rode a substantial boom in exports. The trade balance, which had been a source of concern during the late 1990s due to the overvaluation of the *real*, soared into the black on the back of a commodity boom that lost strength before the 2008 financial crisis (see figure 2.4). Yet the perennial trade deficits that bedeviled Cardoso's Real Plan during the late 1990s did not return because of the continuing strength of exports of manufactured goods and natural resource-based manufactures (Castro 2008). As inflation targeting by the Central Bank kept prices in check, the monetary authority was able to reduce base interest rates to 7.25 percent by late 2012. These conditions allowed Brazil to weather the world financial crisis afterwards, posting in 2010 the highest annual growth rate since 1986. Dilma Rousseff continued Lula's macro-economic policy and even expanded spending in order to prime the pump of the economy to prop up flagging growth levels in 2011–13.

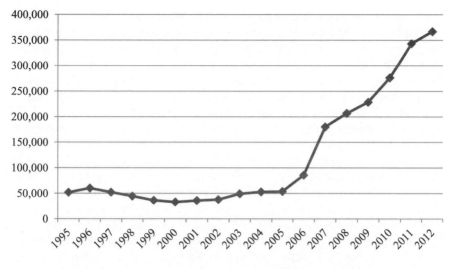

Sources: Santana (*2012*: table 10.5); Central Bank of Brazil.

Figure 2.3 *Total foreign currency reserves, 1995–2012 (US$ million)*

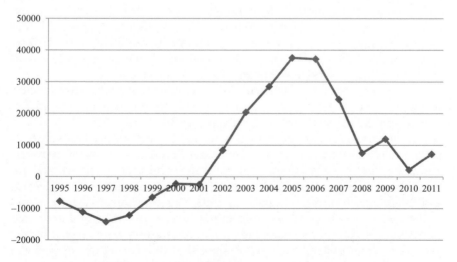

Source: IMF, *Direction of Trade Statistics*.

Figure 2.4 *Trade balance, 1995–2011 (US$ million)*

Whether as a renewed commitment to Keynesian principle or, as I argue in chapter 5, an embrace of a continued developmentalist growth paradigm, the PT presidencies greatly enlarged the role of the state in the economic development of the country. Following his re-election in 2006, Lula embarked on his most ambitious public policy in terms of spending, the Growth Acceleration Program (*Programa de Aceleração do Crescimento*, PAC). During its first phase (2007–10), the PAC sought to invest over half a trillion *reais* (R$504 billion) in mostly infrastructure and energy projects. Approximately 54 percent of the total came from the public sector and 46 percent from the private sector. More than two-thirds of these monies were allocated to energy infrastructure. The PAC used tax rebates and abatements to promote private investment in these and other strategic sectors, including telecommunications infrastructure. Through strategic use of the BNDES and public pension funds, especially the Fund for the Guarantee of Time in Service (*Fundo de Garantia do Tempo de Serviço*), the government realized investments in housing, building 1 million new units to affect 4 million families under the *Minha Casa, Minha Vida* (My House, My Life) program. The PAC also contributed to thousands of projects in urban transport, electrification, and sanitation. A spin-off program, known as *PAC das Crianças* (the PAC for Children), built new community resource centers and paid for counseling, education programs, clinics, and workshops for abused and abandoned children. Having been put in charge of the PAC, Dilma Rousseff was closely associated with the program in the public mind. She would be elected president several months after the launch of PAC-2, which called for an additional R$958.8 billion between 2011 and 2014 in urban and social planning, infrastructure, and energy. Given Dilma's background as energy minister during Lula's first term, it is not surprising that she has paid special attention to this field, with R$621.1 billion of PAC-2 being focused on clean and renewable energy sources and further exploration and development of oil production.

If economic policy, and particularly development *projects*, represented a strength of the PT presidencies, much less was accomplished in the area of *reform*, and particularly political reform (Pereira 2012: 781). Cardoso also struggled with this area, most notably in that he might have done more to make use of the convenient timing of corruption scandals immediately preceding his rise to the presidency. In the early 1990s there were two massive scandals involving national politicians – Collor's campaign finance debacle and the budget committee scandal of 1993. The latter involved bribery and kickbacks in the sale of patronage spending by seven members of the congressional budget committee, who, being of short stature, were labeled by the press the "seven budget dwarves." Despite shocking revelations of personal enrichment by elected officials, no significant reforms of campaign finance or the congressional budgetary process followed these scandals during the Cardoso administration, though oversight functions of the congressional budget process were strengthened.

Brazilians were reminded of this failure during Lula's first term, when again several scandals erupted, afflicting the highest levels of government. The most significant of these was the *mensalão* (literally, big monthly retainer) scandal, which was uncovered in the Brazilian winter (the North American summer) of 2005 through a parliamentary committee of inquiry (*Comisão Parlamentar de Inquérito*, CPI) that was investigating charges of corruption in the postal service. Roberto Jefferson, a prominent federal deputy in the clientelistic Brazilian Labor Party (PTB), revealed that Lula's government was bribing federal deputies using campaign funds and the services of a complicit businessman, Marcos Valério de Souza, in return for their votes on legislation the administration wanted passed. The spreading investigation uncovered startling evidence of the coincidence of bribes and votes over a two-year period. Several legislators, including Jefferson, and PT leader and Lula's chief of staff, José Dirceu, stepped down.[6] But many more individuals, among them legislative staff and senior officials in the Lula administration and party leaders such as PT president José Genoino and PT treasurer Delúbio Soares, were implicated in the vote-buying scandal. Despite all of this, no evidence surfaced of the president's personal involvement.[7] Shortly after the case was finally brought before the Supreme Federal Court (*Supremo Tribunal Federal*, STF), in late August 2012, the court ruled that Dirceu, Genoino, and Soares were guilty of the crime of bribery.

Unlike the Collor and "budget dwarves" scandals, which were about personal enrichment, the *mensalão* scandal was about politics. The need to engage in vote-buying emerged from the limited options the Lula administration had for composing the same kind of legislative coalition that Cardoso enjoyed. Lula opted to expand his cabinet from twenty-one to thirty-four posts, but he doled out almost 60 percent of these portfolios to PT notables, leaving him with fewer cabinet positions to pass to potential partisan partners in the legislature. In part, the move was designed to strengthen factions within the PT that were disposed to forming alliances with center-right parties while also giving those with hard-left tendencies within the party more posts than they could expect in a smaller cabinet. Still, the ideological diversity of the legislative parties in the pro-government coalition, and the fact that the administration still lacked the required 60 percent supermajority to pass constitutional amendments through the Chamber of Deputies, created incentives to try extraordinary measures. The government distributed larger amounts of patronage outside its parliamentary coalition than within it, reflecting the desperation to sustain a large enough majority. Vote-buying was a means of greasing the wheels further, since neither cabinet posts nor the distribution of patronage were sufficient in themselves to maintain a governing majority (Pereira, Power, and Raile 2011).

The *mensalão* scandal was the most significant of a series of corruption scandals that came to light during the 2000s. Others were even more outlandish. For example, in 2006, dozens of federal deputies were accused of diverting money from the sale of overpriced ambulances to municipalities in a scandal dubbed the "case of the leaches" (sanguessugas). In yet another scandal that implicated the PT, petista mayors and city councils throughout Brazil were accused of setting up kickback schemes to funnel money back to the party. These cases of "second cash box" (caixa dois) were for years associated with politicians of the clientelist parties, so the connection to the PT, with its reputation for clean government, was a shock. Yet, despite the parade of bad deeds, little reform emerged in response. Each case brought forth a CPI that would investigate and issue stern rebukes and even recommendations that politicians be removed from office. The CPIs that took on the massive mensalão and sanguessugas scandals asked for expulsion in over 100 cases, but not one deputy was formally prosecuted and tried before 2010 (Taylor 2011; Pereira, Power, and Raile 2011). Politicians regularly resign before being formally charged, thereby preventing the removal of their political rights and allowing them to run again after a time. The coming to light of so many scandals has not led to substantial changes in legislation or practice to prevent politicians from getting away with their misdemeanors. Despite the mensalão scandal, for example, electoral legislation still maintains a weak oversight system, and the electoral courts remain too understaffed and underfinanced to verify the claims made on the financial statements submitted by candidates and their parties (Taylor 2011: 168–9). Merely enforcing the laws that are already on the books against fraudulent campaign spending declarations would go a long way to undercutting corruption.

Despite the corruption scandals that plagued the end of his first term, Lula was re-elected. The causes of this have been well studied, with the primary explanations settling on how targeted conditional cash transfers to the poor helped win Lula the overwhelming majority of votes in the electoral districts of the least developed states, most of them in the Northeast region (Hunter and Power 2007; Zucco 2008). In a voter-level study, Rennó (2007) finds that memories of Lula's good management of the economy simply overrode the importance of scandals in the retrospective view of voters. Those who were concerned with corruption plumped for Lula anyway. Whatever the causes or meanings of these choices, Lula's return to the Planalto (presidential palace) after 2006 set the stage for the deepening of a developmentalist project with notable anti-poverty inflections. But it did few favors for the effort to enhance elite accountability and democratic quality. If anything, the consolidation of high levels of governability and improved policy governance were accompanied by limited improvements in the quality of democracy. The implications of this inattention to the need for political reform were felt once again during Dilma Rousseff's first term, when corruption scandals forced the resignation of her chief of staff, Antônio Palocci, and later six other ministers. Dilma took advantage of these openings to clear out her predecessor's associates and install her own, though she did not take the opportunity to address the problem of corruption in any new ways.

The history of the reform agenda underscores the role of gradualism, moderation emerging from a less ideologically charged politics, consensus on points of good policy governance, and, under the PT presidencies, a recognition of when a return to expansive and ambitious economic and social policies is warranted. Over the long arc of the almost thirty years that Brazil has been democratic, political leaders and civil society have contended with a number of recurring challenges and, sooner or later, dealt with most of them in turn. Appreciating the turnaround means understanding how much Brazil has changed during this time. The first years following the regime represented inauspicious beginnings, as the presidency went to a friend of the military in José Sarney, and many like-minded politicians in the *Centrão* would shape a good part of the new constitution in 1987–8. Hyperinflation and failed stabilization, corruption scandals and presidential impeachments, stagnating growth and ever higher proportions of the population falling under the poverty line were all reasons to dread the future during democracy's first decade. Yet, even during Brazilian democracy's darkest hour, governments and bureaucracies found ways to move forward with structural reforms such as liberalization and privatization.

Although Cardoso's political success in winning the presidency twice can be credited to his successful Real Plan, the process of governing was a tough, long struggle of alliance-building and maintenance. Many of the seeds for the current improved governability of Brazilian politics were planted during this time. Also significant was the continuation of the structural reform program, which, I will argue, strengthened the economic bureaucracy and much of Brazilian industry and agribusiness years before the export boom of the 2000s. This is what is meant by institutional change as "layering," the creation of conditions for further adaptation and innovation in a later phase. Of course, the best example is the Real Plan, which re-created the Brazilian economy and laid the groundwork for the socio-economic and political changes that would occur later. This, more than any other factor, makes 1994 the single year that marks the beginning of the turnaround.

To be sure, most of Lula's successes and those of his successor, Dilma, have been their own. Upon taking the presidency, Lula was faced with a looming financial crisis that he deftly avoided. Rather than turning to the nationalists and protectionists in his party, he embraced Cardoso's promises to the IMF and the international financial markets. Had he made choices more in line with his preferences when he was a candidate for the presidency in 1989 or 1994, things would not have gone as smoothly for the economy. Given Lula's commitment to the logic of progressive continuity of policy, Brazil was poised to make the most of favorable international conditions such as increasing commodity prices and a flow of capital to the so-called BRIC countries. And Lula did more than his predecessor in pursuing a more robust role for the state in the economy and in social policy. His failures were due to what he did not do: he did not do enough to address the weaknesses of government oversight, poor regulation, and lack of transparency that hide malfeasance and outright corruption in the political system. The vulnerabilities of the web of accountability in Brazil represent one aspect of the dimension of the turnaround that is least developed: the quality of democracy.

CHAPTER THREE

Improving Governability

No other area of Brazilian politics has received as much scholarly attention as the macro-political – specifically the interplay between the presidency and the legislature in the process of making policy. It is in this area, due to the institutional design of the political system, that scholars of Brazil have proven to be the most pessimistic about the country's democracy. In the years immediately following the drafting of the 1988 Constitution, the political system seemed to manifest all of the maladies scholars feared would risk the governability of the nascent democracy: too many parties, conflicts between presidents and the legislature, the inability of governments to pass meaningful reform on account of gridlock, and the occasional corruption scandal to undermine public trust in the system. The Brazilian experience seemed to affirm the accuracy of these pessimistic macro-political analyses until the Cardoso government. During Cardoso's terms, and then under the PT presidencies, disconfirming evidence and alternative interpretations of the available data emerged to contest the pessimistic accounts of democracy.

I argue in this chapter that the evolution of the scholarship has demonstrated that governability may improve without fundamental changes in institutional design. Observers of governability have made progress in understanding it in the Brazilian context when they have adopted meso-institutional and multidimensional approaches, even when the focus has remained on the arenas of the presidency and the congress. Yet even these analyses have suffered from an insufficiently broad perspective on inter-institutional effects and the role of the larger political-economic context. I argue in the second part of this chapter that the larger debate has ignored major lurking variables, such as non-institutional factors regarding parties and the ideological convergence of the political class that contributed to improved governability. In short, scholarly debates about macro-political institutions illustrate some aspects of Brazil's turnaround while also demonstrating how the bias for focusing on one dimension of politics is altogether too limiting.

Macro-Political Institutional Design and Governability: From Pessimism to Optimism

It is only recently the case that scholars of Brazilian politics have been able to look back on the last twenty years and comprehensively trace the evolution of the multidimensional debates concerning macro-political institutions. Timothy Power (2010a) has written the most cogent presentation of the debate, and I will use his framework here. Power argues that the debate has had three phases:

1 a pessimistic stage focused on the perverse effects of open-list electoral rules, a high effective number of parties, weak partisanship and party leadership, and incoherent ideologies;
2 a more optimistic stage focused on the powers of the president and central-ized legislative procedures; and
3 a convergent stage in which both optimistic and pessimistic tendencies have focused on the role of inter-party alliances.

The first phase coincided with the first decade of Brazil's post-1985 democ-racy, and it was led by both North American *brasilianistas* and Brazilians who were deeply skeptical about the governability of the country, based on the persistence of weak parties and an excessive number of "veto players," both institutional (e.g., divisions between the presidency and the bicameral legis-lature, highly decentralized federalism) and partisan (e.g., a high effective number of parties). The pessimism of these scholars focused on what several of them saw as the "difficult combination" of multipartism and presidential-ism, a macro-political configuration virtually to guarantee that no executive's party could expect to claim a majority of seats in the assembly, thereby pro-ducing inter-branch conflicts and polarization (e.g., Mainwaring 1991, 1993; Lamounier 1992, 1994). And these problems were especially evident in Brazil after electoral support for the pro- and anti-military parties that dominated during the 1967–84 dictatorship, ARENA/PDS and MDB/PMDB, respectively, began to disperse to lesser parties following the transition to democracy. The weakness of restrictions on moving among parties and the existence of few impediments to the creation of new parties led Brazil to have one of the highest effective number of parties in the world (Amorim Neto and Cox 1997: 169–70).[1]

The key problem in Brazil's macro-political institutional design is a set of electoral rules that combine open-list proportional representation (OL-PR) ballots in districts with high district magnitude (i.e., many candidates compete for each seat). Pessimistic views concerning governability in Brazil were influenced by David Mayhew's (1974) well-known observation of an intimate connection in the United States between the rules of the electoral system and politicians' behavior. Mayhew held that, in electoral systems that create strong incentives for politicians to cultivate a personal vote, these same politicians, once elected, are difficult for party leaders to discipline in the legislature, since they merely have to secure patronage ("pork") for their electoral districts to retain their seats.

Brazil's OL-PR system created the strongest conceivable incentives for per-sonal voting. In OL-PR, voters decide among multiple candidates for multiple seats for the lower house, the Chamber of Deputies. With a total of 513 seats available, the number of seats filled per electoral district is based on the district magnitude, which is a function of population and a fixed floor of eight seats and a ceiling of seventy seats.[2] These rules apply to all of the twenty-six states that act as single, at-large electoral districts. In contrast to a closed-list PR system in which the party leadership determines the order of candidates on the list, and hence their probability of capturing a seat, voters in the open-list system may allocate their votes to any individuals located anywhere on the list. Those that receive the most votes – that is, they are *bom de voto* – are placed high on the list when seats are allocated. Voters may opt to vote for a party instead of an individual (*voto de legenda*), but few Brazilian voters do.[3] The dominant strategy of the electorate is split-ticket voting, in which an estimated 70 percent of all voters engage regularly (a: 1).

The chief implications of this electoral system for governance of the legislature were clear: candidate-centered, split-ticket voters would produce a political class dominated by personalist politicians focused entirely on how politics could benefit them as individuals. Perhaps no other scholar showed a more single-minded pursuit of these possibilities than Barry Ames (1995a, 1995b, 2001, 2002), whose work on the congress showed that the legislative process is driven by the personal preferences of *individual* politicians and not parties. Ames (1995b: 407) argued that "deputies . . . value their own incomes first, reelection second, and public policy a distant third." Consequently, presidents face costly options when trying to muster legislative support. They must buy each vote through the distribution of patronage ("pork-barreling") or use pork to acquire campaign finance (Samuels 2002), since they cannot rely on forging viable coalitions with party leaders. A primary resource is government jobs, with the presidency responsible for some 120,000 appointments, the most of any presidency in the world (Pereira and Acosta 2010: 650).[4] The doling out of government jobs to political supporters – a practice known as *empreguismo* in Brazil – is a staple of patronage politics. The costs are also partly immeasurable, as presidents can assess the price of patronage beforehand and simply take legislative items off their agenda, never proposing much needed reforms in the face of such costs (Ames 2002: 186).

To observers concerned with democratic governability, the prevalence of candidate-centered, split-ticket voting had dire consequences for the organizational integrity of political parties. The supremacy of the individual politician meant that parties had no real influence on campaign politics or legislative procedures – that they were "feckless," undisciplined, and lacking a meaningful collective identity (Mainwaring 1995, 1999). With the exception of government-financed airtime on television during the election season and the rare use of expulsion, parties have few instruments to shape the behavior of politicians. National party offices are particularly weak, since they do not control the subnational nomination processes that place candidates on the ballot. With the exception of the PT among the major parties, national party offices do not distribute much campaign finance, nor do they provide any volunteers. In the congress, party leaders, even when they were willing to do business with presidents, could not deliver their rank and file on key votes.

From the perspective of sitting deputies, those that were *bom de voto* were especially likely to freewheel for pork, using parties as electoral vehicles by switching to organizations that could maximize their re-election and access to patronage. The less electorally vulnerable the deputy, the more likely they are to ignore the dictates of their party leaders and shop for a party with easier electoral quotas to gain/keep a seat (Desposato 2006a).[5] For example, Ames (2002) showed that party leaders' recommendations on contested votes in the Chamber of Deputies had little effect on how co-partisans voted.[6] If roll-call votes demonstrated a high degree of partisan unity it was an optical illusion explained by the costly distribution of pork (Ames 2001).

Ideological commitment is one way that parties can influence the actions of their rank and file, but Brazilian parties, with few exceptions, lack ideological cohesion. This was reflected early during the democratic period, when the catchall parties in the center formed the so-called *Centrão* that dominated in the Constituent Assembly of 1987. These parties – PMDB, PFL, PSDB – were the largest legislative parties during the 1990s. Arguably, they had little that differentiated them ideologically from one another, so voters could not easily use ideological handles to decide among them (Lucas and Samuels 2010).

The indiscipline and lack of ideological cohesion of parties, combined with excessive fragmentation of the party system, made the policy process unpredictable. Since presidents could not know what the level of support might be for any proposed piece of legislation, executives would have to buy votes by distributing patronage (Santos 1997). For scholars such as Ames, Mainwaring, and Samuels, the success of piecing together legislative coalitions was less important than the *costs* of doing so. These costs were most appreciable when inflation and public debt were high and the threat of a fiscal crisis hung over Brazilian democracy like a sword of Damocles.

Brazil's vexed experience with economic reform during the first decade of democracy was often blamed on the set of perverse incentives created by multipartism and presidentialism. Following Ames (2001), the basic view was that the inability of presidents to secure legislative majorities meant that reform would be difficult to pass. To enact reform legislation, presidents would have to part with side payments to too many individual politicians and subgroups of parties, effectively "buying" votes for each round of reform. Making the task more difficult, most major reforms required changing the 1988 Constitution, which necessitated two two-thirds majority votes in both chambers of the congress. To complicate matters further, the bicameral congress does not have a conference committee to hammer out differences between the two houses during the process. Up through the beginning of the Cardoso presidency, observers of Brazilian politics typically claimed that the failure of macro-economic stabilization, fiscal and tax reform, and the "mother of all reforms," political reform, was the result of the costs of collective action given poor policy-making institutions (cf. Haggard and Kaufman 1995). Paralysis, gridlock, political instability, and the venality of individual politicians, several of whom were thought corrupt, coincided with the continuation of hyperinflation, yawning deficits, gargantuan debt obligations, and "robust federalism" in which state governments engaged in profligacy and were bailed out by the federal government on a regular basis (Samuels and Mainwaring 2004; Samuels 2003a).

As compelling as it was to conclude that the multiple, dysfunctional logics of institutional design in Brazil appeared to threaten governability, chapter 2 shows that democracy persevered and the policy-making process moved forward after Fernando Henrique Cardoso was elected president in 1994. Most notably, Brazil's chronic hyperinflation was stabilized and the process of structural reforms expanded. The advent of such inconvenient facts for the pessimistic approaches caused other scholars to question why, in a country fulfilling virtually all of the conditions for institutional failure and a "crisis of governability," the reform pathway did not break down. Political scientists, especially those in Brazil, began to ask to what extent formal institutions really did raise the costs of governing or whether there were heretofore undetected factors that stabilized the system (cf. Pereira and Mueller 2002). These scholars took another look at the Mayhewian premise of the electoral connection by studying partisan discipline in the congress, not only in the post-1985 democracy but in the period 1945–64 and in the upper house, the Senate, which has a different set of electoral rules.[7] Multiple studies measured the degree to which co-partisans voted together on the same pieces of important legislation in the Chamber, employing a simple coefficient known as the Rice score.[8] Comparisons of Rice scores over time found varying levels of partisan discipline across parties (Amorim Neto and Santos 2001). Given that a constant cannot explain a variable, these scholars reasoned that the unchanging parameters of the open-list electoral system were not sufficient to determine these variations (cf. Santos 2002: 238; Lyne 2005: 194). Differences between the constitutions of 1946 and 1988 suggested alternative causes. The latter gave more extensive legislative powers to the presidency. The rules of the congress in the two periods were also different, in that the post-1989 legislature empowered party leaders to set the legislative docket, manage committee membership, and represent their rank and file in peak-level negotiations (Figueiredo and Limongi 2007). The pessimistic approaches had not accounted for these differences, so they missed the reasons why the Brazilian policy-making process could become much more governable over time (Pereira and Rennó 2003). In one clever test of the effects of the OL-PR system, Scott Desposato (2006b) compared roll-call vote unity in the Chamber with the Senate, where members are elected by majority votes in their states. He found that, despite an electoral system that should favor party discipline, the Senate had lower vote unity scores than the Chamber. All of this raised some doubts concerning the Mayhewian premise at the heart of pessimistic claims about Brazilian political institutions.

Such observations paved the way to a second phase on the debate concerning institutional design in which scholars laid out a more optimistic view of how the Brazilian policy-making process works. These scholars turned to the powers of the presidency as outlined in the 1988 Constitution and emphasized to the ways in which presidents could compensate for the coordination problems presented by multipartism. Spearheaded by the work of Argelina Cheibub Figueiredo and Fernando Limongi (1995, 1997, 1999, 2000, 2002), numerous studies in this vein underscored the congress's constitutional preference to delegate some legislative powers to the presidency. At the same time, this work highlighted the capacities of party leaders to organize votes in the Chamber of Deputies through a parliamentary executive known as the *Colégio de Líderes* (Council of Leaders).[9] One strand of research focused on the fact that the executive branch originated more than 85 percent of all legislation after 1988 and that upwards of 72 percent of all legislation initiated by the president was approved by the congress between 1988 and 2006 (Pereira and Acosta 2010: 646; Figueiredo and Limongi 1995, 2000). This is in contrast to the democracy of the 1946–64 period, when only 43 percent of all legislation came from the president and two-thirds of all executive-initiated bills suffered defeats (Santos 1997; Amorim Neto and Santos 2002: 95). Another strand of research concentrated on the fact that parties appeared disciplined in their overall voting patterns within the legislature, with those nominally supporting the president and those in opposition acting accordingly in roll-call votes (Figueiredo and Limongi 1995, 2000; Lyne 2005). The higher Rice scores of the post-1988 period became a basis for investigating a series of centralizing procedures within the congress (Santos 1997). These empirical findings defied the expectations of the pessimistic approaches regarding the combination of OL-PR, multipartism, and undisciplined parties. Finally, Figueiredo and Limongi (1999, 2000) emphasized how the *Colégio* centralized power through control over committee assignments and agenda-setting powers over the legislative docket.

Other scholars emphasized the governability-enhancing aspects of the Brazilian policy-making process. Causal pride of place was given to the ability of presidents to dispense patronage, a practice that President Cardoso derided as *fisiologismo* but implemented skillfully during his time in office (Alston and Mueller 2005; Santos 1997, 2002; Amorim Neto and Santos 2001; Melo 2005; Santos and Vilarouca 2008). But, in addition to the patronage carrot, Brazilian presidents have a stick in the form of a pocket veto that may be used on parts of bills (line-item veto) or the whole piece of legislation (package veto) (article 66).[10] Presidents can also fast-track bills (*pedido de urgência*) through committee, limiting legislative oversight.[11] But, even before utilizing this procedure, the executive has direct influence over the composition and behavior of congressional committees by collaborating with pro-government leaders on the

Colégio de Líderes to assign and reassign members frequently, sometimes on the eve of key votes (Pereira and Mueller 2004; Santos 2002; Santos and Rennó 2004). The agenda-setting powers of the president are constitutionally codified, especially in the crucial area of initiating all legislation concerning the budget, tax policy, and reforming the public administration. The president has the exclusive power to initiate annual budgets.[12] Although party leaders in the congress have control over the *Comissão Mista de Planos, Orçamentos Públicos e Fiscalização*, which is the primary parliamentary oversight body for the budget, the committee's capacities to amend budget legislation are subject to limits set by the president (Pereira and Mueller 2000, 2002). As a counter to Mayhewian expectations of personalism, studies of re-election rates by legislators demonstrated that the system of selective incentives engineered by the president could assure federal deputies of their political survival and, by extending their time horizons, motivate their continued support for the president's legislative agenda (Pereira and Rennó 2003, 2007).

One central focus of the more optimistic macro-political scholarship during the 1990s was the use of decree authorities by the president. The Constitution of 1988 under article 62 gave presidents the power to issue decrees with "the force of law" for up to thirty days if justified by a situation of "urgency and relevance." While this was originally conceived as a governability-enhancing mechanism for dealing with the problem of permanent minority presidentialism, executives from Sarney to Cardoso interpreted the powers to issue "provisional measures" (*medidas provisórias*) in expansive ways. Three paraconstitutional interpretations greatly expanded the legislative abilities of these presidents. First, executives were free to define what "urgency" meant, allowing them the discretion to initiate decrees. Second, the Supreme Court upheld the right of presidents to apply decrees to the broadest range of legislation, except annual budgets and constitutional matters. Most crucial, it allowed presidents to reissue decrees not previously rejected by the congress. In practice, modest changes to rejected bills could be added and then the legislation could be reissued. Congress was also limited in its powers to amend *medidas provisórias*, since any such attempt required one-fifth of all deputies in the Chamber to comply with a measure to initiate it. During the first thirteen years of Brazilian democracy, presidents used provisional measures so frequently that, by one count, there was a situation of "urgency" each week (Pereira, Power, and Rennó 2008: 6). The congress attempted to change this in September 2001 by passing Constitutional Amendment 32 (*Emenda Constitucional 32*, EC-32), which limited reissues to one time and set the maximum period that a decree could be valid to 120 days (a maximum of sixty days after first being introduced and another sixty days after the one and only reissue). But EC-32 also mandated congress to act on a decree within the first forty-five days or require the issue to go to the top of the legislative docket automatically. The reform had the unintended consequence of enabling Cardoso towards the end of his second term and Lula during his first term to rely even more on decrees, since such initiatives necessitated congressional action more immediately. As table 3.1 demonstrates, the monthly average number of provisional measures increased through 2007, when Lula's PAC accounted for a large number. But EC-32 did not have a lasting effect given declining monthly averages after 2007. Through late 2012, Dilma Rousseff's presidency used provisional measures much less frequently than her predecessors. In any case, the use of decrees reinforced the legislative powers of the presidency, especially the agenda-setting capacity, which, along with other constitutional and partisan mechanisms in the presidential "toolbox," compensated for the drawbacks of multipartism in the legislature and enhanced governability.

Table 3.1 Provisional measures by administration

Administration	Period	N	Monthly average	Total	Monthly average for term
Fernando Collor	March–Dec 1990	76	8.00		
	Jan–Dec 1991	9	0.75		
	Jan–Oct 1992	4	0.44	89	2.92
Itamar Franco	Oct–Dec 1992	4	1.33		
	Jan–Dec 1993	47	3.92		
	Jan–Dec 1994	91	7.58	142	5.26
Fernando H. Cardoso I	Jan–Dec 1995	30	2.50		
	Jan–Dec 1996	41	3.42		
	Jan–Dec 1997	34	2.83		
	Jan–Dec 1998	55	4.58	160	3.33
Fernando H. Cardoso II	Jan–Dec 1999	47	3.92		
(pre-EC-32)	Jan–Dec 2000	23	1.92		
	Jan–Sept 2001	33	3.67	103	3.12
(post-EC-32)	Sept 2001–Dec 2002	102	6.80	102	6.80
Lula I	Jan–Dec 2003	57	4.80		
	Jan–Dec 2004	73	6.10		
	Jan–Dec 2005	41	3.40		
	Jan–Dec 2006	69	5.80	240	5.00
Lula II	Jan–Dec 2007	69	5.75		
	Jan–Dec 2008	40	3.33		
	Jan–Dec 2009	27	2.25		
	Jan–Dec 2010	42	3.50	178	3.70
Dilma	Jan–Dec 2011	36	3.00		
	Jan–Aug 2012	21	2.63	57	2.70

Sources: Santos and Vilarouca (2008: table 4.5); Presidência da República, Casa Civil, Subchefia para Assuntos Jurídicos (www.planalto.gov.br).

Coalitional Presidentialism

If the president can set the agenda and legislate, the president can also use these powers more continually to sustain a governing coalition in the congress. Following on the work of Abranches (1988), the seminal, comparative work of Shugart and Carey (1992) and Cheibub, Przeworski, and Saiegh (2004), and extended studies of Brazil by Meneguello (1998), Santos (2002, 2003), and Figueiredo (2007), scholars began to see a consistent pattern of "coalitional presidentialism" (*presidencialismo de coalizão*).[13] Unlike presidentialism in its purest form, coalitional presidentialism has the executive share power with the assembly in ways that allow the branches to form alliances based on inter-party collaborations and the strategic distribution of cabinet posts to party leaders. This forms the institutional framework that enables the management of voting blocs on select pieces of legislation. Taken together, the logic of coalitional presidentialism approximates the alliance politics of parliamentary systems (Figueiredo 2007: 198). The result of this scholarship was the initiation of a third phase in the debate on the macro-political configurations of Brazilian politics and policy-making. This phase took on a convergent (or synthetic) character by combining several of the elements of the pessimistic and optimistic camps (Power 2010a).

Although on the surface it would seem that the logic of coalitional presidentialism contradicts the seemingly unilateral logic of presidential decree authorities, especially as these were originally outlined in article 62, the actual use of decrees by Brazilian presidents tended to be consistent with coalitional presidentialism. It should be noted that congress retained the power to amend the constitution and revise decree authorities as it did in 2001. Knowing that, presidents could not bypass the legislature and engage in unilateral legislation typical of "hyperpresidentialism" (Negretto 2004). Given that decrees can satisfy the preferences of legislators as well as executives, presidents used decrees to shape the legislative docket of congress as one of several tools to manage coalitions on legislation in the assembly (Figueiredo 2010; Figueiredo and Limongi 1999).[14] As such, the power is highly contingent on the president's support in the congress, the leadership of the *Planalto*, the macro-economic context, and the timing of electoral cycles. Empirical studies by Amorim Neto and Tafner (2002) and Pereira, Power, and Rennó (2005) underscored these factors by showing that the congress was willing to delegate to particular presidents under favorable conditions but not to the *presidency* as a branch of government.[15]

The use of decrees was contingent on several factors that presidents could have a hand in determining in collaboration with political party leaders in the congress. Two factors emphasized by scholars of coalitional presidentialism are the composition of cabinets and the management of floor voting blocs in the assembly. Building from Abranches (1988), Octavio Amorim Neto (2000) was the first political scientist to test systematically in the Brazilian context the premise taken from the European parliamentary literature that the *proportionality* of the distribution of cabinet portfolios to the party seat shares of ministers is a factor in determining support for the president's legislation in the assembly. Using this measure, Amorim Neto designed a variable he called *cabinet coalescence*, which was based simply on the difference between the percentage of seats held by ministers' parties in the Chamber of Deputies and the percentage of cabinet portfolios held by those same parties. A similar measure, used in table 3.2, is the percentage of ministers divided by the per-

Table 3.2 Presidential–legislative coalition characteristics, 1988–2012

Coalition	Duration in months	Start date	% pres. party	% govt. coalition	% ministers /% seats
Sarney	17	10/1988	41.4	63.0	0.77
Collor 1	7	03/1990	5.1	29.7	0.19
Collor 2	4	10/1990	6.1	30.5	0.25
Collor 3	14	02/1991	8.0	33.2	0.19
Collor 4	6	04/1992	6.2	42.2	0.42
Franco 1	11	10/1992	n/a*	60.0	0.48
Franco 2	5	08/1993	n/a	59.6	0.44
Franco 3	11	01/1994	n/a	55.3	0.20
Cardoso I 1	16	01/1995	12.5	56.1	0.56
Cardoso I 2	32	04/1996	16.6	77.2	0.59
Cardoso II 1	38	01/1999	18.3	73.9	0.64
Cardoso II 2	10	03/2002	18.2	45.2	0.46
Lula I 1	13	01/2003	18.2	42.9	0.59
Lula I 2	12	01/2004	17.7	62.4	0.53
Lula I 3	4	02/2005	17.7	57.7	0.54
Lula I 4	2	05/2005	17.7	58.3	0.53
Lula I 5	19	07/2005	17.7	69.6	0.53
Lula II 1	3	01/2007	16.0	60.0	0.54
Lula II 2	29	04/2007	16.0	68.0	0.62
Lula II 3	16	9/2009	15.4	63.0	0.63
Dilma 1	14	1/2011	17.2	63.5	0.64

Note: *Itamar Franco left his party, the PMDB, and continued to serve without a party affiliation.

Sources: Figueiredo (2010: table 6.1); Figueiredo (2007: table 6); Amorim Neto (2012a); Aramayo and Pereira (2011); Argelina Figueiredo, personal communication (Dec 2012).

centage of their party seats. The data show a relationship between cabinet coalescence and other descriptive indicators of coalitional ties between the presidency and the congress and how these varied over time. As expected, the Collor and Franco governments had weak legislative alliances compared with the Cardoso, Lula, and Dilma administrations.

Amorim Neto went a step further to test whether presidents who forged coalitions based on high cabinet coalescence reaped the fruits of these ties with higher approval of their legislation before the congress. His findings of a positive correlation between cabinet coalescence and the floor voting discipline of parties with cabinet ministers suggested that there were, indeed, pro-government coalitions at work in the assembly. Attention then turned to the ways in which presidents could manage their legislative coalitions. Amorim Neto and Tafner (2002) and Pereira, Power, and Rennó (2005) found that *medidas provisórias* are instruments of legislative coalition management by presidents with higher cabinet coalescence rates. At lower rates, the use of decrees may serve only to worsen relations with the assembly, threatening governability between the branches. Notably, the one government that singularly failed to manage a legislative coalition by distributing cabinet portfolios strategically, the Collor administration, relied heavily on *medidas provisórias* but suffered high levels of congressional gridlock and opposition.[16] Thus this *bête noir* for the pessimistic approaches to Brazilian macro-political institutions was the exception that proved the rule: governability relies on the president's use of her expansive "toolbox" of legislative powers to manage a consistent pro-government coalition in the congress (Figueiredo 2010; Raile, Pereira, and Power 2011).

For political parties, the main implications of coalitional presidentialism were that there were two party systems: electoral and legislative. In the electoral arena, the incentives for politicians to cultivate a personal vote were manifest, and coalitional presidential scholarship following along the lines of the research of scholars such as Octavio Amorim Neto and Carlos Pereira did not dispute these findings. But, in the legislative arena, contrary to the work of Barry Ames (2001), politicians would vote according to the alliances formed by their party leadership and the president; that is, legislators would identify themselves either as pro-government or as members of the opposition.[17] Once again, understanding the president's powers to legislate was crucial, because the fiscal resources to maintain clientele networks were imbedded in annual budgets that, according to the 1988 Constitution, were under the purview of the presidency to design, propose, and implement. Ames's (2001) emphasis on the use of targeted pork played a key role in managing coalitions. Pereira and Mueller (2000, 2002, 2003) and Alston and Mueller (2005) found that federal deputies would trade pro-government votes for the president's approval of budgetary amendments favoring their municipal bailiwicks, thereby linking their parties' avowed allegiances to the government with their voting behavior.[18] Ames (2002) and others contested these findings, arguing that such *appearances* of discipline overlook the weakness of partisanship, but this mattered little to scholars of coalitional presidentialism, who underscored the governability-enhancing effects all the same (Raile, Pereira, and Power 2011). More important, these scholars reasserted the importance of pro-government and opposition orientations, which were consistent not only in terms of the internal unity of parties and coalitions in roll-call votes but also in terms of inter-party and inter-coalitional divisiveness between parties allied to the government and those in the opposition (Lyne 2005, 2008; Amorim Neto and Santos 2003).

Coalitional presidentialism seems to explain a lot about the way governability has improved since 1995 in Brazil, despite the continuation of electoral incentives for individualistic behavior. Some scholars have concluded that it provides the "unifying framework" for understanding governability (cf. Power 2010a; Santos and Vilarouca 2008). Yet even these authors agree that the framework does not answer all questions. One issue regards measurement. Given a variety of indicators, as depicted in table 3.2, it is not clear what mixture and what degree on any of these metrics constitute a "strong coalition government." Whereas some scholars highlight the proportionality between ministries and party seat shares (cf. Amorim Neto 2000, 2002; Amorim Neto and Tafner 2002), others underscore the degree of partisanship, inter-party difference, and legislative experience as valid indicators (cf. Meneguello 1998; Lyne 2005, 2008; Figueiredo 2007), and still others highlight the way in which presidents manage coalition goods such as cabinet portfolios and targeted pork (Raile, Pereira, and Power 2011; Alston and Mueller 2005). Since several of these factors show up as statistically significant in the various regression analyses, it is difficult to understand the causal weight of some of the predictors. But they beg a fundamental question, since these differences might be thought of as the extent to which presidential coalitions must be created and managed and to what extent they are inevitable aspects of presidentialism with multipartism. The latter may not describe the Brazilian experience on account of the different strategies pursued by presidents (Amorim Neto, Cox, and McCubbins 2003; Zucco 2009: 1089), but some authors in the "coalitional presidentialism" school see a more permanent and systemic dynamic, and that is most often due to the use of different indicators (e.g., Figueiredo and Limongi 2002). But, even if "partyness" varies with each government, there is no consensus in the scholarship on what explains why some governments create workable coalitions (e.g., Cardoso 1 and 2; Dilma) and why others fail (e.g., Collor) or struggle (e.g., Lula 1).

A second question concerns interpretation of the evidence. The central claim in the scholarship is that coalitional presidentialism improves governability by enabling collaboration between the two branches of government. But there is no agreement as to which branch is the main driver of legislation. Some scholars interpret the evidence as incontrovertibly in favor of legislative leadership (cf. Figueiredo and Limongi 2002). Others see the presidency as being in control of the process (cf. Pereira and Mueller 2003: 755–6; Alston and Mueller 2005). While the president cannot use the threat of dissolving the legislature when policy disputes emerge, a toolbox is available for cajoling, coercing, and outright buying of votes. This is especially true of the power over the national budget, which is not constitutionally an area subject to decrees. The president has the power to propose the annual federal budget (*Projeto de Lei Orçamentária Annual*) *and* she retains the power to implement its provisions with a high degree of discretion by controlling the Ministry of Planning, Budget and Management. These points are consensual among scholars, but then interpretations differ on how these powers are employed. One view holds that passing the annual budget requires a horse-trading of votes in the congress, with the institutional framework giving presidents all of the discretionary power. Executives can veto in part, or as a whole, amendments proposed by deputies. The president also retains discretion over outlays from an array of federal agencies and public firms, most notably the BNDES, the Central Bank, and the *Caixa Econômica Federal*, to name a few. By contrast, congress has true discretion over only 2 percent of spending (Pereira and Mueller 2002). Another view is that these powers are contingent on agreements with the *Colégio de Líderes*, without whom the president cannot truly enact budgets (Figueiredo and Limongi 1999, 2002). Complicating matters further, pessimistic scholars claim that this debate within coalitional presidentialism scholarship is about legislative proposals that went forward, not those that were never attempted due to the president's expectations of costs in securing legislative passage – a phenomenon of "non-decisions" that is well documented in press accounts in Brazil (Ames 2002: 189–90). Overall, this debate remains unresolved.

Differences in interpretation present fundamental challenges to the state of the art on presidential–legislative relations in Brazil. If presidents have the advantage, then this makes the benefits of coalitional presidentialism for governability more uncertain. Some scholars, following delegation theory, hold that the advantage of the presidency is systemic. They argue that the president, who is the agent in the delegative principal–agent relationship, has better information than the congress. Such information asymmetries by themselves may be problematic, as they have been throughout Latin America, where governability crises, especially since the 1980s, have tended to be associated more with imperial presidentialism (i.e., "hyper-presidentialism," "exaggerated presidentialism") than with overly fragmented assemblies (Cox and Morgenstern 2002). Other scholars underscore the contingent nature of the many assumptions of coalitional presidentialism, making presidential supremacy more of a variable. For example, we might accept that, during periods of high cabinet coalescence, legislators may still be well served by the president's proactivity, but, during periods of low cabinet coalescence, the agenda-setting powers of executives may approximate the feared unilateralist presidency or the resulting gridlock may endanger governability. As in the United States (Neustadt 1960), presidential styles may contribute to inter-branch conflict. Bargains struck at one time may obsolesce as presidents become lame ducks during their second terms, which is a limitation that is confirmed empirically in the Brazilian case (cf. Pereira and Rennó 2007: 679). Raile, Pereira, and Power (2011) find that presidents may develop varying levels of sunk costs in designing coalitional cabinets and then either under- or overproduce pork to manage their coalition subsequently. Something like this happened between the Cardoso and Lula administrations. While Cardoso could use patronage in the way predicted by coalitional presidentialism, the role of pork-barreling changed afterwards. The discontinuity in the use of pork and cabinet positions under Lula's presidency and the attendant vote-buying corruption scandals of 2005 suggest no structural bias in favor of a particular style of governance that is consistent with the parameters of coalitional presidentialism (Pereira, Power, and Raile 2011; Zucco 2009). Conceivably, all of this suggests that governability can be undermined when even a few of the conditions that undergird coalitional presidentialism are unavailable, bringing down the house of cards in dramatic fashion. The risks inherent in the absence of more institutionalized forms of partisan discipline and ideological cohesion in the legislature remain a concern for the system.

Third, the focus on governability is problematic for democratic quality since, as the next chapter makes clear, the ability to govern in a stable political system does not guarantee or even require that the elites within that system be fully accountable to one another and even less so to their constituents. Some scholars of coalitional presidency worry that the legislature may become a reactive body stripped of its independence and oversight functions (Amorim Neto 2006). More fundamentally, the emphasis given to the distribution of material rewards and offices to coalition "partners" explicitly rejects the notion of trust or common cause among elites. Support is bought, whether by coalition or particularistic goods, and, where this is prevalent, the preferences of constituents can be ignored on behalf of securing power after elections are done. This is a dangerous precedent for elite accountability, since governments can avoid answering for misconduct by buying the necessary support. It should be recalled that the parliamentary inquiry into the *mensalão* scandal was almost undermined in the early stages by the furious attempts of the Lula administration to use budgetary allotments to create incentives for deputies not to support the inquiry. If Brazilian democracy has become more mature due in great measure to the stabilizing effects of coalitional presidentialism, then the results may be of a low-order, low-intensity equilibrium – a steady state of dubious democratic quality.[19]

Fourth, coalitional presidentialism does not address the issue of whether the policies that emerge from this system are better at achieving their aims than policies that would emerge from a purer form of presidentialism or even parliamentarism. The expectations of pessimistic approaches were that the prevalence of personalism in the congress produces an oversupply of parochial legislation that aids deputies' bailiwicks while undermining the pursuit of universalistic public goods. Although empirical studies that classify legislation have shown that bills dealing with national policies and public goods outnumber parochial initiatives (cf. Figueiredo and Limongi 1999, 2002; Lemos 2001; Amorim Neto and Santos 2002, 2003), the discussion has stopped short of evaluating policy outcomes in a more comparative manner.

Putting aside the issues of democratic quality and policy governance and returning to the explanatory power of coalitional presidentialism, we might still ask to what extent this master frame ignores structural and contextual factors that explain the maturation of Brazilian democracy. Two in particular present time-inconsistency challenges. First is the demonstrated shift in the ideological orientations of the political class away from polarization and towards greater conciliation around principles of market-oriented policy and modest welfare-enhancing programming. As I argue below, these tendencies partially pre-date and subsume the Cardoso administration – the government most authors agree initiated coalitional presidentialism. It might be more useful to think of coalitional presidentialism as endogenous to a process of de-polarization within the political class that is part of a single twenty-year sequence of structural adjustment that started with Collor and continued through the PT presidencies (Power 2008: 102). Second is the actual performance of macro-*economic* policy as a precursor to the development of a coalitional presidential macro-political system. It should be remembered that the end of hyperinflation with the *Plano Real*, which was initiated as the *unidade real de valor* plan in 1993 while Cardoso was Itamar Franco's finance minister, preceded the consolidation of the coalitional presidential system. Several years before Cardoso's anti-inflation plan, the Sarney and Collor governments had already begun a process of structural adjustment. A number of nagging issues that could have otherwise become the focus of distributional conflict within the political class were settled by the stabilization of prices and the consolidation of the structural reform agenda, most importantly, privatization and liberalization of the economy. Timothy Power (2008: 84) refers to this confluence of factors as something akin to the "rebooting of the [post-1985] democratic regime," a process that made the authoritarian-era cleavages of Brazilian politics obsolete. More important, the "reboot" seems a *sine qua non* for the emergence of coalitional presidentialism, and several of the scholars who subscribe to the master frame admit it explicitly by beginning their analysis of governability effects after 1995 (e.g., Pereira, Power, and Rennó 2008: 15), focusing entirely on Cardoso's government (e.g., Pereira and Mueller 2003: 743; Nicolau 2000), or simply arguing that his government was the pre-eminent case of coalitional presidentialism (e.g., Amorim Neto, Cox, and McCubbins 2003). This suggests that structural and macro-economic policies succeeded in changing the context, reducing the costs of the selective incentives presidents used to manage legislative coalitions. Coalitional presidentialism may be more a consequence than a cause of changes in Brazilian politics.

The contributions of the debate concerning the macro-political institutions of Brazilian democracy greatly enriched our understanding of a major dimension of the country's politics. It took conclusions about the "weakness" of parties and the legislature and found heretofore lurking variables, additional factors to consider that explain the paradox of why the country did not sink into a crisis of governability as several other Latin American countries did during the 1990s. But no debate, no matter how expansive, on what amounts to a single dimension of Brazilian politics can explain the progress of democracy and policy governance. The next section focuses on subsets of the debate on macro-politics – underexplored and unexplored areas that in some cases have become the focus of new research.

Political Parties and Ideological Convergence of the Political Class

The work on coalitional presidentialism had imprecise implications for understanding Brazil's political parties because it suggested that parties could be weak and strong simultaneously. Based on electoral rules, patterns of campaign finance, and the personalist orientations of campaigns and the electorate, the incentives to cultivate an individual vote and eschew partisanship were evident and, with notable exceptions, such as Santos (1999b) and Figueiredo and Limongi (2002), largely uncontested by coalitional presidentialism scholarship (Desposato 2006b: 1018). However, there was no necessary Mayhewian electoral connection to the behavior of politicians in the congress. There, the centralization of decision-making and the coalitional logic of the uses of presidential power militated against the fragmenting effects parties experienced in the electoral arena. The inescapable implication was that the institutions governing the powers of congress, the presidency, and the design of the electoral system all formed exogenous and sometimes paradoxical incentives shaping the behavior of the political class. But this left parties too often as an afterthought. Scholars of coalitional presidentialism largely elided the organizational distinctiveness of parties, their varying levels of ideological cohesion, and their history. This work tended to understand parties as the minimal embodiments of collective action strategies that served individual politicians in their efforts to exert leverage vis-à-vis the executive (cf. Santos 2002: 243, 2003). To the extent that party preferences mattered, they were organized simply as "pro-government" and "opposition" – the distinctiveness of partisan differences within these groupings not being very important for understanding the legislative process. For scholars emphasizing the role of legislative leadership through the *Colégio de Líderes*, political parties were mere instruments linking leaders and their rank and file, and their internal discipline was manifest in roll-call voting statistics (cf. Santos and Rennó 2004; Nicolau 2000). Their internal discipline was based on rules distributing rewards and costs to their members. The pessmistic scholars also failed to explain why even the catchall parties became more seemingly disciplined over the 1990s or why leftist parties such as the PT were highly disciplined from their inception but were able to shift their policy preferences over time (Samuels 2004). The mixed evidence led Amorim Neto (2006: 142) to the conclusion that the debates on macro-politics relegated the understanding of Brazilian parties to the status of "an unresolved enigma."

Empirical changes forced a rethinking of some of this scholarship as the coalitional presidential logic that relied on the pre-eminent case of the Cardoso administration and variations of the same *Centrão* political class gave way to the rise and evolution of the PT and the Lula presidency. For much of the post-transition democratic period, the PT embraced a self-identity of socialism and radical politics mobilized with a mass base (Keck 1992; Meneguello 1989; Avritzer 2009: 46–61; Partido dos Trabalhadores 1998). Following Lula's second loss in a presidential contest in 1994, the party initiated a period of introspection that led to a prolonged and somewhat halting process of moderation in the socialist program and culminated in the distribution of the June 2002 document titled "Letter to the Brazilian People." The document signaled to foreign markets more than just to the Brazilian people that Lula and the PT were prepared to adopt the Cardoso-era agenda of macroeconomic reforms and a commitment to price and exchange-rate stability with a moderate welfare policy aimed at alleviating poverty. Gone were the erstwhile calls for radical land reform, renunciation of the external debt, and the vitriol once reserved for "neoliberal reforms." All of this was aimed at assuaging the concerns of international financial markets. That this shift occurred at all given the nature of the PT during the first decade of Brazilian democracy is extraordinary, but even more important was the debate that ensued to explain its causes and its meaning.

How could such a stalwart radical party that had shown increasing ability to win local office, and come close to winning the presidency in 1989, make such a fundamental change? One view was that its electoral success created incentives that interacted with its internal institutions to moderate the party's platform. Samuels (2004) argued that the internal institutions of leadership recruitment and accountability to the rank and file were the distinguishing factors that explained the transformation of the PT. In the PT, party delegates are elected from the municipal to the national level, with each successive layer of delegates voting for the next level. The party's success during the 1990s in winning mayoralties expanded the ranks of pragmatists among party delegates by forcing many to deal with the realities of governing. Between 1985 and 2000, the number of PT mayors went from three to 187 (ibid.: 1015). As more *petistas* entered governments, they formed alliances outside the party, often cemented with the power of government resources such as public-sector jobs. Social movements allied to these figures also saw incentives to moderate and work with their associates in power. The emerging network of pragmatic party rank and file gave Lula and other moderates a broader set of strategic choices to take the party in a different direction. Had more radical elements remained in positions of influence within the PT, Lula would not have been able to move as he did.[20] Hunter (2010) disputes this bottom-up narrative, arguing instead that Lula engineered more of the change top-down. Beginning in the mid-1990s, Lula's faction within the PT, *Articulação*, moved to isolate hard leftists imbedded in the middle-tier bureaucracy of the party, to elect more moderates to the National Directorate, and to make the party more vertical in its structure (ibid.: 127–45). This effort culminated in the implementation of a Process of Direct Elections (*Processo de Eleições Diretas*) that empowered rank-and-file activists and supported leadership concerned with governing into the top echelons of the party (Ribeiro 2009, 2010).[21]

Resolving this debate is not as important as underscoring how the contending versions of Lula's rise to the presidency and the PT's transformation under his leadership challenge several premises of the work on macro-politics in Brazil. Lula's late conversion to his predecessor's macro-economic policies and the PT's seemingly cooperative support for a presidential agenda that was at odds with its two-decade-old platform raised questions concerning partisan ideological change that were not at the center of the scholarship on partisan discipline or electoral incentives. Before this point, ideological coherence was given little attention, and when it was attended to it was noted only in the case of the leftist parties, which were treated as exceptional in this regard. In his exhaustive study of the Brazilian party system, Scott Mainwaring (1999) tempers the conclusion that individual politicians are the chief agents of representation more than their parties by pointing to exceptions such as the PT. Further consideration of the matter seemed secondary, since the main leftist parties commanded no more than 10 percent of the seats in the lower chamber during the ten years following the transition to democracy. But even more important parties during the Cardoso administration, the conservative parties such as the PFL, evinced more discipline than the catchall parties of the center right (Lyne 2005: 198). Such differences across parties begged the question of whether partisan ideology mattered either inside or outside the congress, but the pervasive concern with discipline and the classification of pro- and anti-government "coalitions" crowded out these considerations.

When ideology was used to categorize parties, the focus tended to be on the empirical experiences that defined the organizations, usually within a particular timeframe, thereby making them obsolescing methods for studying ideological change. In these treatments, "right" and "left" were situational rather than systemic qualities of the party system. So "the left" was identified as parties and candidates that supported the transition to democracy and, subsequently, an expansion of popular participation and civil, political, and economic rights (Keck 1992; Baiocchi 2005). Similarly, Power (2000) operationalized the conservative right in terms of support for the bureaucratic-authoritarian regime. He found that ARENA/PDS veterans were opposed to reforms that would strengthen political institutions. These conservative interests preferred, instead, to maintain erstwhile channels of access to patronage, and they oriented their loyalties to executives – presidents, governors, and mayors – and downplayed allegiances to parties or platforms.

Using the more conventional method of ideal-point estimates of ideological scoring based on the similarity of legislators' voting records (the W-Nominate scores taken from American politics; see Poole and Rosenthal 1985), the results belied the importance of neat ideological categories (Leoni 2002). For example, W-Nominate scores had the PSDB in the center during the forty-eighth and forty-ninth legislatures (1987–90 and 1991–4) but on the far right, along with the PFL, in the fifty-first and fifty-second legislatures (1999–2002 and 2003–7). The pattern was understandable only by framing the results with reference to the dynamics of pro-government and anti-government coalitions. In other words, ideological orientation offered only limited explanatory power for legislative behavior, especially when compared to the role of presidential distribution of pork (Zucco 2009).

These operationalizations of left and right in Brazil were obsolescing by design. As the generation of politicians that participated in the transition aged and conditions changed, parties reoriented their thinking. Parties engaged in strategic alliances with some conservative parties, such as the PL (*Partido Liberal*) and the PP (*Partido Progressista*) allying with the PT and the once center-left PSDB moving to the right (though not the extreme right) in maintaining periodic alliances with the DEM (*Democratas*, the former PFL since December 2007). Far from denying the importance of ideology, these observations required a fuller unpacking of parties in terms of their ideological flexibility and evolving orientations.

In any party system, politicians choose parties because they have like-minded members. In ideologically coherent parties, the collective can more efficiently coordinate their efforts on behalf of a common agenda. Party labels also communicate cognitive shortcuts to voters that identify the membership's policy orientations, thereby reducing the costs for individual politicians of explaining what they stand for (Aldrich 1995). These points apply not only to parties such as the PT but to all of the major organizations in Brazil. Of course, not all studies of parties elided these aspects. Scholars such as Aline Machado (2005), Rogério Schmitt (2000), and Mona Lyne (2005) found high levels of ideological cohesion among the alliances that formed the basis for coalitional presidentialism. Hunter's (2010) work on the PT demonstrated that ideology still mattered in the internal workings of parties and that these dispositions could and did change over time in response to new opportunity structures.

With the exceptions noted above, pessimists saw very little evidence that the parties were ideologically consistent. Scholars who focused on individual political ambition took preferences as a constant. These studies dispensed with ideology entirely by concentrating on legislators' dispositions to pinpoint their ambition on gaining extra-legislative executive positions (Santos 1999a; Samuels 2002, 2003a). Yet, even here, conservatives were more inclined this way than leftists, who value more their collective efforts in the legislature. Ideology also played a secondary role in the work of much of the coalitional presidentialism scholarship because of its emphasis on material connections between presidents and parties in terms of cabinet portfolios and budget amendments. Still, these scholars noted a propensity for like-minded parties to stay in the same coalitions (cf. Lyne 2005). Figueiredo and Limongi (1995) began their analysis of partisan unity in roll-call voting by delineating the consistency of parties to cluster in predictable left–right groupings.[22] Using the same data, Leoni (2002) applied a statistical method adapted to mapping ideological orientations among parties in a legislature, confirming earlier distributions of the Brazilian parties along a left–right axis. Desposato (2006a: 75) found that deputies during the 1990s were five times more likely to enter an ideologically proximate party than one that was further afield.

Such extensive empirical work still failed to detect how the ideological orientations of individual politicians and parties could change or read the data as indicating virtually no change over time (cf. Leoni 2002).[23] By contrast, the experience of the PT underscored the role of the flexibility and evolution of ideology in singular organizations, suggesting that there was probably more temporal variation in other parties and across the party system. A breakthrough came in a unique series of surveys of legislators conducted by Timothy Power in 1990, 1993, 1997, 2001, 2005, and 2009 and now organized as the Brazilian Legislative Survey (BLS). The BLS surveys provide indicators of ideology that are exogenous to legislative behavior, thereby clearing away the bias of W-Nominate scores by coalition politics (Zucco 2009). The iterated nature of the surveys allowed scholars to compare the evolving perceptions of politicians of left and right and their placement not only of themselves and their parties but also of other parties (i.e., non-members) on a ten-point scale.

Using the BLS data, Power and Zucco (2009, 2012) illustrated the evolution of ideological orientations across the main parties. Their measures track precisely what historical-institutionalist studies such as Hunter's (2010) found, in that the PT and the PSDB shifted from their respective positions on the left and center left to occupy more proximate locations in the center. Yet the overall ordering of the parties on the left–right scale shows considerable stability over time. Figure 3.1 maps the estimated positions on the conventional ten-point left–right gamut for all of the major Brazilian parties. The points within bands are stacked from the oldest survey (1990) to the most recent (2009), and they include 90 percent confidence intervals for each

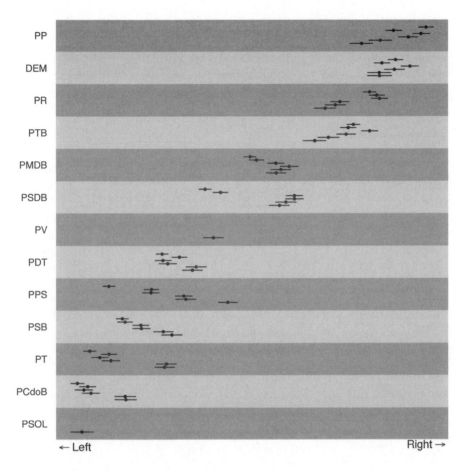

← Left   Right →

Notes: Older observations are towards the top and more recent observations towards the bottom of each band.

PP: *Partido Progressista*; DEM (formerly PFL): *Democratas*; PR: *Partido da República*; PTB: *Partido Trabalhista Brasileiro*; PMDB: Partido do Movimento Democrático Brasileiro; PSDB: *Partido da Social Democracia Brasileira*; PV: *Partido Verde*; PDT: *Partido Democrático Trabalhista*; PPS: *Partido Popular Socialista*; PSB: *Partido Socialista Brasileiro*; PT: *Partido dos Trabalhadores*; PCdoB: *Partido Comunista do Brasil*; PSOL: *Partido Socialismo e Liberdade*.

Source: Power and Zucco (2012).

Figure 3.1 *Ideological positions of the Brazilian parties, 1990–2009*

party-year unit of analysis. The figure demonstrates that the placement by non-members of the four largest parties – PT, PSDB, PFL/DEM, and PMDB – shows the shift of the PT to the center and the PSDB to the right, thus reducing the ideological distance among these parties. This is confirmed by figure 3.2, which uses the Sani–Sartori ideological distance scores with the BLS data.[24] It is clear that there has been a convergence towards the middle of the ideological spectrum so that ideological distances even at the extremes (e.g., PT–PFL) have fallen.

The available data provide some basis for the idea that there has been ideological convergence or a weakening of already anemic ideological self-placement. Using the BLS data, Lucas and Samuels (2010) argue that ideological coherence remains indistinct for parties other than the PT, and especially for the non-leftist parties. One can accept this as a blessing in disguise in the sense that ideological polarization, which did play a role in presidential contests such as the 1989 race, has been replaced by more practical orientations for the political class. As Power and Zucco (2009, 2012) suggest, and as Hunter's (2010) study of the PT confirms, the realities of governing in Brazil require a reconfiguration of alliance patterns that favor a softening of ideology and an embrace of pragmatism (Power 2008). The PSDB engineered a shift to the center right which created the alliance possibilities that sustained Cardoso's legislative agenda. The PT experienced a similar transition, though more quickly, just before Lula's election to the presidency. Since that time, the overall pattern of ideological convergence across the political class has been evident, with a weakening of erstwhile cleavages between left and right, pro-military and anti-military, and pro-statist and anti-statist. Whether this

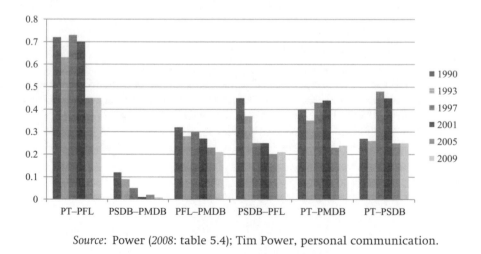

Source: Power (*2008*: table 5.4); Tim Power, personal communication.

Figure 3.2 *Sani–Sartori ideological distances, 1990–2009*

is "convergence" or simply a weakening of already anemic ideological self-placement, the de-polarizing results are the same.

The evident decline of ideology in shaping legislative behavior beginning with the Collor government provides further evidence that the inter-branch and inter-party alliances that explain the continuity of coalitional presidentialism under Cardoso had antecedents and non-institutional correlates. If pessimists were correct that the electoral and party system along with "robust federalism" create multiple veto points and veto players, the convergence of ideology reduced the likelihood that these vetoes would be exercised (Power 2008). The evident convergence of ideological orientations in the political class might well be as powerful a determinant of the more governable system Brazil now enjoys than any of the more variable factors that have been used to explain presidential–legislative relations. As we will see in the chapters to come, ideological convergence of the political class plays a role in other dimensions of the Brazilian political system, including the economic and social reform agendas.

The political institutions of Brazilian democracy are distinctive and have evolved historically in ways that mean theoretical insights from American politics (such as the Mayhewian assumptions about politicians' behavior) do not fit entirely well over time (see Santos 1999a). If the debates about coalitional presidentialism and the party system have generated any insights, the most useful have to do with appreciating the diversity of incentives, policy preferences, and sources of power that shape the behavior of political representatives in Brazil (cf. Figueiredo and Limongi 2002: 305). Of course, this complex reality requires further parsing by scholars, but the field must take care not to become too insular. Major aspects of the political party system, ideology, and the transformation of federalism have received less attention due to the focus on one dimension of macro-politics above the others: the relations between the presidency and the national congress. The adoption of "meta-frames" has also served to undercut explanatory power, whether it has been the Mayhewian view, delegation theory, or coalitional presidentialism. All of these approaches have been guilty of ignoring lurking variables and failing to move beyond the dependent variable of governability. These approaches have also focused more on proximate institutional causes and have largely ignored the changing context that made these institutions perform as they did.

CHAPTER FOUR

Accountability, Participation, and Good Governance

The review of work on macro-political institutions shows that Brazil has achieved a high, perhaps unexpected, level of governability since the transition to democracy in 1985. But the constancy of institutions and their day-to-day predictability, as well as the willingness of elites to play by the rules of the game, guarantee a measure only of stability, not of quality. If we turn to other dimensions of Brazilian democracy, there is good news and there is bad news. On the positive side, Brazilian democracy retains strong procedural dimensions, including free and fair elections and robust levels of participation, both at the ballot box and through a highly organized and vibrant civil society. On the negative side, political identities of partisanship and ideology that could otherwise give voters and their representatives a sense of connectedness are weak. Too much of the oligarchical and authoritarian past lingers, including pervasive vote-buying in the poorer states and at the local level, the unfairness and politicization of the courts, corruption, and illegal police violence against innocent and guilty alike. Just as patronage is often the currency of political coalitions among parties and the executive and legislative branches, material benefits distributed to poor voters form the lifeblood of clientelist politics. In their most developed configuration, these networks produce lasting political machines. As elites operating in all areas of the polity – elected offices, the public bureaucracy, and public security – privilege themselves and assume impunity from accountability, Brazilian democracy weakens.

This chapter moves beyond the macro-political debates discussed in the last chapter to analyze the quality of Brazil's democracy. It should be recalled that pessimistic and most coalitional-presidential approaches to macro-politics assumed that the representative link between politicians and their voters was weak. Since members of congress can increase the probability of their own election (or re-election) by distributing material rewards and cutting deals with co-partisans and other allies to deliver voters, they do not rely on providing a programmatic alternative to the electorate in return for their vote. To become so concerned with the stability of this low-intensity democracy rather than its quality is unsatisfying. In order to go beyond these concerns with governability and analyze the quality of democracy, it is essential to consider four major dimensions: elite accountability, government responsiveness, voting and the electorate, and participation.

The accountability of elites to citizens, defined here as their answerability to the public for institutionally inappropriate or illegal actions, is a centerpiece of democratic quality. Although corruption is a persisting problem in Brazil, consuming an estimated 2 to 5 percent of GDP and sapping the public's trust in democracy (Power and Taylor 2011a), illegal actions are not the only means through which politicians violate expectations of official accountability. Politicians routinely renege on campaign promises, elide oversight to pursue private interests, and misuse their office to protect their personal interests and those of close supporters.

Accountability as a dimension of democratic quality is also manifest in other spheres of the polity in terms of the responsiveness of governments to popular preferences. Accountability relies on non-elites having a say, perceiving differences among the choices presented to them during elections, and retaining the ability to elect and subsequently to remove their representatives. Voters who can discern differences among their choice of candidates and parties, and especially those who maintain an ideological or partisan link to these choices, are better able to select their preferred governing programs from the panoply of candidates and parties. Elites must be accountable too between elections. So the capacity of organized civil society to exert oversight and demand responsiveness is a crucial participatory pillar of democracy.

The main analytical assumption of this chapter is that the four dimensions profiled together here form a composite, multidimensional concept of the quality of Brazilian democracy. The central argument is that these dimensions have not all improved during Brazil's turnaround. In keeping with the principle mentioned in chapter 1 that "not all good things go together," I show in this chapter how some aspects of democratic quality have advanced while others have eroded or stagnated. In some cases, the factors that make one dimension stronger also weaken other dimensions. This inconsistency is best expressed in two paradoxes: (1) the continuity of oligarchical forms of doing politics in the face of a more participatory and organized civil society and (2) the advent of good governance in various areas of policy-making in the absence of significant improvements to procedural democracy.

The first paradox contrasts the notable achievement of how Brazil became Latin America's largest democracy and, after nearly thirty years, one of the region's most long-lived, and yet, despite extensive mobilization and participation of citizens, the country has not experienced enough fundamental changes in how the political system is governed. As the last chapter showed, the core practices of the political class remain the same as they have been during much of the country's political history. Material exchanges, when not forming the currency of well-developed clientele networks, serve only to reward the same groups of leaders. I have employed the term "oligarchical" to describe this order to make the connection to the past more evident (Montero 2005, 2011). And whether one ascribes to either the pessimistic or the more optimistic view of political institutions, the *troca de favores* among elites remains the essence of how politics are done in Brazil. Yet it is also true that civil society organizations (CSOs) and participatory politics have emerged since the Constitution of 1988 to complement in powerful ways the system of political representation. The contradiction of a more participatory democracy with the persistence of oligarchical forms of politics is a paradox. Without disregarding the real advances made by civil society, it suggests that more robust and varied forms of participation and aspects of representation are not sufficient for generating more fundamental changes in Brazilian politics overall.

The second paradox contrasts the improved performance of government in several key areas during the recent administrations of Fernando Henrique Cardoso, Lula da Silva, and Dilma Rousseff with the absence of notable improvements to procedural democracy. In this regard, I underscore the way in which good policy has worked against strengthening procedural democracy by diverting attention away from much needed reforms in this sphere. While Cardoso and the PT presidencies have been credited rightly with engaging in social and industrial policies that have contributed to Brazil's turnaround, their governments have done little to improve the quality of the vote. Their record regarding the empowerment of civil society is better in areas such as healthcare and affirmative action, where movement politics have proven important (see chapter 6), but less effective in environmental politics. Efforts to engage civil society organizations consistently were more prevalent under Lula's presidency than Cardoso's.

Elite Accountability

Elite accountability in liberal democracies relies upon both horizontal and vertical forms of oversight, governance of law abidance, and the ratification of mandates and power. This section focuses on the horizontal dimension that requires the answerability of public officials to one another (Mainwaring 2003: 11). Horizontal accountability is manifest through the workings of intra-state institutions, most prominently the judiciary, the executive and the legislature, and national and subnational oversight agencies that enforce regulations on public officials. These institutions monitor, investigate, and sanction officialdom through what Guillermo O'Donnell (2003) calls the "legal institutionalization of mistrust." I address the vertical dimension in two subsections below that are concerned with voting and popular participation, the two key components of *social accountability* (Peruzzotti and Smulovitz 2006).

As the last chapter established, a great deal of scholarly attention has focused in recent years on the relationship between the presidency and the congress, but the driving concern of this work has been governability and not elite accountability. The debate between optimistic and pessimistic variants of the macro-political scholarship did not just elide accountability, it settled on aspects of inter-branch relations that made governability possible but accountability problematic (Power 2010a). Whether one is a pessimist or a proponent of coalitional presidentialism, the dynamics of governance between the presidency and the congress remain contingent on the right combination of cabinet assignments, budgetary understandings, and ideological mix of "pro-government" and "opposition" forces. By contrast, elite accountability requires more constant, collective rules of the game that effectively monitor and sanction presidents, parties, and individual politicians from violating the terms of shared power (O'Donnell 2003). This difference was captured well by the cautionary tale of the *mensalão* scandal during the first term of Lula's presidency. Lacking sufficient cabinet appointments to keep a majority of support in the congress, PT leaders resorted to bribery that became a wider network of pay-to-play transactions to buy votes for the government's legislation. By contrast, elite accountability must be systemic and ongoing, based on an emerging "web of mechanisms of accountability" that is not as dependent on how well presidents manage coalition dynamics (Mainwaring 2003: 30).

Worse still, coalitional presidentialism weakened accountability mechanisms that were created to provide additional, direct oversight functions. The 1988 Constitution empowered the congress to form Parliamentary Investigative Committees (*Comissões Parlamentares de Inquérito*, CPIs) to exert parajudicial oversight over the presidency and its own members and report their findings to the Public Prosecutorial Service (*Ministério Público*, MP) for civil or criminal prosecution.[1] As pro-government coalitions have increasingly become the basis for inter-branch operations, CPIs have been used less frequently to investigate the government, except in cases in which scandal pressures the government to take the initiative (Taylor and Buranelli 2007: 70; Sadek and Cavalcanti 2003). More frequently, CPIs are used as bargaining chips in negotiations between the pro-government and opposition coalitions (Figueiredo 2010). It should be recalled that the CPI that eventually uncovered the *mensalão* scandal was almost undermined as a result of the government's use of its budgetary discretion to undercut support for the inquiry. More typically, only one in five CPIs issues a final report; most result in no further investigation, let alone prosecutable charges (Power and Taylor 2011b; Taylor 2009: 165–6). When matters come to a dead end, the Brazilians say that it has all "ended with pizza"[2] (*acabar em pizza*), a typical outcome for CPIs.

The politicization of accountability mechanisms such as CPIs is done largely out in the open as a tactic of governments trying to get their legislation through congress. Less visible is the way that campaign finance operates in Brazil. Brazilian politicians tend to have long careers, stretching across subnational and national office. They therefore garner strong incentives to cultivate long-term relationships with financiers, who are not limited in the amounts they may legally provide to individual candidates. Nevertheless, they are also often willing to fund campaigns by providing kickbacks to incumbents through a "second till" (*caixa dois*), in which excess payments are channeled to politicians or their parties (Taylor 2010: 98–9). Donors can be individuals, parties, or corporations, though private firms are the biggest contributors by far (Samuels 2001a: 34–5). Such exchanges are best viewed as "investments" that are repaid in the form of policy outputs (pork) for the investor (Samuels 2002, 2006b). Due to the closeness and long-term nature of these ties, contributors and candidates know one another well. Often they develop friendships or already enjoy ties fortified by kinship. David Samuels (2001a, 2002) has found that these conditions help to explain why there is a strong statistical correlation between the provision of pork by deputy and the distribution and continuation of campaign contributions. Politicians then reap a reward in improved job security, as money contributes strongly to candidates' vote totals in congressional races (Samuels 2001b). Campaign finance transactions involve systemic injection of private interests into public policy that produce perverse incentives (cf. Pereira, Rennó, and Samuels 2011).

In other ways, the rules governing the accountability of the political class have become harder even as the pork–campaign finance nexus and conflicts of interest have continued. Congressional elites empowered oversight mechanisms to handle the accounting of public monies after the 1993 budget corruption scandal. The Federal Accounting Tribunal (*Tribunal de Contas da União*, TCU), which has origins as far back as 1890 and was reconstituted by the 1988 Constitution, became more active after the budget scandal. As a constitutional agent of the legislative branch, it provides oversight and investigates cases involving presidential and congressional accounts. The TCU has been particularly active in the last ten years in imposing sanctions, including suspension of the rights to hold elected office, on public officials it finds guilty of misconduct.[3] More generally, the post-1993 climate led to more data on public accounts becoming more widely available to the public (Figueiredo 2007: 183–6). State and municipal auditors (*Controladoria Geral da União*, CGU) have been active since 2001 in investigating official malfeasance and handing their findings to the state and federal MPs. The CGUs have added tremendously to the general move to make public accounts transparent by distributing data acquired through regular audits and by enabling new anti-corruption legislation, which affects not only subnational governments that fall within the CGUs' oversight but also the federal government, itself often deeply involved in subnational spending and budgeting (Speck 2011). The need of subnational governments to adhere to the spending limits and budget transparency requirements of the Fiscal Responsibility Law (*Lei de Responsabilidade Fiscal*) has reinforced the CGU's activities since 2001. Furthermore, the chief tax-collection agency, the *Receita Federal*, routinely collaborates with the *Ministério Público* to bolster its investigations, which has broadened the network of oversight over official accounts. Finally, in June 2010 the congress passed the Clean Record Law (*Lei Ficha Limpa*), which proscribes any candidate with a conviction in an appeals court (i.e., politicians with "dirty records," or *fichas sujas*) from running for office.[4]

The result of the institutional hardening of accountability mechanisms during the last decade of democracy has been that corruption and other forms of official misconduct have been detected more consistently. Periodic TCU and CGU audit reports, not to mention the occasional CPI, have implications for officeholders, who are dissuaded for running for re-election if the taint of corruption goes public (Rennó 2011). This has affected even the most cohesive interest groups in the legislature. For example, in their study of evangelical deputies, Reich and dos Santos (forthcoming) find that a disproportionate number were involved in the *mensalão* scandal in 2005. They show that virtually half of the evangelists in congress (the *bancada evangélica*) either failed to win re-election or decided not to run again in large part because of the pall cast on evangelical deputies by the scandal. However, detection and prosecution are two different processes. The latter requires that the courts take up where oversight bodies leave off.

The Judiciary

The judiciary retains extraordinary powers to sort out legal conflicts, but the courts are limited to acting only in areas of policy and law that are brought before them. Unlike the legislature and the presidency, the judiciary is a reactive branch, but it too faces its own problems of poor governability, weak accountability, and even corruption. Its complex federal structure and still evolving powers contribute to its problems. At the apex of the judiciary are the Supreme Federal Tribunal (*Supremo Tribunal Federal*, STF), the highest court of appeal, and the Superior Justice Tribunal (*Superior Tribunal de Justiça*, STJ), both of which interpret constitutional questions and act as the highest courts of appeal. The STJ acts as the superior appeals court for the lower courts of appeal, which are organized into five regional federal tribunals staffed by 130 judges. There are 560 courts of first instance, the equivalent of 94 district courts in the United States, staffed by 990 judges (Arantes 2005: 236). Local electoral judges and the regional electoral courts at the state level adjudicate cases involving misconduct of elections, with appeals going to the highest electoral court, the Superior Electoral Tribunal (*Tribunal Superior Eleitoral*, TSE).

The judiciary faces several major challenges, the first of which is its gigantic caseload and its inefficiency. This problem begins with the STF, where judges do not control the docket and must hear all appeals. Each decision applies only to the parties of the case and does not enjoy *erga omnes* (direct effect towards all). And, most important, the STF does not have the power to establish a precedent for the whole system (*stare decisis*). The caseload that moves slowly up the juridical ladder is massive at the bottom and only barely less so at the appellate and higher court levels. Dilatory appeals are common, lengthening procedures to an average of eight to ten years (Taylor 2009: 159).

The electoral courts must monitor over 350,000 candidates and upwards of twenty-nine parties in each national election at multiple levels of the federation. The judges, who do a tour of duty of only two years in the electoral courts from the regular judiciary, must manage their workload with under-staffed and poorly budgeted offices (Taylor 2011: 167–8). And, even though the TSE's decisions cannot be easily appealed, politicians in the dock have been effective in gumming up the works by appealing on constitutional grounds, thereby shifting their cases to the regular judiciary, where they can wait years before they are tried.

One of the virtues of Brazilian democracy – a robust participatory political culture – which I discuss in greater detail later in this chapter, contributes to the inefficiency of the judicial system and introduces problems of poor governability. Brazil has become a litigious society during the democratic period. An estimated half a million cases are brought against the federal government each year. Arantes (2005: 237) estimates that each judge's share amounts to over 5,000 cases! Large numbers of these cases are generated by civil society organizations and non-governmental organizations (NGOs) that seek to overturn or delay implementation of federal legislation. The Direct Action of Unconstitutionality (*Ação Direta de Inconstitucionalidade*, ADIn) is par-ticularly effective in this regard. The 1988 Constitution sanctioned the use of ADIns to allow official institutions – for example, federal prosecutors, the branches of government, state governors, and organizations with a national representative function, such as the national bar association, political parties, and labor unions – to challenge the constitutionality of any measure. Yet ADIns have been used excessively during the democratic period (Taylor 2008: 78–83). The ADIn gives even the smallest parties in the congress the ability to delay the legal force of bills, and these have been the organizations to make most use of them. Arantes (2005: 243) estimates that parties with less than 5 percent of the seats in congress drafted one-quarter of all of the ADIns brought between 1990 and 2003. A common practice of parties in the opposition in congress is to file ADIns against bills that were passed by the majority. When it was in opposition to Cardoso's government, the PT engaged in this practice, one party members themselves called "juridical guerrilla warfare," by filing broad judicial challenges throughout the lower courts.

Given the volume of ADIns, the STF has considered more constitutional challenges to legislation than any other high court in the Western hemi-sphere (Taylor 2008: 13–14). This represents a considerable power, as injunc-tions issued against legislation can suspend implementation of a law or strike a law from the books if it is deemed unconstitutional. Once issued, injunc-tions are not subject to appeal and remain universally binding. Fortunately, the high court has a record of exercising its authority in a measured way. Injunctions to suspend a law are issued no more than 24 percent of the time, while injunctions of unconstitutionality are issued only 11 percent of the time (ibid.: 79).

The increasingly political nature of some of the cases the courts hear also reflects the fact that the judiciary has become more involved in the most political of arenas: elections. Beginning in 2002, the STF ruled that party coalitions across the state and federal levels had to be the same. This involved the judiciary in the composition of coalitions, which, as the last chapter showed, is a central piece of legislative politics in Brazil. This action encouraged the presidency, the legislature, and subnational governments to become more involved in filing cases (Arantes 1999: 91–2). Before each election, contending parties and candidates often file complaints with the courts. Most of these cases involve accusations that the opposing candidate or party is illegally on the ballot. One estimate for the 2002 race showed that an average of thirty-two legal actions were filed for each of the 1,654 executive and legislative offices up for election (Arantes 2005: 246).

The Brazilian judiciary has become more professional and technically adept during the democratic period, but its personnel can become unaccountable and even brash in the way that they violate the law. More than the garden-variety conflict of interest is at issue in some cases. One example from the brash file was the case of Judge Nicolau dos Santos Neto (a.k.a. "Lalau"), a federal magistrate who was exposed by federal tax authorities and the MP in 1999 as the author of an $80 million kickback scheme in which he conspired with private contractors to overprice the construction of the regional labor court building in São Paulo. The case inspired the Lula government to organize a broad-based sting operation led by the federal police, and known as *Operação Anaconda*, to root out other cases of corruption in the judiciary and the state police forces.

The problems besetting the judiciary seem to represent not only a weakness of elite accountability but also another source of anemic governability in Brazilian politics. Fortunately, the political class has not been blind to the need to address these problems. Matthew Taylor (2008: 29–30) counts no fewer than forty proposed reforms of the judiciary between 1988 and 2004. One of the most notable occurred in 1993 during the Itamar Franco administration. To clear judicial obstacles to reform legislation, congress gave the STF the power to hear Declaratory Actions of Constitutionality (*Ação Direta de Constitucionalidade*) brought by the president, congress, or the attorney general. These allow the court to declare any law constitutional, voiding all lower court actions against it.[5] More than a decade later, in December 2004, another transformative reform passed the legislature. This reform was the culmination of a series of scandals involving the judiciary (e.g., the Lalau case and others exposed through *Operação Anaconda*). The legislation strengthened the principle of *stare decisis* at the STF and STJ and made appeals more difficult. Under Constitutional Amendment 45, two-thirds of the judges on the STF may invoke a "summary of binding effect" (*súmula de efeito vinculante*) to establish a precedent binding on all other courts. The reform also established an oversight body, the National Judicial Council (*Conselho Nacional Judicial*), to exert greater administrative control over the lower courts and to enforce rules proscribing nepotism and conflicts of interest. Despite the *súmula de efeito vinculante*, lower court dockets remain overwhelmed with cases.

The MP and the Federal Police

The courts alone are insufficient to exert oversight without an empowered and autonomous prosecutorial force, beginning with the *Ministério Público* at the federal level and its offices in all of the states.[6] The 1988 Constitution represented a watershed in strengthening the MP as an autonomous "fourth branch of government" along with an emerging body of civil law that defends collective rights (Arantes 1999, 2003, 2011; Kerche 2007). The scope of the MP is broad, encompassing the oversight of the administration of public policy at all levels of the federation, including constitutional matters and both individual and group rights. It has standing to file an ADIn at the STF against any of the branches of government, and it does so as an autonomous body. Only the MP can prosecute a case before the STF and the STJ. It can also dispose of a wide assortment of procedural actions, such as public civil actions (class-action lawsuits) and civil summary proceedings. Given the sweeping federal structure of the judiciary, the MP has extensive personnel – 9,662 state and 338 federal prosecutors – though the national coverage of the MP puts a strain on the workload of the federal office (Taylor 2009; Cavalcanti 2006). These appointments are meritocratic and life-long. Consequently, the MP has been quite active throughout Brazil. One recent study estimates that it is pursuing over 4,000 cases against public officials, in fourteen of the twenty-seven states (Arantes 2011: 198). The ease of access for regular citizens is also notable. In recent years, state-level MP offices have processed complaints from individuals and groups who started the process via the internet or through a phone call (Sadek and Cavalcanti 2003: 216). All of these powers and processes make the MP the prime mover in prosecuting official wrongdoing in Brazil.

The federal police supply a complementary function to the MP, acting as a judiciary police in support of the work of federal courts and the MP. Like the MP, the federal police are empowered by the 1988 Constitution though, unlike the MP, are subordinate to the president. Their functions are diverse, including protecting the property of the federal government, though their primary role during the democratic period has been to investigate crimes with interstate and/or federal dimensions. In this role the federal police count on a staff of just over 11,000, including detectives, forensics experts, crime-scene analysts, and other assorted professionals in criminology, who are carefully vetted according to tight admissions standards (Taylor 2009: 163). Their range of activities requires that they act as partners with the federal judiciary, which retains the sole power to authorize the federal police to engage in tactics such as wiretapping or arresting suspects. In recent years, the federal police have been most effective in exposing scores of cases of corruption through their various sting operations. Arantes (2011: 201) reports that over 600 such operations occurred between 2003 and 2008, each cleverly named to represent the case. For example, one operation focused on fraud in the bidding for blood byproducts within the Ministry of Health and was dubbed "Operation Vampire."

Even as these institutions of oversight and prosecution have become more robust in the last decade of democracy, the political class has found ways to slow their progress, especially in the courts. The use of writs of *habeus corpus* from higher courts and dilatory appeals typically keep accused officials out of jail. A law passed in 2002 restricted the MP from prosecuting elected officials, such as mayors, governors, and federal legislators, who are indicted for malfeasance at any level other than in the high courts. This move damaged efforts to strengthen elite accountability, not just because it delayed proceedings by adding to the already clogged dockets of the high courts; the law restricted the state-level MPs from bringing cases against corrupt officials. This is a major reason why the cases of official malfeasance that are prosecuted represent a small percentage of those that might otherwise be pursued (Figueiredo 2010). The MP's chief weakness is that the investigatory powers it does retain – for instance, the use of techniques such as wiretaps and "midnight raids" to gather information – have been challenged by other institutions (Taylor and Buranelli 2007: 64–5). One prominent example that was a cause of the massive demonstrations in 2013 was the congress's attempt to limit MP investigations through a constitutional amendment (*Proposta de Emenda Constitucional* 37/2011), which was ultimately defeated on a vote of 430 to 9 on June 25, 2013. Still, the MP cannot guarantee convictions or even trials if the courts do not comply. Time and time again investigators finding evidence for misconduct recommend that dozens of officials lose their elected positions, only to see the courts fail to follow through (Taylor 2009, 2011).

The Media

If prosecutors and the courts represent formal systems of oversight and sanctioning, the media constitute the most important source of informal monitoring and reputational sanctioning. The independent media represent a non-electoral form of vertical oversight that can enable the enforcement of elite accountability between elections – a kind of "social accountability" (Peruzzotti and Smulovitz 2006). In Brazil, the media, and particularly television and radio, have tremendous influence on how voters think about politics, but the fourth estate is not as independent as theories of societal accountability require. More than 85 percent of respondents in surveys report that they get most of their political information from television (Boas 2005). Broadcasters are also trusted more than political institutions themselves (Porto 2003). This influence has, at times, allowed major networks, such as the largest, O Globo, to frame elections, especially presidential races, in favor of their preferred candidate. The most notorious case was O Globo's biased coverage in 1989 of the presidential race between Collor and Lula, which had a statistically significant effect on the vote in Collor's favor (Boas 2005). Such results only verify what has long been known about the media in Brazil: that it filters information for voters and that the bias of newscasts in particular has an effect (Lima 1993). Judging from the accusations hurled against O Globo for conservative reporting during massive national demonstrations in 2013, the Brazilian public has become much more aware of media bias and is more willing to condemn it.

A related question is whether investigative journalism performs the function of an effective watchdog. While media exposés of official corruption have become more common in the last decade, often enraging the public, this kind of journalism has done more to erode public trust without necessarily leading to the kinds of institutional changes that would strengthen the web of elite accountability (Porto 2011). The press has produced more favorable results when it has acted in tandem with official oversight and investigatory authorities. Informative media accounts are essential for translating complex investigations for the public, who have neither the time nor the inclination to study the matter in great detail (Taylor and Buranelli 2007: 75). Press reports can also affect the political class more directly. For example, media coverage of occasional CPIs, combined with street protests and the campaigns of civil society organizations, have proven useful at times for focusing public attention and leading politicians to change their behavior or even leave office (Lemos-Nelson and Zaverucha 2006). By imposing reputational costs on politicians in particular, the media may be said to have the ability to sanction wrongdoing (Porto 2011: 112; Pereira, Rennó, and Samuels 2011). This is true at the national level and in reference to the major national broadcasters, who can saturate major markets with negative information about a politician, but it is also true at the local level, where candidates seeking re-election find their chances greatly reduced if they are the focus of an investigation that is covered by local radio (Ferraz and Finan 2008).

The press as watchdog imposing reputational sanctions works well if media organizations are autonomous from politicians. However, at the local level, direct political control of the media represents an insidious threat to the media's supervisory role. Politicians have strong incentives to control local radio stations, since using the airwaves in favor of their own campaigns or those of their allies is a powerful asset that boosts vote shares for these candidates (Boas and Hidalgo 2011).[7] Maintaining political control of big commercial broadcasters is a difficult trick, since these are based in large urban areas. Their transmissions are not as local as those of the 2,168 community radio stations, which have a shorter reach but can be manipulated more easily by local political machines.[8] Boas and Hidalgo (ibid.: 870) note that up to 78 percent of all towns have no other local AM/FM broadcasters, so a monopoly over community radio is equal to local dominance of the airwaves in much of Brazil. Article 21 of the constitution established that all radio broadcasters, including the small, informal community radio stations, must apply for a federal concession license. Without authorization, they are prohibited from advertising or forming networks. This means that only those with commercial profiles or political connections are viable (Nunes 2004: 65). Empirical work has shown that the Ministry of Communication's approval rate for radio license applications is twice as great for incumbents than it is for other politicians (Boas and Hidalgo 2011). Since there are few limits on how many broadcasters a politician or political group may purchase, the concentration of ownership can resemble oligopoly in some states (Bayma 2001). As a spoil of power, this advantage reinforces the monopoly of clientele networks tied to local political machines and political bosses.[9] The extent of this effect is widespread in Brazil. Nunes (2004: 64–5) reports that, in cities such as Fortaleza, in the poor northeastern state of Ceará, only five of fifty known community radio broadcasters are non-political.[10] The best estimates indicate that somewhere between 30 and 35 percent of all community radio stations are controlled by politicians directly or indirectly through family members or associates (Lima 2008). In addition to these stations, there are an estimated 10,000 illegal or "pirate" radio broadcasters, and as many as 20 to 30 percent of these are in the hands of politicians or their confederates.[11] The phenomenon is so extensive that journalists in Brazil have given it the evocative title of "*coronelismo eletrônico*" (cf. Bayma 2001; Lima 2008).

The Police and Civil Society

Brazilian society during the democratic period has tolerated gross injustices carried out by officials who could rely on juridical inefficiency, corruption, or simple indifference to grant them a veneer of impunity. While malfeasance by politicians is a persisting problem, the most egregious forms of official misconduct and subsequent impunity in Brazil involve security forces. Some police, both on and off duty, regularly commit crimes by contracting out their services as enforcers and even assassins. These *justiceiros* and *milícias*, as they are known as individuals and groups, are used in urban centers, such as Rio de Janeiro, but also in less developed states and towns, where they are often employed to quell landless peasant and urban shantytown (*favela*) mobilization (Hinton 2009). The actions of these privatized security forces can often be brutal, but this is rivaled by the violence sometimes undertaken by special operations police known as Police Pacification Units (*Unidade de Polícia Pacificadora*) in their "pacification" efforts in urban *favelas*. Finally, an overall indicator that official security forces are largely unaccountable in Brazil is the fact that police are among the most frequently indicted public officials in corruption scandals (Arantes 2011) – though, sadly, this is probably just the tip of an iceberg.

Efforts under the Lula administration to promote less heavy-handed and non-violent forms of crime prevention such as community policing are significant, but they were hampered by the fragmentation of public security management among and within the twenty-seven states. Each state controls its own police forces, which are divided between an investigatory police known as the *polícia civil* and the uniformed military police (*polícia militar*), though they cooperate infrequently (Pereira 2008: 194–5). Accountability mechanisms for these forces are weak, given that internal affairs procedures are not independent of the police force and external oversight by the MP depends on the gathering of evidence of corruption by the *polícia civil*, who have little control over what the military police do. The autonomy of the military police in this regard is troubling, given the high number of homicides this force is accused of committing but for which it is seldom prosecuted. One notorious case involved an ex-colonel of the military police in the state of Acre who became a federal deputy. Hildebrando Pascoal was convicted in November 2006 on multiple counts of homicide after prosecutors discovered that he ran an organized crime ring in his Amazonian home state that trafficked in drugs and regularly committed murder. Pascoal was dubbed the "Deputy of the Chainsaw," after his favorite tool for executing his victims. We know about Pascoal because he was ultimately brought to justice, but such instances are rare, since prosecution for crimes committed against the poor is not a common outcome.

Perhaps the most pervasive challenge to strengthening elite accountability comes from the citizenry. Despite the advent of periodic protests and media-inspired movements against corruption, individual citizens still report in surveys that they prefer an efficacious and dishonest representative to a clean one who is less competent (Almeida 2006: 44–5). This orientation is captured by a phrase associated with a legendary two-time governor of São Paulo (1947–51 and 1963–6) Adhemar de Barros, whose most enthusiastic supporters campaigned for him on the slogan "he steals but he gets things done" (*rouba mas faz*). In their study of voters' propensities to punish corrupt politicians, Pereira, Rennó, and Samuels (2011) find that 42 percent of candidates besmirched with corruption allegations were re-elected in 2006. This is no small number. By the end of the 2000s, upwards of one-third of the members of congress were involved as defendants in criminal cases (Taylor 2011: 164). Of course, this is not to say that all Brazilian voters are accepting of corrupt politicians. The tendency to adopt the *rouba mas faz* perspective interacts with the educational level and socio-economic status of the citizen. The poor and less educated are more willing to accept corruption by an incumbent as long as their evaluations of the state of the economy are positive (Almeida 2008). Media coverage and the resonance this gives to salient cases can also change this calculus (Ferraz and Finan 2008), but the low confidence that Brazilians have for the courts suggests that even voters that care about corruption do not expect to see the guilty tried (Taylor 2009).

These are important questions that rely on more than a consideration of institutions.

Government Responsiveness

Whether it is through the media or non-governmental organizations or official oversight institutions, elite accountability cannot be vibrant if citizens are not able to detect whether their representatives are abiding by the promises they made to the voters during their campaigns. This is the first dimension of government responsiveness. The other is the capacity of voters to punish representatives who renege on their promises (Manin, Przeworski, and Stokes 1999; Peruzzotti and Smulovitz 2006; Stokes 2001; Powell 2000; Diamond and Morlino 2004).

The baseline for government responsiveness is what citizens expect from their political system in terms of solutions to problems they perceive as significant. Table 4.1 contains the responses of Brazilian citizens who participated in the Latin American Public Opinion Project surveys of 2006, 2008,

Table 4.1 Citizens' views of the most serious problems facing Brazil, 2006–2010 (percentage of respondents indicating issue as a problem)

	2006	2008	2010	Average
Violence	18.83	17.42	15.77	17.34
Unemployment	20.59	13.50	12.19	15.43
Healthcare	9.29	17.69	14.14	13.71
Corruption	13.56	10.94	8.61	11.04
Lack of personal security	6.95	4.52	4.71	5.39
Violent crime	4.44	5.27	4.14	4.62
Lack of education	2.26	4.19	3.98	3.48
Inequality	2.26	3.17	4.96	3.46
Poverty	3.43	2.57	4.06	3.35
Drug use	1.00	3.58	4.23	2.94
Politicians	2.18	1.42	1.95	1.85
Economic crises	1.09	1.22	2.44	1.58
Drug trafficking	0.67	1.01	2.52	1.40
Environment	0.42	0.61	1.67	0.90
Inflation	0.25	0.88	0.98	0.70

Source: Latin American Public Opinion Project (LAPOP) surveys, 2006 (N = 1,195), 2008 (N = 1,481), and 2010 (N = 2,461).

and 2010 and were asked to indicate the top problems facing their country. Although there is variation over time, citizens underscored economic problems, healthcare, and issues of personal security as their major concerns. Over the period of study, unemployment and corruption became less and healthcare more of an issue, while violence remained significant, with little change over time. What is obvious is that citizens are concerned most with everyday problems that are of immediate interest to them, such as the availability of affordable healthcare. Larger questions such as redressing inequality and poverty or enhancing environmental sustainability are not on their minds to the same degree.

These results resonate with other national surveys which consistently show that Brazilians judge their leaders with a clear set of personal priorities in mind (Almeida 2008). On the economy, the governments of Cardoso and the PT presidents scored highly, though Cardoso performed less well years after his Real Plan ended hyperinflation and the country suffered an energy crisis in 2001–2 and the fallout of the Argentine financial crisis. Brazilians care deeply about their personal freedom, and they define democracy in those terms, speaking often of freedom to choose leaders, to speak, and to organize. Brazilians favor an activist state in the economy and in the area of social policy, but they oppose such activism if it threatens personal liberty (Montero 2011: 129). In this regard, the developmentalist economic policies profiled in chapter 5 and the focused social policies discussed in chapter 6 match these expectations well.

Government responsiveness can be evaluated in terms both of what citizens want (policy outcomes) and their preferred means (policy process). This distinction underscores how responsive government is a double-edged sword. Too much of a focus on policy outputs veils the need to improve the procedural quality of democracy. Good governance in terms of results might even excuse leaders from strengthening institutions that enhance accountability, popular participation, and the quality of elections. Generally, voters have viewed the presidencies of Cardoso, Lula, and Dilma as responsive, but their responsiveness in some key areas, such as social and economic policy, veiled their inaction in other areas, notably the need for political reform, improvements in personal security, and more transformative policy such as land reform. For example, Lula ended his presidency as the most popular leader in Brazilian history, with high approval for his economic and social policies. More than 52 and 42 percent of respondents to the 2010 LAPOP survey gave his government the highest marks for managing the economy and combating unemployment, respectively. But 45 percent gave Lula's government the lowest marks for addressing the problem of personal insecurity, and more than half rated his government well below average for combating corruption. It is notable that almost a quarter of all respondents claimed that his government had done "absolutely nothing" to address corruption, and this view was registered well after the *mensalão* had ceased to be a subject of the daily news.

Neither Cardoso nor Lula was re-elected based on their efforts to strengthen the procedural quality of democracy – just on their policy outputs and particularly actions affecting the economy. Ironically, Lula's re-election in 2006 did not strengthen the PT as a national party or otherwise reconfigure the political system in favor of programmatic government, so it is not surprising that the popular view of Lula's responsiveness is focused more on economic and social policy and less on political reform and improvements in the web of accountability.

Yet even when referring to popular policy outputs, voters are not always pleased with the process for producing these results. These processes do not coincide with citizens' expectations of how their democracy should work. Policies such as the Real Plan, the various industrial policies of the three presidencies, and the *Bolsa Família* and its predecessors were conceived of by technocrats working out the details ensconced from popular oversight or input; they were designed in fairly closed institutions such as the *Banco Central*, the National Development Bank (BNDES), the ministries of the Economy and Social Development, and the presidential palace (*Planalto*). Given the way that processes of policy-making and political campaigning discount the input of the public, it is not surprising that, despite the view that governments have delivered in key areas, the impression Brazilian voters have of the political class and political institutions is negative. According to the annual Latinobarómetro surveys, Brazilian voters distrust politicians and parties, and the official stations they occupy in the legislature and in executive office (president, governor, and mayor), at rates exceeding 70 percent (Moisés 2011). Turning back to the 2010 LAPOP survey, almost a third of respondents declare that they have little or no confidence in Brazil's political institutions and almost a quarter have virtually no confidence in the electoral process. These sentiments were clearly confirmed during the massive national demonstrations of 2013, as the political class came in for the most harsh and bitter criticism by the protesters.

Such widespread disaffection suggests that efforts to encourage greater popular participation in government are crucial to broadening the role of the state in civil society. On the municipal level this has happened through the expansion of participatory councils. According to Brazilian law, up to 40,000 councils are possible in the country, but recent surveys have shown that there are more than 75,000.[12] At times, Brazilian governments have raised expectations about scaling up such local participatory politics. For example, Cardoso placed his wife, Ruth, a highly respected anthropologist and scholar of social movements, at the forefront of the newly created Council of the Solidarity Community to build networks of communication with civil society organizations (CSOs). Yet this process was not sustained (Friedman and Hochstetler 2002: 29–30).

Lula's presidency proved far more responsive to popular participation in government. His administration scaled up the existing Economic and Social

Development Council (*Conselho de Desenvolvimento Econômico e Social*) and attempted to forge ties to CSOs early in his first term. He created eleven and restructured nine of the sixty-four councils in existence (Faria 2009: 164–5). In some areas, such as the environment, his and Dilma's commitments to developmentalism strained relations with ecological movements (Hochstetler 2008: 43–4). But in other areas Lula accelerated the creation of national conferences and employed them as the initiators of policy ideas, especially following the *mensalão* affair, when the president was eager to ease the pressure of the scandal (Avritzer 2012). Yet even these efforts could not be taken too far. Many of the union, landless peasant, environmental, and non-governmental organizations that had once participated in the Economic and Social Development Council could no longer accept neoliberal macro-economic policies or tolerate periodic efforts by the government to work out separate deals in the congress without the input of CSOs. The corruption scandals that bedeviled the Lula administration in 2005 were the *coup de grâce* for many CSO networks, suggesting that representative democracy was flawed.[13]

Voting and the Electorate

The Brazilian electorate, at over 135 million, is the largest in Latin America, and its impressive turnout, which has averaged 80 percent since the transition to democracy, makes it one of the most participatory (see table 4.2).[14] Yet turnout is merely a rudimentary indicator of the quality of elections. Much more important is the way that citizens understand their choices, how they ponder the implications of their decisions in terms of policy outputs, and how they make sure that their representatives will be accountable for the

Table 4.2 Characteristics of the electorate, 1982–2010

Year	Size of electorate	Total no. of voters	Percentage	Total abstention	Percentage
1982	58,871,378	48,455,879	82.3	10,415,499	17.7
1986	68,576,451	65,133,227	95.0	3,443,224	5.0
1989	82,056,226	70,250,194	85.6	11,806,032	14.4
1990	83,820,556	71,940,913	85.8	11,879,643	14.2
1994	94,743,043	77,660,795	82.0	17,082,248	18.0
1998	106,053,106	83,280,755	78.5	22,766,744	21.5
2002	115,184,176	94,741,120	82.3	20,442,672	17.7
2006	125,827,049	104,779,065	83.3	21,047,984	16.7
2010	135,804,433	111,193,747	80.6	24,610,686	19.4

Source: Tribunal Superior Eleitoral.

promises they make during campaigns. Each of these dimensions is complex, involving not only the cognitive abilities of voters but the nature of the messages they receive from parties and candidates. Ideally, a democratic electorate should benefit from what Gary Cox (1988) calls the "efficient secret," a term he uses in his analysis of the emergence of parliamentary democracy in Great Britain during the nineteenth century. Voting in this context involved a choice not just of personalities and parties but of governing programs – indeed, of particular cabinets and legislative leadership organized as parties or coalitions of like-minded parties. Over time, the rules governing the legislature and elections favored party-building elites and the government programs they represented and not the interests of individual politicians (who were once appropriately known as "private member MPs"). By contrast, the Brazilian open-list PR electoral system, as chapter 3 showed, encourages voters to choose individual candidates and not parties, favoring the personal characteristics and material promises that politicians make to their constituents. Picking up on Cox's idea, Shugart and Carey (1992) label Brazil's system as one that retains an "inefficient secret." The last chapter showed that this does not necessarily mean that the legislature cannot centralize many of its functions governing policy-making, but the implications for voters are different. I argue in this section that the weakness of partisanship and the dominance of personalism undercut the link between citizens and programmatic government.

The growing availability of political surveys of Brazilians has allowed more social scientists to test propositions about how the electorate makes choices. Of course, the amount of research on these questions is far outweighed by the more voluminous attention given to macro-political institutions (Samuels 2006a), and it is from this literature that the main propositions about the Brazilian electorate have been derived. These can be grouped onto two dimensions: (1) the strength of partisanship – that is, to what extent voters identify with particular parties – and (2) the coherence of ideologies in the electorate – to what extent voters share consistent political orientations and worldviews among social groups and like-minded political candidates and parties. Both of these dimensions are central to understanding how the Brazilian voter suffers from a form of the "inefficient secret."

Partisanship

As was noted in the last chapter, Brazilian voters harbor preferences for choosing individual politicians rather than parties, so partisan orientations are weak and split-ticket voting behavior is the dominant approach taken (Carreirão and Kinzo 2004: 156; Ames, Baker, and Rennó 2008a). Since party labels impart very little useful information to the average voter, as many as 50 to 60 percent of the electorate tends to ignore candidate partisan affiliations (Venturi 2010; Carreirão and Kinzo 2004).[15] Ames, Baker, and Rennó

(2008: 5) note that, in one survey in 1999, only 36 percent of respondents could correctly identify the party of the president (Cardoso), and that was shortly after he was re-elected in 1998. Moreover, in keeping with the expectations of the "inefficient secret," the typical Brazilian voter does not make choices based on their desired government or government program. Voters are motivated by local rather than national issues, and they rely on information gathered from social networks in their neighborhoods as well as candidates' campaigns (Ames, Baker, and Rennó 2008a; Ames, García-Sánchez, and Smith 2012). They develop preferences for candidates based on casual conversations with neighbors and family members that form "information cascades" capable of forming opinions prior to an election (Baker, Ames, and Rennó 2006).

Once again, the PT is an exception, as figure 4.1 demonstrates. Supporters of the PT (*petistas*) are more likely than supporters of all of the other parties to self-identify as partisans (Samuels 2006a; Ames, Baker, and Rennó 2008a; Mainwaring, Meneguello, and Power 2000: 196–7). Samuels and Zucco (forthcoming) report that almost 60 percent of all party identifiers are *petistas*. And as the figure shows, the PT is the only party to have gained an appreciable number of party identifiers since the democratic transition (Samuels 2008). While only 8 percent of voters identified themselves as *petistas* in 1989, by 2010 more than a quarter of the electorate did (Venturi 2010: 200). The rela-

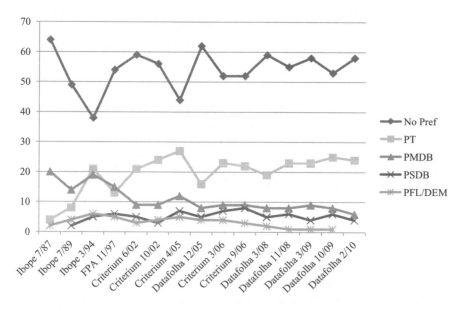

Source: Venturi (*2010*) using various national polls.

Figure 4.1 *Partisan preferences as a percentage of the electorate, 1987–2010*

tive strength of *petismo* over time is in doubt, as some scholars saw it decline even during Lula's presidency (Carreirão 2007a: 319; Ames, García-Sánchez, and Smith 2012), while others view additional dimensions to the developing partisanship of the Brazilian voter with Lula's election. In a series of controversial articles and a book, André Singer argued that Lula's re-election in 2006 showed the electoral significance of the rise of a new lower-middle class that identifies with Lula but also increasingly with the PT. This "subproletariat" came to compose a larger and growing share of the PT's support base (Singer 2009, 2010, 2012).[16] Singer bases these conclusions on aggregate electoral and survey data showing a significant increase in Lula and PT supporters between 2002 and 2010 among the lower two quintiles of the population divided by household income. A related finding is that more of Lula's supporters were to be found in the poorer states of the Northeast in 2006 than in 2002 (Hunter and Power 2007), but Singer (2010) also notes that, by 2010, this was also true for the party (see also Venturi 2010: 206–7). In the Southeast, and even in his home state of São Paulo, middle-class voters abandoned Lula, though poor neighborhoods supported him. While Singer (2009, 2010, 2012) argues that the class and regional shifts in the support base of both Lula and the PT suggest an emerging constituency with ideological consistency, empirical studies at the individual voter level demonstrate that voters' affiliations to *lulismo* and to *petismo* belie the existence of an ideological or partisan coherence that is predicated on demographic stratification (Holzhacker and Balbachevsky 2007; Samuels 2006a).[17] In their six-wave, two-city surveys of neighborhood respondents, Ames, García-Sánchez, and Smith (2012) demonstrate that there was little partisan or ideological consistency among Lula's supporters in 2006. Rather, social conversations and neighborhood networks tended to explain the continuity of his support.

That social context is a proximate determinant of voters' choices underscores the extent to which the electoral system encourages personal support for politicians, the tendency of campaigns to focus on personalities, the emphasis on material benefits to constituents, and the prevalence of vote-buying in large parts of the country (Santos and Vilarouca 2008). The proliferation of parties and the large size of electoral districts reinforce the tendency of voters to deal with the information overload by referring to the personal qualities of the candidates and to rely on the opinions of family members and neighbors to form their views (Ames, Baker, and Rennó 2008b: 109–10). The very structure of the ballot, which has not changed much even as Brazil moved from paper to electronic balloting, puts emphasis on voters having a well-formed picture of personalities. Voters are presented with lists of candidates and their electoral numbers, with few opting for a straight party-line vote. Politicians' names (which can take on bizarre profiles, such as "Wolverine" and "Bixa Muda"), campaign promises, and even colorful facts about their lives determine whether voters select them, but seldom the party to which they are affiliated.

One can blame the electoral system for the weaknesses of partisanship, but attention must also be drawn to the intermediaries that transmit partisan messages: political parties. Putting aside the question of the strength of parties in the legislature (chapter 3), there is less of a debate about the weakness of parties in the electorate (Baker, Ames, and Rennó 2006: 385). In their study of the PT, Samuels and Zucco (forthcoming) find that it is virtually alone among the Brazilian parties in forming ties to its constituents through cultivating the support of civil society organizations and thereby creating the conditions for mass partisanship. Although the debate over macro-political institutions established that even the catchall political parties could be internally disciplined in the legislature, these organizations remain largely inchoate with respect to their constituents. Their ideological incoherence undermines any attempt to forge stronger partisan identities (Mainwaring 1999; Ames 2001).

All of these institutional causes for weak partisanship are exogenous to voters themselves, so they do not shed light on the individual-level orientations which cause them to engage, by and large, in split-ticket voting and personalism. After all, the ballot structure *does allow* citizens to select party-line options, so the fact that so many refrain from doing so begs the question (Ames, Baker, and Rennó 2008a). Earlier studies of the Brazilian electorate interpreted the voters' penchant for personalism as evidence of their "irrationality" (Silveira 1998), impulsiveness, and absent-mindedness, since most could not remember their choices (Kinzo 1992). The popular belief that *o povo não sabe votar* ("the people don't know how to vote") is shared by large segments of the middle class (Souza and Lamounier 2010: ch. 6). However, empirical work has found a correspondence between voters' approval of the president and their opinions of economic reforms such as privatization, suggesting an issue orientation among voters and an ability to reflect on their choices of candidates based on these assessments (Baker 2002; Almeida 2008). More recent analysis of the available survey data shows that voters are localists; they see their choices through the lens of local issues and they support candidates that have a local following (Baker, Ames, and Rennó 2006). When straight-ticket voting occurs, it is purely by accident. As Ames, Baker, and Rennó (2008a) suggest, these are cases involving a local personality who just happens to share the same party with a well-known presidential or gubernatorial contender.

The inequalities of the education system play their own role, with many scholars, although they are split on the matter, finding a positive correlation between education levels and partisanship. There is inconsistent statistical support over time and across partisan organizations for the proposition that more educated voters are more partisan (Carreirão and Kinzo 2004: 147–50; Carreirão 2007a: 322–5; Kinzo 2005). And, once again, while the effect is stronger for the PT than for the other parties, it is not robust (Samuels 2006a), or there is a negative correlation (Samuels 2008).[18] This is partly explained by the corruption scandals of 2005, which accelerated the loss of support among more educated voters in the Southeast and South (Singer 2010). Still, it is not clear that education level affects the relative issue orientation of voters' choices (Baker 2002). Engagement in political discussion in a social context is a stronger predictor of voter choice than education alone (Ames, García-Sánchez, and Smith 2012). But, here again, the relationship is not straightforward. Souza and Lamounier (2010: ch. 6) find that middle-class Brazilians employ the benefits of their education to become involved in political discussion more frequently and, consequently, are better informed and more engaged.

Ideology

While voters do not tend to orient their political views by party, there is a debate as to whether they retain consistent ideological orientations. Some scholarship in Brazil has shown that voters' self-identified ideologies are real and long lasting. Singer (1999) compared ideological self-placement in a series of surveys between 1989 and 1994 and found ideological continuity in voters' orientations.[19] More recent studies show, however, that the depth and meaning of these ideological orientations are quite shallow. First, most studies of ideology demonstrate that voters fail to locate their attitudes correctly on a conventional left–right scale.[20] Part of the problem is that most respondents, across education groups, do not understand "left" and "right" and cannot explain consistently their meaning (Carreirão 2002a; Almeida 2001, 2006). Typically, fewer than 20 percent can correctly place the major parties on the conventional left–right gamut (Carreirão 2007a: 316). More voters that self-identify as "right wing" report a preference for the leftist PT than one would expect (ibid.: 318). Second, even when ideological orientations are properly understood, they are far from being the deep-seated dispositions that govern voter choice in many advanced capitalist countries, especially in Europe. For example, comparisons of self-identity responses on multiple waves of the Brazilian National Election Study (*Estudo Eleitoral Brasileiro*) between 2002 and 2010 show volatile increases and declines in the percentage of respondents claiming an ideological identity, with consequent inconsistency in such orientations predicting voting behavior (Carreirão 2007a). When data about self-identity in Brazil is tested using more rigorous techniques that control for differences in education, social class, and religion, the importance of self-identified ideology as a predictor of voter choice disappears altogether (Carreirão 2002b, 2007b; Holzhacker and Balbachevsky 2007). This is in contrast to the far more consistent patterns seen in more ideologically cohesive polities. The difference is partly the result of class structures and the role of race, religion, and age, which make up more deep-rooted societal cleavages that have sustained ideologies in advanced capitalist countries since World War II (Lipset and Rokkan 1967). By contrast, such social cleavages have not created either clear or lasting partisanship in Brazil (Mainwaring and Scully 1995). The overall sense from the current scholarship, notwithstanding Singer's thesis, is that ideological stability is a weak and inconsistent predictor of voter behavior.

One salient indicator for the weakness of ideology (and partisanship) in the electorate is a high level of volatility over time (Mainwaring 1998). This can be captured by the Pedersen index, which measures the net change in the distribution of party vote shares between electoral cycles. The index ranges from 0, signifying no change in vote shares, to 100, which indicates that all votes migrated across parties. Table 4.3 pools Pedersen values for presidential and legislative elections across sixteen Latin American countries, listing them from the largest average volatility scores to the smallest. Brazil figures among the first six countries by combined average but among the first three by presidential elections. This profile is consistent with the endemic use of split-ticket voting (Baker, Ames, and Rennó 2006; Silveira 1998), with fluid cleavage structures, and electoral rules that encourage personal voting (Roberts and Wibbels 1999).

Table 4.3 Average electoral volatility in Latin America, 1978–2000

Country	Volatility in presidential elections	Volatility in legislative elections	Combined average volatility
Nicaragua	51.3	47.7	49.5
Peru	39.9	49.6	44.8
Panama	26.7	46.6	36.7
Ecuador	37.7	29.2	33.5
Venezuela	37.8	28.9	33.4
Brazil	**38.4**	**23.0**	**30.7**
Bolivia	27.3	27.6	27.5
Paraguay	24.7	16.1	20.4
Argentina	23.0	14.1	18.6
Dominican Republic	18.5	18.1	18.3
Mexico	20.0	15.7	17.9
Chile	21.8	10.0	15.9
Colombia	13.2	10.8	12.0
Uruguay	11.5	11.2	11.4
Costa Rica	8.7	11.9	10.3
Honduras	6.2	7.9	7.1

Source: Roberts (n.d.).

Given the volatility of the electorate and the mixed evidence for ideology as a predictor of the vote, we have few solid insights into how political orientations work in Brazil. More frustrating is that what empirical studies have shown is unsurprising. The most concrete results from the balance of studies show that self-described "leftists" tend to support Lula and are more educated, but that no issue area necessarily predicts their orientation (Ames and Smith 2010; Samuels 2006a). Poorer voters tend to self-place as "on the right" or "centrist" (Carreirão 2002a: 198). Voters that evince a low level of ideological self-identification (or who do not respond to the question) are more likely to vote for the right.

One complication in the available studies is that some citizens respond while others do not. Carreirão (2002a) was one of the first Brazilian scholars to find varying response rates in ideological self-placement surveys across education groups, with the less educated many times less likely to self-place. The non-response tendency is more of a concern in panel surveys that, by their nature, compare responses over time from the same respondents. It is primarily in these kinds of studies, which are rare in Brazil, that the determinants of non-response can be assessed. Notably, Ames and Smith (2010: 21–2) have conducted the most extensive study to date on these dynamics, and they show that education level, political knowledge, and the relative polarization of political candidates' own placement on the ideological spectrum determine whether voters self-place their identity at all.[21] Most interesting, Ames and Smith's results suggest that gender plays a role, as women are less likely than men to self-place. These are foundational questions which suggest that the standard survey does not pick up all of the complexity of Brazilian voting behavior and political orientation. But, as Ames and Smith suggest, there are consistent patterns that further study can clarify.

Better understanding of political ideologies among voters would help strengthen systems of representation and elite accountability. The congruence of ideological preferences between voters and their representatives is one of the ties that bind the electorate to the politicians for whom they vote. In order to mobilize their constituents, politicians and their parties must transform their programs into symbols and ideas that speak to citizens' interests. Voters are able to differentiate more capably among political actors based on the symbolic labels that ideologies represent. And representation and accountability are enhanced when voters can identify with the worldviews of their partisan choices (Rosas 2005). But there is little evidence that this has happened in Brazil. Comparing responses among 1,401 voters in a six-wave, two-city study between 2002 and 2006, Ames and Smith (2010) demonstrate that citizens self-place in a bimodal pattern, opting for either left or right, preferring center left and center right. By contrast, Power and Zucco (2009) show that political elites in the congress tend to avoid self-placement on the right and claim centrist or leftist positions more consistently.[22] Although I have argued that a less ideologically polarized elite has enhanced governability, the claim here is not that a more polarized electorate would enhance the quality of democracy. Rather, a greater correspondence of ideologies between voters and parties would make the electorate's choices more identifiable, enhancing the prospects for the kinds of programmatic government invoked by Cox's (1988) "efficient secret."

Weak ideological ties are due to many of the same reasons as to why partisanship is anemic. First, the number of parties coupled with low elite polarization complicates the voters' task to identify clear ideological bedfellows to support (Lucas and Samuels 2010). Second, as the last chapter showed, ideological divisions within the political class are becoming less well defined over time. Ideological convergence within the political class undermines the voters' sense of distinctions among parties. Since ideological frames take time to form, this trend has slowed and made more inchoate the coordination of elite and voter ideologies. Third, elite and party ideologies have been a moving target over the last twenty years. The moderation of the PT is a case in point. Both the degree and the speed with which this transition occurred seemed to some PT voters, especially those on the far left, a stunning betrayal of principles. Not surprisingly, many traditional supporters and organization allies turned away from the party soon after Lula's government initiated its economic and social agenda (Hunter 2010). Yet, as Samuels (2008) has shown in his study of *petismo* between 2002 and 2007, PT partisans were also on the move. More extreme leftists, disenchanted with the corruption scandals of 2005, abandoned the party to support the far-left opposition. The average remaining *petista*, as well as most new affiliates, represented a more moderate view. The effect was a washing out of ideological self-placement as a salient predictor of support for the party.

Given that the Brazilian electorate cannot rely on partisan and ideological cues to identify their representatives, how does the average voter make a decision? The available studies seem to offer what amounts to an emerging meta-frame for understanding the Brazilian voter, and it is simply that social networks tend to shape how citizens make their political choices. Given weak partisan and ideological orientations, they tend to gather information about candidates from friends and relatives in their immediate social context and then employ these bits of data as cognitive shortcuts to make their decisions (Ames, García-Sánchez, and Smith 2012; Baker, Ames, and Rennó 2006). At the presidential level, much evidence suggests that conversations tend to revolve around evaluations of the last government's handling of the economy (Carreirão 2002a; Rennó 2007). These findings underscore the importance of location – where voters live and how the social *milieu* in which they are imbedded can shape their perspectives on politics.

The inability of voters to relate to partisan programs or to think in consistent ideological terms in ways that correspond to the orientation of political elites belies the idea that Brazilian parties can organize political life. What we know about mass partisanship and ideology contrasts sharply with the views of coalitional presidential and other scholars about the relative strength of parties (Samuels 2006a: 20). Moreover, the weakness of the quality of the vote in the face of substantial challenges to elite accountability and government responsiveness puts a lot of pressure on the fourth dimension of democratic quality: popular participation.

Popular Participation

The value of popular participation was imbedded in the 1988 Constitution not only in terms of representative democracy through elections but also in terms of direct democracy through referenda, plebiscites, popular initiatives and councils (Cavalcanti 2006). By any measure, Brazilian civil society is vibrant and takes advantage of these and many other opportunities to mobilize around issues of importance. The transition to democracy in 1985 brought a wide range of political activism to the fore. Urban social, women's, and landless peasant movements joined Afro-Brazilian, workers', environmental, and consumer movements (Alvarez 1993; Keck 1992; Hochstetler 2000; Hanchard 1996; Avritzer 1995). Although their focus was particular to their issue agenda, as a whole these movements contributed to what Evelina Dagnino (1998) has called the master frame of expanding citizenship (*cidadania*) through social mobilization around the "right to have rights." This reflected awareness on the part of the leaders of civil society organization (CSOs) and non-governmental organizations (NGOs) that they should make the political and social rights protected by the 1988 Constitution the focus of their claims. A parallel development was the focus on what Leonardo Avritzer (2002) has called "participatory publics" – namely, the deliberative processes among CSO networks to guarantee transparency and accountability in policy-making (Wampler 2012: 346). On an everyday basis, CSOs interact with official institutions such as the federal and state MPs, as well as the media and wider networks of NGOs, to form participatory publics (Cavalcanti 2006; Wampler and Avritzer 2004). Together these participatory forces provide great potential for societal accountability and for assuring that public policy responds to the needs of the poor (Peruzzotti and Smulovitz 2006; Donaghy 2011).

The first challenge social mobilization faced following the transition was sustainability. After the heightened awareness of the first several years following the transition had passed, movement activism dwindled, as groups broke off to form their own NGOs and other issue-focused CSOs, though the splintering created new cross-cutting networks that remained vibrant during the 1990s (Alvarez 1993; Hochstetler 2000). The establishment of popular councils (*conselhos populares*) in major municipalities such as Porto Alegre and Belo Horizonte in the early 1990s held the promise of providing one means of institutionalizing participation by opening up government decision-making, particularly on the budget, to popular oversight.[23] Almost a quarter of

Brazil's population lives in cities that have participatory budgeting (*orçamento participativo*) (Wampler and Avritzer 2005; Avritzer 2009). In participatory budgeting, ordinary citizens take part in government-sponsored meetings to set the priorities for the next municipal budget cycle, specify public policies they prefer, and elect delegates to advocate for these in further negotiations and committees involving CSOs, government officials, and other delegates. Where it has been practiced, this process has improved notably the transparency of public accounts, and it has encouraged the creation of horizontal ties among CSOs, enabling alliances and weakening clientele networks (Wampler and Avritzer 2004, 2005; Wampler 2012; Abers 1998; Avritzer 2009). Nevertheless, the effects for encouraging and sustaining participation are mixed. Some studies showed that the participatory budgeting experience in Porto Alegre increased CSO membership (e.g., Abers 2000: 166; Santos 1998), but other studies of the same case (cf. Baiocchi 2005) and elsewhere in Brazil showed no consistent increases in individual membership, activism, or autonomous self-organization (Nylen 2002, 2003; Baiocchi, Heller, and Silva 2008). In his studies of participatory budgeting in Belo Horizonte, Nylen (2002) finds that the process empowers citizens who are already engaged in movement politics; it broadens associational life and undercuts clientelism, but it does not mobilize the unorganized (Wampler 2007b; Baiocchi, Heller, and Silva 2008). The Porto Alegre case also contains several *sui generis* characteristics, such as less entrenched and weaker forms of clientelism that made implanting participatory budgeting and subsequently enhancing popular participation much easier (Goldfrank 2007: 161). These and other studies suggest that the primary payoff for participation comes in the form of more extensive organized group behavior, especially by elected delegates, as participatory budgeting reinforces and extends existing CSO networks (Wampler 2007b, 2012; Baiocchi 2005; Avritzer 2002, 2009).

As with voting, the degree and quality of participation diverge in Brazil. Regardless of the device used, popular participation can be insufficient. For example, during the 1980s, a sustained grassroots effort by public healthcare officials to create a universal right to health bore fruit when it was enacted in the 1988 Constitution. The movement's members, known as the *sanitaristas*, called for a nationalization of all healthcare to protect this right, but they were no match for medical business interests and conservative politicians, who opposed what they saw as an attack on the private sector (Hunter and Sugiyama 2009: 42–3). The result was the continuation of uneven quality and access in healthcare (Weyland 1996), though the movement eventually achieved notable gains under the Health Ministry of José Serra (1998–2002). Local health councils today form the most widespread example of participatory advising to policy-making in Brazil (Avritzer 2009: ch. 6), though much is still left to be done in this area (see chapter 6). In other areas of policy, inclusion in decision-making proved more important than activism. In housing, for example, the relative strength of local CSOs mattered less than the mere participation of representatives of civil society groups on housing policy councils (Donaghy 2011). Since 2003, more and more local participatory frameworks have been scaled up to the national level in the form of policy conferences. Although such conferences were used as early as Vargas's government, Lula expanded their use in areas such as healthcare, human rights, education, food, and public security, affecting subsequent policy-making (Avritzer 2012). These examples underscore the fact that participatory politics have often achieved change and have been integral to the web of accountability in Brazil. But generating sustainable, positive outcomes depends on the existence of civil and political societies that interact in a way consistent with participatory policy-making (Avritzer 2009). Participation is insufficient without help from policy-makers and institutions.

Participation can also be engineered or captured by political elites for their own purposes. The aforementioned story of the politicization of community radio is a good example. More pervasive still is the frequent use of material rewards to channel popular will, thereby undercutting the autonomy and protagonism of civil society. Brazil has seen many social movements and nongovernmental organizations that have succeeded in broadening participation, but the sustainability of these experiences has been variable. Who participates is another relevant dimension. Even when social movements have retained the ability to mobilize women and ethnic minorities, formal institutions have failed to respond with a similar broadening of representation. This problem reflects a core contradiction in Brazilian political institutions. On the one hand, the system provides many opportunities for individuals and groups to organize and exert voice, but the costs of sustaining participation are too high for those with little means or few opportunities (e.g., women and blacks). In the electoral arena, for example, large districts, proportional representation, open-list ballots, low thresholds, and the proliferation of small parties improve the chances for women to gain seats in the legislature. But these same conditions put a premium on individual candidates raising enough money and garnering the support of subnational political interests (Htun and Jones 2002).

Clientelism represents the most fundamental threat to the development of an autonomous base for self-mobilization. *Troca de favores* narrows the polity to patrons and clients, thereby undercutting autonomous organizations (Abers 2000). Participatory budgeting has fought this tendency by enabling citizens of modest means to organize autonomously from politicians and parties (Goldfrank 2007). Empirical studies of participatory budgeting show that citizens who are involved feel they can affect the allocation of public resources without the intervention of politicians (Wampler and Avritzer 2004). They also report a greater motivation to learn and advocate more on behalf of issues that move beyond the local to include broader questions of public policy (Abers 1998; Baiocchi 2005). More consistent have been findings that show that participatory budgeting delegates have engaged in collective action to break down the private deals with government officials that used to dominate municipal policy-making in many parts of Brazil (Wampler 2007b, 2012; Baiocchi, Heller, and Silva 2008). Nevertheless, clientelism can function beyond the point at which policy choices are decided. Popularly approved funds are not always spent as intended on policies intended to benefit the poor. Many of the same surveys of participatory budgeting that show some effect in its favor also report that funds are often directed to bolster the electoral strength of incumbent parties or captured for political use by elites once citizens taking part approve of budget priorities (Goldfrank and Schneider 2006; Wampler 2007a, 2008).

Empirical work on CSOs and how their networks have expanded in the last decade of the democratic period suggests that CSO leaders value coordination with other CSOs as a primary strategy for securing public policy resources both within and outside of participatory frameworks such as participatory budgeting. These lessons are reinforced by prominent examples of how CSOs cannot rely too heavily on even sympathetic public leaders. The best case was presented shortly after Lula became president, an event that in itself galvanized social movements, especially on the left. Yet, as was pointed out above, Lula's embrace of his predecessor's economic reforms struck the CSOs backing him and the PT as a betrayal of principles (Hunter 2010). Other CSOs saw Lula's commitment to social reform through programs such as *Bolsa Família* as insufficient for generating income distribution and land reform demanded by unions affiliated to the *Central Única dos Trabalhadores* (Unified Workers' Central) and the landless peasant movement (*Movimento dos Trabalhadores Rurais Sem-Terra*), respectively. Environmental CSOs that called for prohibitions on genetically modified organisms in agriculture were largely excluded from the composition of farm legislation (Hochstetler 2008: 48).

In a country with many inequalities, it is no surprise that participation is another dimension in which Brazil's inequalities are played out. The poor are especially vulnerable to the material incentives that bind clients to patrons and allow local political bosses to generate support for politicians involved in the larger *troca de favores* fueling the exchange of patronage in the political system (Bezerra 1999). These ties repress autonomous participation, and, since they reflect social inequalities in Brazil, it is not surprising that women, ethnic minorities, and the poor are less likely than men, whites, and the middle and upper classes to participate in organizations such as political parties or to enter electoral contests as candidates themselves. One obvious indicator of this disparity is that more than 80 percent of the members of the political class hold advanced university degrees, a sure sign of how a combination of access and privilege has defined who enters the political class (Araújo and Alves 2007).

Although the 1988 Constitution declared that men and women are equal in Brazilian society, access to power has been unequal in the democratic period. Even though half of the electorate is composed of women, and

Brazilian law after 1997 requires that up to 30 percent of candidates for office must be female, women hold only 8.9 percent of the seats in the congress, the lowest percentage in the region save for Panama. Quotas fail due to lack of enforcement and frequent backsliding by party leaders, thus watering down the effect of the regulations (Araújo and Alves 2007: 535–6). More progressive legislation depends on the emergence of leftist parties and the weakening of conservative political forces such as the Catholic Church, which has often intervened in matters involving reproductive rights and abortion (Htun and Power 2006).

Until recent affirmative action initiatives in the federal universities, the historical exclusion of Afro-Brazilians from higher education was a major and unattended cause of the paucity of political representatives of black or mixed race (Johnson 2008). It is notable that black and mulatto Brazilians outnumber whites but are underrepresented in the ranks of the political class. Lula appointed four Afro-Brazilians to his cabinet and one to the STF, who became the chief justice, but blacks and mulattos held fewer than 10 percent of seats in congress (Mitchell 2009). Popular conceptions of race are at the core of the explanations for this. Non-whites are typically stereotyped as inept and irrational, not only by whites but by light-skinned blacks and mulattos (Sheriff 2001). At least one major survey undertaken in Rio de Janeiro about racial attitudes confirms that voters are less likely to support Afro-Brazilian political candidates due to perceived lack of education and social class status (Bailey 2009). Voters also fault prejudice as a strong impediment to non-whites seeking political power. And this is a catch-22 because, in order to gain power, Afro-Brazilian leaders believe that they must eschew talk of race and embrace class-based and community-specific issues (ibid.: 91). Addressing racial prejudice is thereby left to white Brazilian leaders.

Given all of the challenges CSOs face with governments of different orientations that have proven unresponsive to calls for greater popular participation, that have preferred to co-opt or buy support, and that have exposed the limitations of once encouraging experiments such as the *orçamento participativo*, it is not surprising that these groups have increasingly turned away from seeking partnerships with national and subnational governments. Kathryn Hochstetler (2008) notes that a broad array of CSOs have learned a bitter lesson after two decades that the political class will not share power and negotiate with civil society or address the continuing inequities in representation that exist by engaging in transformative political or socio-economic reform.

If the quality of Brazilian democracy depends on the integration of institutional changes in favor of stronger forms of elite accountability, government responsiveness, improved electoral decision-making, and popular participation, then this chapter provides mixed support that the country has engineered a sufficient turnaround. To be sure, Brazil's "web of accountability" is more developed today than it was even ten years ago, and the pace of change provides a basis to be optimistic. Especially notable is the institutional development of investigatory and prosecutorial powers as reflected in the MP, the *Controladoria Geral da União*, and federal and state auditors (Power and Taylor 2011b). The popular councils have proven to be essential sources of societal accountability in local government. But too many essential pieces of the web are weak: the investigatory functions of CPIs are overly politicized, monitoring by the media and CSOs can be compromised by self-interest, and the courts provide poor enforcement. All too often, the impressive institutional apparatus of accountability makes matters *acabar em pizza*. Other pillars of a high-quality democracy, such as the capacity of the electorate to select programmatic governments and the inconsistent responsiveness of government, are too underdone to support the claim that Brazil is prepared to engineer an acute upgrade to its democracy.

As with other dimensions of Brazil's turnaround in recent years, much work remains to be done. The institutions that compose the "web of accountability" need to be strengthened and more effectively coordinated so that the three key functions of monitoring, investigation, and sanctioning are done routinely and do not depend on the right configuration of political forces in the legislature or the advent of embarrassing scandals that shock the system into reform. Regarding the electorate, the balance of findings demonstrate that the partisan and ideological identity of the average voter is ill-defined, though, as with the evolution of macro-political institutions, scholars now know more about how these orientations take shape. The key seems to be education and the equality of access to it, factors that are closely associated in Brazil and elsewhere with more sophisticated political citizenship. In that regard, the economic and social changes engineered in recent years through the advent of good policy (some rather innovative) hold out some hope of shifting the foundations of the political system so that they generate a higher quality democracy in the future. These economic and social policies are, respectively, the focus of the next two chapters.

CHAPTER FIVE

The Renewed Developmental State

Brazil has never adopted neoclassical economic thinking systematically. Arguably, the country never had a proper "neoliberal era," even as presidents Sarney, Collor, and Cardoso liberalized trade, privatized major sectors, and employed fiscal reforms to contain the growth of public debt. Nor did Brazil ever have an autarkic economy. As a country imbedded in what Cardoso and Faletto (1979) once called the "semi-periphery" of international capitalism, it had choices that were not available to smaller and more dependent economies in Latin America. From 1940 until 1980, Brazil responded to the challenges and opportunities of global economic change by creating an enduring developmentalist model in which the state coordinated ties through official finance and regulations on foreign investment and domestic industry to produce import substitution and a scaling up of the industrial sector (Evans 1979). The result was the largest industrialized economy in Latin America. According to the standard narrative about Latin America during the 1980s, the debt crisis and the crisis of import-substitution industrialization (ISI) ended this state-centered development model (Cavarozzi 1992; Frieden 1991) and replaced it with a neoliberal policy paradigm known as the "Washington Consensus," which called for sweeping macro-economic stabilization and structural reforms (Bresser-Pereira 2006; Williamson 1990). Yet Brazil remained quite different from other Latin American countries that adopted neoliberal reforms more completely. Even the first, more liberalizing governments, despite Collor's rhetoric, never dismantled the main institutions of the developmental state, and developmentalist thinking continued in major institutions of the economic bureaucracy (Sikkink 1991). Instead, these institutions were repurposed to promote the competitiveness of many of the same firms and sectors that had been favored by ISI.

This chapter will argue that Brazil has followed the path of several developing country economies, such as China, India, Vietnam, Taiwan, and South Korea, in that it has continued with a heterodox, pragmatic policy mixture that has deviated in important ways from the Washington Consensus (Rodrik 2007; Boschi 2011; Diniz 2011). Even as trade policy was liberalized and the first three democratic governments engaged in significant privatization of some state industries, Brazilian policy-makers continued to employ *statist* institutions, policy mechanisms, and policy goals. Yet this was not simply a continuation of statism as it had been practiced since the 1950s. The developmentalist state after 1985 phased out most import-substituting policy mechanisms and made a transition to a more market-oriented statism. The policy repertoire moved well beyond the export promotion and foreign investment attraction devices that were practiced in other Latin American economies such as Chile, Colombia, and Mexico (cf. Kurtz and Brooks 2008). Brazilian developmental policies redefined over the course of the first decade of democracy the purposes of many of the institutions and actors – state banks, public firms, and technology institutes – that played a central role in the import-substitution industrialization period. Yet the same sectors and firms that were the targets of ISI-oriented policies remained the champions of the new developmentalism during the democratic period. In short, market-based reforms did not dilute statism. Rather, statist priorities reshaped market-oriented policies.

In trying to place the Brazilian experience in the larger context of the development of other rising emerging markets such as China, India, South Africa, and Russia, scholars after 2000 began to focus on the role of economic policy beyond the Washington Consensus. Increasingly, more attention was turned to the strategic role of the state, and, with that, the term "new developmentalism," or "neodevelopmentalism,"[1] became more commonly used to describe Brazil and the other BRICSA countries[2] (cf. Khan 2007; Khan and Christiansen 2011). These ideas resonated strongly in Brazil, where the Washington Consensus never became the rallying point of a sustained neoliberal political project as it was in Mexico and Argentina under democratic rule and Chile under authoritarianism. Brazil was not just a latecomer to neoliberalism, it was a limited practitioner (Boschi and Gaitán 2012: 54).

The argument in this chapter is not that Brazil adopted a new model called "neodevelopmentalism" but that it continued statism. What was fundamentally new was the transition from inward-oriented ISI to an outward-oriented and competitiveness-centered market approach. This narrative runs counter to the view that the developmentalist state weakened and succumbed to the Washington Consensus or simply eroded its capacity to generate growth. As with the study of political institutions, there is a pessimistic view of the Brazilian state's ability to recapture the developmentalist capacity it enjoyed between 1940 and 1980. Kurt Weyland (1996, 1998, 2000) has been most consistent in articulating this alternative view. He emphasizes the fragmentation and lack of internal coordination of state agencies as well as their tendency to be captured by business and clientele networks. Particularly threatening to developmental capacity was the fiscal crisis of the state as a result of burgeoning public debt, receding tax receipts, and the continuation of unsustainable levels of profligate spending by states and municipalities during the 1990s.

Such pessimistic views of Brazilian state capacity have a basis in observations of development institutions during the 1980s and most of the 1990s, but, as the analysis below will show, the foundation for a more ambitious structural policy was being laid during these years. This was true not just because of the continuation of major developmentalist organizations such as the National Development Bank (BNDES) and its repurposing in the context of a more market-oriented economic policy, but because it was based on the reversal during the 1990s of many of the elements of fiscal crisis that pessimists opined would end Brazilian developmentalism once and for all (see chapter 2). The capacity of the state to promote development increased during the 2000s, most noticeably as the PT presidencies expanded the activities of developmentalist institutions in the economy. Thus the study of the renewed developmental state verifies the usefulness of taking a holistic and multidimensional view of the Brazilian state. Clientelism remains a continuing limitation on its efficiency, but it has not debilitated it as pessimistic approaches argue.

The persistence of what Veiga (2009) calls the "national-developmentalist paradigm" is based on official preferences for enhancing the competitiveness and performance of national firms based in the domestic economy. These incentives trump both practical and ideological arguments for designing policies meant to make the overall economy internationally competitive and more efficient. The importance of these preferences is confirmed by several facts in the Brazilian experience. First, it is not only that the public banks, particularly the BNDES, survived the privatization wave in Latin America during the late 1980s and the 1990s, but that the latter actually ran Brazil's privatization program. The retention and growth of the public banking sector gave the country a comparative advantage in maintaining a national-developmentalist paradigm in comparison to other Latin American economies (Stallings and Studart 2006). Second, the industrial sectors most favored by import-substituting policies – infrastructure, automobiles, rubber, plastics, electronics, and capital goods – remained favored by trade and industrial policies before, during, and after the period of trade liberalization that was most acute between 1987 and 1994. These sectors were already integrated into global capital, as they retained the largest share of foreign direct investment (FDI) inflows before the liberalization of the early 1990s, and they would remain the chief recipients of this investment after 1994, when the most intense period of trade liberalization ended. The sequencing of their adjustment in the post-ISI era reflects the priority of policy. These firms did not liberalize to adjust; they reconverted as the economy was liberalized and they internationalized once their reconversion in the domestic economy was consolidated.

The renewed developmentalist state is reactive in that it is based on the recognition that Washington Consensus reforms are insufficient to promote competitiveness and growth (Bresser-Pereira 2005, 2006; Bresser-Pereira and Nakano 2002). This is a homegrown, pragmatic set of responses by policymakers over time to the opportunities and constraints governing economic development in an age of globalization (Santana 2012). It also reflected in Brazil a reaction by prominent economists, many of whom had experience during the Cardoso administration, to revive the premises of their own structuralist and Keynesian training following the debt crisis.[3] The result was a line of thinking that deviated from the more ardent embrace of free-market ideology under the Mexican presidents of the 1980s and 1990s (Centeno 1994), the Carlos Menem presidency in Argentina during the 1990s (Teichman 2001), and the long-held dominance of neoliberal thinking among economic policy-makers in Chile (Silva 2008).

Brazilian statism in the neoliberal era differs from the "simulated market" approach that grafts only some reactive statist mechanisms, most prominently export promotion, onto a generally market-oriented policy.[4] It is unlike what Kurtz and Brooks (2008) call "embedded neoliberalism" – namely, a mixture of supply-side interventions such as export support, public employment, and macro-economic priorities of capital and trade account openness. Brazil is pursuing a far less open form of liberalism and a far more determinate form of statism in this hybrid formula. Whereas "embedded neoliberalism" describes a "general strategy of state-mediated international economic integration," the Brazilian state is fostering more than "mediation" and with a focus not exclusively on external competitiveness. Even in the latest phase of growth, exports represent on average only 14 percent of Brazil's GDP, with commodity exports composing half of these (Santana 2012: 220).

A more useful distinction is to be found in Atul Kohli's (2006a, 2006b) notion of "pro-business" policies. Using his sustained study of India as a basis, he finds that pro-business strategies develop from real-world experiences in South Asia and depend on "variations in how states are organized and in the institutionalized relationship of the state to the private sector" (2006a: 1253). Pro-business strategies manage demand and supply constraints for sectors and/or firms. The policy repertoire is broad, employing a variety of tools that are directed as part of an intentional choice by governments to favor some firms and sectors over others (Rodrik 2007: 119; Kohli 2006a).

Whereas neoliberalism takes for granted the efficiency gains accrued from an open trade regime, Brazilian developmentalism recognizes the need to improve productivity through the use of technology in order to compete more effectively with imports and find external markets in sectors that are export-oriented. While much attention has focused on Brazil's export of commodities, less has been placed on the growth of import volumes in medium- to high-technology sectors that have invested in capital goods to increase productivity (Santana 2012: 221–2).

To the extent that there was a neoliberal experience in Brazil, developmentalism continued within its parameters, operating in a manner that was sensitive to the sustainability of macro-economic stability (Boschi and Gaitán 2012). On the one hand, this means eschewing closed-market policies such as

ISI and, on the other, maintaining a commitment to price stability and inflation control. This reflects not an ideological commitment to orthodoxy but
a strategic concern with enabling the state to have sufficient fiscal capacity
to engage in industrial policy (Bresser-Pereira 2006).

Much of the recent scholarship on Brazilian neodevelopmentalism claims
that the model relies not only on industrial and macro-economic policies that
promote and sustain growth but also on social policies that increase income
equality and reduce poverty (cf. Boschi 2011; Boschi and Gaitán 2012: 50). In
this regard, Brazilian scholarship is both too focused on its own experience
and not focused enough. For scholars of developmentalism who draw from
comparative studies, reducing poverty and inequality is better understood as
an *outcome* of statist policies. This scholarship argues, in my view persuasively,
for a focus on the *process* of transforming productive structures, as in increasing productivity and sectoral or firm-level competitiveness (Chang 2011).
Brazilian neodevelopmentalist scholarship also tends to overclaim the role
of social policy. As this chapter and the next one will show, welfare policies
have at times had a demand-side effect but have not been well integrated into
the policy framework as a strategic component of the renewed developmentalist state. One of the striking aspects of industrial policy in Brazil after 1987
is the *absence* of a transformative labor market and of social welfare policies
linked intentionally to official economic strategies (Bianchi and Braga 2005).
This by itself is a contrast to the broad-based approach applied during the
Vargas, Kubitschek, and bureaucratic-authoritarian periods. Where social
policy reform and innovative programming begins to play a role in national
politics during the Cardoso and, especially, the Lula and Dilma administrations, its focus is on poverty alleviation and not the labor market. No fundamental reforms of Vargas-era labor market laws were passed during the 1990s
and 2000s, despite the advent of the first labor-backed presidency with Lula
in 2003 (Hall 2009).[5]

The apparent decoupling of industrial and labor market policy and industrial policy-making and labor-backed politics was a function of a more purely
statist institutional logic in the Brazilian case. Industrial policy was already
focused at the time of the transition to democracy on particular firms that
faced few remaining human capital or collective bargaining challenges.
Some of these firms sloughed off the problems of collective bargaining with
unions during the privatization process by offering workers shares and
buyouts that undermined organized labor. Firms that had not undergone
privatization engaged in productive restructuring and even internationalization while being shielded by Vargas-era corporatist labor codes. Consequently,
the labor confederations and sectoral unions would not play a role as a movement advocating for linking social welfare and labor market policy to industrial policy. Union pension funds would even have a major hand in financing
the very industrial policies that elided labor market reforms. Statism proceeded by embracing fiscal discipline and macro-economic stability while

targeting support to strategic sectors and in alliance with pension funds managed largely by union bureaucracies and domestic and transnational capital.

This chapter argues that Brazilian developmentalism has evolved a distinctly pro-business approach that is not just an ad hoc reaction to the limitations of neoliberal reform or the challenges of globalization, but a continuing, pragmatic strategy to enable producers to compete internationally and at home. Under the PT presidencies especially, the model has achieved its most consolidated form by producing marked improvements in private investment, the adoption of new technologies, and contributions to aggregate growth (Santana 2012). I note in the next section in greater detail the ways in which the renewed developmentalist state differs from the ISI-focused statism of the pre-1985 period. The subsequent section focuses on the performance of the system under the Lula and Dilma presidencies.

The Differences between ISI-Focused Developmentalism and Post-1985 Developmentalism

From the first stages of import-substitution industrialization during Getúlio Vargas's *Estado Nôvo* (1937–45), the focus of industrial policy was on the creation and expansion of industries, with an early emphasis on heavy industrial sectors such as steel, chemicals, utilities, and resource-based manufactures emanating from extraction. After 1950, a proliferation of policies and governing institutions coincided with a long period of industrial expansion driven by a deepening of ISI (Suzigan 1978; Moreira 1994). The average annual growth rate of the economy between 1951 and 1981 stood at 6.6 percent, much higher than the 4.6 percent of global growth and approximating the higher levels of Japan and other East Asian developmental states such as Taiwan and South Korea (Maddison 2003). Several of the core agents that I discuss below were created during the ISI period: BNDES (1952), Petrobras (1953), Finep (1967), and Embrapa (1972), among others. At the same time, the state encouraged foreign direct investment in sectors with acute needs for capital and technology, though eventually every industrial sector hosted FDI (Evans 1979; Baer 2008).

It should be underscored here that no central institution or driving logic "organized" Brazilian industrial policy during the ISI period. Rather, as Wilson Suzigan (1978) observes, developmentalist policies were casuistic and decentralized, responding to sectoral needs in practice while in theory being driven by the directive to promote overall economic growth. This logic was contradicted by the advent of the Latin American debt crisis in 1982 and the acute recession and capital flight that the region suffered subsequently. Industry as a percentage of GDP fell from 33.7 percent in 1980 to 29.1 percent in 1993 and did not increase notably from that point (Pinheiro, Giambiagi, and Gostkorzewicz 1999: 14). Given that the previous structure governing industrial policy was never as centralized as it was in a number of the developmentalist states of East Asia, what Brazilian planners endured during the 1980s was less a crisis of a particular agency or set of agencies than a challenge to redirect goals for each sector. These priorities received more attention than the policy instruments used during the ISI period (see Grupo Interministerial 1986). In this way, the crisis of ISI did not become a crisis of industrial policy, as the institutions and agencies that were once responsible for this economic policy continued, albeit with fewer resources (Erber and Vermulm 1993: 40; Rua and Aguiar 1995).

In the subsections that follow, I detail several of the core dimensions in which the industrial policies of the developmentalist period after 1985 differed from the erstwhile ISI-focused developmentalist model and note an evident periodization to the statist experience that emerges on each of these dimensions. First, it is clear that, while the Sarney and Collor administrations were the most open to liberalization and structural adjustment, they kept the main agents and instruments of industrial policy intact (Suzigan 1986, 1992; Rua and Aguiar 1995). More importantly, policy documents from these administrations show a level of innovative and pragmatic thinking that would be reflected in later iterations of industrial policy frameworks (see Grupo Interministerial 1986; SEPLAN 1986; Presidência da República 1991). With the exception of how privatization policy was implemented, these administrations did little to put these ideas into practice, not primarily on account of ideological opposition but because of the persistence of macroeconomic instability (Castro 1990, 1995).

Second, the advent of price stability with the Real Plan in mid-1994 allowed several erstwhile ideas concerning industrial policy to be implemented. Most notably, the BNDES, which had artfully managed the first industrial restructuring of key sectors such as steel, petrochemicals, and mining during the privatization process, expanded the scope of its disbursements to finance new investment (Além 1997, 1998). With the benefit of a decade of successful stabilization and the restructuring of private firms with a renewed commitment to improving productivity and innovation systems, the Lula administration was able to follow a broader and deeper industrial policy that included the internationalization of major producers in the Brazilian economy, an intensive infrastructure-building strategy, and an expansive energy strategy (see Presidência da República 2003). Lula created new coordinating bodies, notably the Brazilian Agency of Industrial Development (*Agência Brasileira do Desenvolvimento Industria*) and the National Council for Industrial Development (*Conselho Nacional do Desenvolvimento Industria*). The Council for Economic and Social Development (*Conselho de Desenvolvimento Econômico e Social*) brought business, labor, and other NGOs into a forum to help the administration develop policies and legislation. Dilma Rousseff capitalized on this broadened vision for industrial policy by linking these policies further into the new funding made available by the PAC-2.

While I emphasize a level of continuity from the ISI period among policy mechanisms and institutions, the scale, purposes, and performance of post-1985 developmentalism differ. I detect four areas of distinctiveness:

1 an emphasis on the competitiveness of existing industries rather than on the creation or vertical integration of the industrial sector;
2 the reduced but still strategic role of parastatals, former parastatals, and the economic bureaucracy;
3 the prioritization of innovation, especially improvements involving technological capacity; and
4 the maintenance of a counter-cyclical orientation to industrial policy within a stricter domain of macro-economic stability.

I argue that each of these four dimensions became a salient part of the policy regime from the advent of democracy in 1985 and evolved along the lines of the periodization profiled above.

Moving from Vertical Integration to an Emphasis on Competitiveness

Industrial policy during the ISI period had a defensive orientation that was designed to create and expand the industrial sector through vertical integration, but it did little to address the competitiveness of these firms in global markets. Gains made in the export sector depended heavily upon exchange-rate manipulation and were not sustainable (Suzigan 1988: 12). The Brazilian economic bureaucracy that emerged following the democratic transition in 1985 was sensitive to the need to rethink industrial policy to account for the realities of ISI's decline. Even during the liberalizing Sarney and Collor administrations, major policy declarations and working papers within the ministries of Economy, Industry, and Planning, and within the BNDES economics department, embraced the theme of moving beyond principles of protectionist, infant industries and improving the competitiveness of domestic industries through the promotion of efficiency gains (Suzigan 1986, 1991; Nardini 1990; Barreto and Arkader 1992; Fritsch and Franco 1993: 27–8). Firms had already during the 1980s begun the process of shifting towards exports where they could, and economic policy-makers recognized the intra-industry nature of import penetration and the ways in which these complex linkages enhanced the export performance of technology- and capital-intensive sectors such as airplanes, steel, chemicals, motors and car parts, and resource-based manufactures such as paper and wood-based products (see Moreira 1999: 298–307).[6] Following the Real Plan's success in controlling runaway inflation, firms began a second and more extensive process of reconfiguring production lines and investing in productivity-enhancing technology (Coutinho and Ferraz 1994; Meyer-Stamer 1997). These trends were recognized and supported by Cardoso's industrial policy, which became the basis for enhanced activity by the BNDES (see Presidência da República 1995; Castro 1995). But the overvalued *real* undercut internationalization as a way of scaling up production and finding new markets. Following the devaluation of the currency in January 1999, the benefits of an export orientation became more accessible. This led to another period of investment in technology to enhance the competitiveness of the industrial sector (Castro 2008: 7).

What is notable for my argument is that, despite the irregular periodization of industry's adjustments and the on-again/off-again promise offered by export markets, the thinking of state agencies once responsible for ISI was focused on enhancing the competitiveness of existing industries rather than on the expansion of the industrial sector as a whole. One hard case that illustrates the continuity in statist thinking was the way that the Collor and Itamar administrations implemented privatization. The National Privatization Program (*Programa Nacional de Desestatização*, PND) in its initial phase (1990–5) dominated the activities of the BNDES, which was charged with the task of providing finance to reconvert the public firms in steel, petrochemicals, and fertilizers prior to their sales (Erber and Vermulm 1993: 49). The thinking of the organizers of the PND was that privatization included a process prior to the auctioning of public firms that involved the productive restructuring of each going concern through financial and industrial policy interventions to upgrade productivity and absorb debt (Tourinho and Vianna 1993).[7] This amounted to an industrial policy in deed and intention, as the view of PND and BNDES leaders was that the chosen modalities of privatization served to reconvert potentially competitive firms (Montero 1998; Castro 1995).

The advent of price stability created another example of a hard case for the continuity of statist thinking. The years just after the Real Plan and leading up to the January 1999 crisis saw an appreciation in the currency that created strong disincentives to export. Nevertheless, BNDES economists focused on the value of targeted finance for productivity-enhancing projects within the largest former beneficiaries of the ISI period (cf. Além 1997). Total BNDES disbursements shot up an unprecedented 300 percent in the first two years of the Cardoso administration (Além 1998). Total disbursements increased their share of gross fixed capital formation by 37 percent over the course of Cardoso's first term (Plattek 2001: 106). Due in part to the overvaluation of the *real*, the bank took a direct role by providing export finance disbursements, which increased by 550 percent, from $890 million in 1996 to $5.86 billion in 2005.

It was only after almost a decade of macro-economic stability, liberalization, and other structural reforms, combined with private firms' productivity-enhancing investments and an increasing export profile for many sectors, that industrial policy could be refocused on the task of scaling up existing sectors, including through internationalization. The stage was thus set for the initiatives of the Lula and Dilma presidencies to broaden the foundations for competitiveness, with industrial policy concentrated on accelerated domestic investment and consumption, together with a strong component represented by the state.

Following on a decade of thinking at the BNDES in particular (Além 1997, 1998; Amann 2009: 197), Lula's industrial policy emphasized internationalization in the clearest way with a combination of export-promotion policies at home and a more aggressive foreign economic policy through multilateral organizations such as the World Trade Organization (WTO) and bilateral ties with major trading partners such as the United States and the European Union. A central part of Lula's trade strategy was the redirection of Brazilian exports to new markets, mostly in developing countries. Notably, during the late 1990s and early 2000s, Brazilian exports to Mercosul declined more strongly than exports to the US and Europe, while trade with non-traditional markets, and especially China, expanded most rapidly after 1997 (Almeida 2011: table 4; see chapter 7). The Lula administration also created a sovereign wealth fund to provide preferential credit to the largest firms pursuing internationalization.

The Reduced but Still Strategic Role of Parastatals and Former Parastatals

Public firms fulfilled a central role in articulating the ISI experience in Brazil. Their creation served several purposes, including the diversification of domestic industry, the protection from foreign ownership of firms in sectors deemed to be essential to "national security" (e.g., oil, aeronautics, and mining), the nationalization of foreign private firms operating in infrastructure (e.g., railroads, utilities, telecommunications), and the nationalization of failing firms and banks (Pinheiro 1999: 151–2; Evans 1979). The crisis of ISI led not to a shift of policy thinking from developmentalism to liberalism but to a sustained interest in converting the policy instruments of the ISI period, and especially the parastatals, to new uses. Evidence for this came early, as economic bureaucrats, soon after the regime transition, mined the cases of the newly industrialized countries of East Asia for ideas concerning industrial policy (cf. Santos Filho and Ferreira Junior 1987; Fritsch and Franco 1990). And, as was evident in the approach to privatization profiled above, parastatals would remain a key part of the strategy, but in new ways.

The privatization program under Collor and Cardoso replaced the structuralist logics governing the use of parastatals. Although the national security justification for public ownership of oil would remain, key parastatals such as Embraer (aeronautics) and Companhia Vale do Rio Doce (CVRD) (mining) were auctioned. Federal bailouts of state-owned banks, including those owned by the state governments during the first half of the 1990s, led to the privatization of most of these financial entities, even as the large federal banks (*Banco do Brasil* and *Caixa Econômica Federal*) continued in public hands (see chapter 2). Whereas the structuralist approach during the ISI era relied on *complete ownership*, this was less important in the renewed developmentalist period. Nevertheless, partial ownership remained a key mechanism for directing privatized firms within the parameters of national industrial policy. This was especially the case with the expanded role of the pension funds linked to the *Banco do Brasil* (Previ), the largest pension fund in Latin America, Petros (Petrobras), and the holding company of the BNDES, BNDESPar. For example, these three public entities maintain 60 percent of the capital of Valepar, the holding company that controls the formerly public mining giant, Vale (formerly known as CVRD). Overall, the state directly or indirectly maintains partial or full ownership of up to 20 percent of all firms listed on the Brazilian stock exchange, the Bovespa (Ban 2013). The government holds golden shares in some of the largest (e.g., Vale, Embraer, Usiminas, CSN, etc.), thereby controlling against major changes in ownership, especially through foreign takeover (Schneider 2009). For example, the BNDES expanded its shares in Vale in 2003 to prevent a Japanese firm from gaining control of half of the company.

These patterns of partial ownership complement the sectoral priorities of the BNDES, so they are vital instruments of industrial policy (Santana 2011: 148). Public finance through the BNDES and support for research and development (R&D) through Finep and the Program for the Development of Industrial Technology shaped the investment possibilities of these firms, which, even when conglomerates such as EBX and Votorantim took little direct aid from the state, were able to recruit executives and engineers from state enterprises such as Petrobras and Electrobras. They could also count on tariff protection in sectors considered strategic by economic planners. Government procurement policies favoring domestic suppliers also aided them in sectors as diverse as construction, energy, and mining. State aid for the largest firms was so pervasive during the presumed "neoliberal era" of the 1990s that scholars took to calling the range of supports a *de facto* "national champions" industrial policy (cf. Schneider 2009).

Under the Lula government's PAC, the parastatals returned to a level of protagonism that they had not seen since the privatization period. But, with its emphasis on combining public and private funds, the PAC required the parastatals to cultivate further their relationships with private firms (Castro 2008: 26). This built on more than a decade of innovation involving the economic bureaucracy and particular sectors in Brazil.

The Prioritization of Technological Capacity

Technological development and capacity received insufficient attention in the industrial policies that preceded the democratic transition in 1985. The emphasis on scaling up industry rather than enhancing sectoral and firm competitiveness made attention to R&D or education policy a tertiary concern (Suzigan 1988: 10). Only with the advent of Sarney's plans in 1985 would technology receive pride of place in the rhetoric of industrial policy statements, but fiscal retrenchment and anemic levels of spending on public R&D undermined putting these ideas into practice (Suzigan 1986, 1991). Rhetoric met practice primarily after the Real Plan.

Both official and academic sources recognized the challenges Brazilian industry faced after 1985 in integrating new technologies and enhancing productivity. Perhaps one of the earliest and most complete studies to take up this question was undertaken by the BNDES in 1988 on the capital goods sector, which at that time was beleaguered. The bank's study revealed that national firms trailed behind foreign-owned companies in automation and especially in the use of computer-aided design and manufacturing. Overall, there were only thirty industrial robots in service in 1985 in the automobile industry (BNDES 1988: 87). In its review of the entire industrial fabric of the country, the BNDES concluded that only the steel firms and Petrobras, the state oil company, had the technological resources and R&D capacity to become competitive internationally. Subsequent academic studies verified the parlous combination of undercapacity, low productivity, and weak internationalization in consumer durables more generally (Suzigan 1991, 1992; Cruz and Silva 1991; Meyer-Stamer 1992; Coutinho and Ferraz 1994; Barros and Goldenstein 1997). Notably, even the most liberal economists, several of whom would serve in the governments of the 1990s, saw these technology/ innovation needs as justifying a refocusing of industrial policy rather than its rejection (e.g., Fritsch and Franco 1990, 1991; Moreira 1994).

The Sarney and Collor governments were active in articulating a concern for innovation and productivity, but price instability and poor funding undermined the programs they proposed (Cano and Silva 2010). Policies such as the Collor-era Brazilian Program of Quality and Productivity (*Programa Brasileiro de Qualidade e Produtividade*, PBQP) cogently spelled out industry's needs, as the BNDES and academics had done earlier, with programmatic goals and funding targets laid out in a way that had not been the case previously. High benchmark interest rates, necessary to fight inflation, undermined efforts to make the PBQP viable, though that did not detract from the correct diagnosis of industry's challenges that were contained in these and other documents (Suzigan 1992; Erber and Vermulm 1993; IPEA 1990).

After the Real Plan, the disbursements and project portfolios of the BNDES and several technology-promotion agencies expanded notably, though the thinking was still very much within the outlines of earlier policy statements such as the PBQP (see Presidência da República 1995). In fact, the Collor-era PBQP continued and became fully integrated into BNDES programming but, more important, into Finep (*Financiadora de Estudos e Projetos*), a public firm created by the military during the late 1960s to finance public–private joint R&D ventures. Its agrarian parallel, the *Empresa Brasileira de Pesquisa Agropecuária* (the Brazilian Agricultural Research Company, Embrapa), was even more active, having accounted for the most rapid improvements in the productivity of agribusiness in Brazil's history since 1983 (Barros 2009).

In the Lula government's *Diretrizes da Politica Industrial* (2003) and the policies that followed (PITCE, PAC, and PDP), technological innovation was integrated more systematically into every aspect of industrial policy than was the case with any of the policies that preceded it (Suzigan, Negri, and Silva 2007). Policy-makers in this case were strongly influenced by the European Union's Lisbon Competitiveness Strategy and its emphasis on "horizontal policies" for promoting innovation (Arbix 2009). Following this model, the 2004 Technical Innovation Law (*Lei de Inovação Tecnológica*) supported private innovation and created new scientific and technical institutes that would take the lead in developing intellectual property and link universities and firms. The Lula administration's other advance on the developmentalist model was to tie innovation to internationalization. The government envisioned transnational production fostering new productive technologies, a more efficient division of labor, and the adaptation of innovative ideas from elsewhere and their application in the Brazilian market (see Presidência da República 2003).[8] Central to the official thinking was an understanding of how innovation and product differentiation shape the terms of trade, thereby linking the concern for innovation to trade strategy. These became explicit priorities of BNDES programming after this time (Almeida 2011: 181). In this regard, productivity-enhancing business-to-business linkages were considered as important as firm-specific improvements. The bank's policy goals also coincided with a notable increase in R&D spending by both the public and the private sector.

Counter-Cyclical Industrial Policy within Macroeconomic Stability

Brazilian industrial policy during both the ISI and the more recent developmentalist periods pursued a counter-cyclical tendency even as it operated under different macro-economic policy frameworks. Under ISI developmentalism, state coordination of private-sector investment continued despite periodic boom–bust dynamics in the larger economy. This was obvious during the two great investment surges of the first statist period, the initial 1954–64 expansion and the military's PND II (1974–9), both of which were the products of indicative planning and were limited only by the availability of capital (Suzigan 1988). Whatever macro-economic instability was created by growth or the manipulation of exchange rates and the price of finance was a secondary concern to economic planners. By contrast, the post-1985 developmentalist period operated under very different macro-economic parameters, though it retained the focus on counter-cyclical intervention. Every one of the industrial policy statements issued between 1985 and 1994 tempered expectations about what the continuation of statist mechanisms could do without a stabilization of prices. This merely recognized that industry continued to stagnate, with most of the former leading firms of the ISI era forced to consider restructuring during a period marked by acute hyperinflationary spirals (Suzigan 1991).

Commercial opening and macro-economic stability set the base conditions but also delimited the outer parameters of what was possible for industrial policy after 1985. A synergistic link developed between price stability and openness with the expansion of industrial policy. Without the former conditions, the increased provision of credit and its association with more private investment would not have occurred (Castro 2008). Under Cardoso's industrial policy, which was the first to have the benefit of price stability, BNDES disbursements expanded notably, though there was no change in direction from the principles outlined in earlier policy statements (see Presidência da República 1995, 1998). In the midst of low growth rates from 1995 to 1999, economic bureaucrats in the BNDES viewed these micro-economic policies as essential for promoting expansion but not so extravagant as to risk inflation (BNDES 1996; Além 1998).

The implicit complementarity between stabilization and more ambitious industrial policy became ingrained when Lula, still a candidate for the presidency in 2002, made an oath embodied in his "Letter to the Brazilian People" to continue Cardoso's economic policies. This shift on macro-economic policy at the apex of the PT had its political logic (see Hunter 2010), but it was also a principle well established in the economic bureaucracy that Lula was to command. By this time, the Brazilian government was firmly committed to a more independent central bank that embraced inflation targeting, the maintenance of surpluses in both current and fiscal accounts, market-determined interest and exchange rates, and increased tax revenues. These principles were recognized explicitly in Lula's and Dilma Rousseff's own industrial policy statements (see Presidência da República 2003; Governo Federal 2008, 2011). Yet it is also notable that developmentalist inflections were available to these governments on several of these macro-economic policies. Fiscal policy would retain strong counter-cyclical tendencies, interest rates would decline slowly, and capital controls would be used selectively to adjust the exchange rate in the event of rapid appreciation of the currency.

Implementing Developmentalism in a Neoliberal Era

In this section, I analyze the evolution of some of the main agents of development policy since the democratic transition. The analysis emphasizes the evolution of the system, but it pays particular attention to how these agents have adjusted their actions under the presidencies of Lula and Dilma. The section is also concerned with indicators of performance of these agents and how the overall system has affected private-sector investment and growth.

The Lula government wasted no time in reviving industrial policy-making as a core focus. The government's *Diretrizes da Politica Industrial*, published in November 2003, outlined dozens of sectoral and thematic priorities that were given fuller treatment in an implementation plan known as the Industrial, Technology, and Trade Policy (*Política Industrial, Tecnológica e de Comércio Exterior*, PITCE) in March 2004. The PITCE outlined fifty-seven measures for eleven priorities, among them policies to spur innovation and focus resources on "sectors of the future" such as biotechnology, biomass, and energy. Exemptions and abatements on production, value-added, and payroll taxes complemented these measures, along with new lines of credit from the BNDES.[9] In May 2008 the Lula government launched a second industrial policy, the Productive Development Policy (*Política de Desenvolvimento Produtivo*, PDP), which added to the PITCE $21 billion in new mechanisms, including technical assistance to firms and government procurement, regulatory, and fiscal policies designed to sustain growth and promote innovation. Additionally, the PDP called on Finep to provide an additional $23 billion and the BNDES to open up $120 billion in non-infrastructural financing at 40 percent lower interest and at double the former maturation period (Cano and Silva 2010: 193).

Public Finance: The BNDES and the Pension Funds

A crucial pillar of statism historically in Brazil is the provision of public finance to firms. As shown in the previous section, the state retained its motivations for acting to promote private investment after 1985. The BNDES, in particular, became the main agent in the provision of long-term finance to private firms – a role it retained from the ISI period. First created in 1952, the BNDES became the chief financier of large development projects in infrastructure, steel, and utilities. By the 1960s it was the chief source of finance for all industries, using its lines of credit to substitute for previously imported capital goods during the military's most ambitious development plan, the PND II (BNDES 2002). As previously mentioned, the BNDES adjusted its mission during the thirty years that followed the winding down of ISI. It maintained its concern for the effects of development and national ownership during the privatization process, which it oversaw. After the Real Plan, it returned to some of its erstwhile functions as a development bank by focusing on the continued reconversion of the industrial sector. The bank became more sensitive to its role as a counter-cyclical entity, providing credit during the low-growth period of the mid- to late 1990s when financial markets were unwilling to do so. Since that time, the BNDES has maintained a pattern in its lending that accelerates faster than economic growth and slows once growth rates approach the high point of the business cycle (Almeida 2011: 176).

A couple of months before Lula's presidency began, the Cardoso administration, through decree 4.418 (October 2002), re-established the BNDES as the chief implementer of the investment policies of the federal government. In 2005, its role in promoting innovation and technology was formalized in an institutional partnership with Finep. With its expanded institutional role during the 2000s, the BNDES became the source of one-fifth of all finance for the private sector in Brazil and the first source for long-term finance (Santana 2011: 145–6; Almeida 2011: 177).[10] During the Lula administration, the BNDES more than doubled its portfolio of investments (Santana 2011: 138). Figures 5.1 and 5.2 show the dramatic rise in BNDES disbursements over the 2000s. Disbursements to industry tracked the overall increases closely. Using data acquired from the BNDES through a Freedom of Information Act request, Kathryn Hochstetler and I compiled a database of all of the bank's loans between 2002 and 2011, coding for sectors and location.[11] This section examines these loan data in greater detail, analyzing the patterns and priorities of the BNDES's initiatives. Subsequently, I discuss how the BNDES extended its activities in the first decade of the twenty-first century, placing a new emphasis on the internationalization of its own activities and those of the firms it financed.

BNDES spending did not just increase quantitatively under Lula; it also became part of an increasingly focused attempt to develop a more ambitious industrial policy. Lula's election energized those technocrats within the bank who saw it as an opportunity to use the BNDES to play a larger development role (Além 2011). Already in 2002, one group discussed how the bank might be used in a "pragmatic industrial policy" that kept basic elements of competition and market opening while using the state to move Brazil to higher

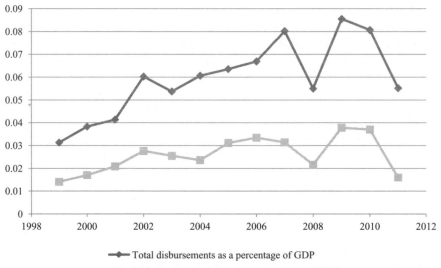

Source: BNDES and IPEADATA.

Figure 5.1 *All BNDES disbursements as a percentage of GDP, 1999–2011*

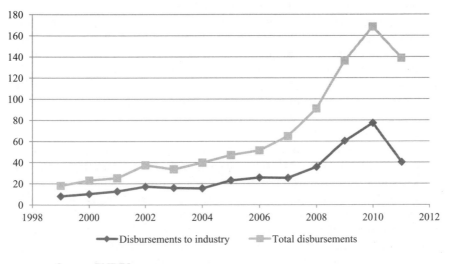

Source: BNDES.

Figure 5.2 *All BNDES disbursements, 1999–2011 (R$billion)*

levels of sustained growth (Além, Barros, and Giambiagi 2002). The main concern, of reducing external vulnerability while keeping inflation low, was repeated in the PITCE Directives, the first formal proposal for a new industrial policy under Lula (Presidência da República 2003). There was a strong tone of needing to build defenses against international markets, which had upended the Brazilian economy between 1998 and 2002 through linked currency, debt, and balance of payments crises. The PITCE stressed expanding exports and paying down debt, as well as "stimulating the sectors where Brazil has a larger capacity or necessity to develop comparative advantages" (ibid.: 2–3). The BNDES's role was to link and facilitate the infrastructure projects that lay the foundation for industrial growth.

Beginning with the Collor-era privatization program, in which they played a key role as domestic financiers and buyers, the public pension funds came to play a major role with the BNDES in supporting the developmentalist economy. The pension funds share with the bank a long-term time horizon and an interest in fortifying domestic firms, many of which are run by boards with pension fund representation. The preference is also logical, given that these funds hold the savings of the middle-class and unionized workers, most of whom have stakes in domestic industries. With total assets in 2007 totaling some $220 billion and three-digit growth since 2002, the public pension funds are also heavily concentrated. The top three funds – the public bank funds (*Banco do Brasil* and *Caixa Econômica Federal*) and the Petrobras fund – command almost 30 percent of all pension fund assets (Santana 2012: 224).

The political management of the pension funds became even more oriented to developmentalist principles with the advent of the Lula presidency. Lula named former union leaders to run the largest public pension funds. Their previous involvement in the privatization process enabled those running the funds to articulate development policy to favor domestic concerns. For example, the pension funds that participated in the privatization of Vale, the global iron ore giant, secured 60 percent voting shares in Valepar, its holding company.

The BNDES drew on its new resources to expand lending greatly during Lula's second term, at rates that were often partially subsidized up to 40 percent. The Hochstetler–Montero database includes 2,115 such loans for the period 2002–11, ranging in size from under 1 million (359) to over 1 billion *reais* (38). Table 5.1 lists the three sectors per year that received the largest volumes and numbers of loans. The list overlaps remarkably with the BNDES priorities since 1952 in energy and infrastructure. With the exception of telecommunications and retail, the list reflects a striking correspondence with the 1958 Targets Program (*Programa de Metas*), showing that the PAC follows a similar set of priorities (Oliva and Zendron 2010: 76; BNDES 2007; see Sikkink 1991: 136–7). At the same time, in terms of the number of loans, the post-1985 pattern shows a greater diversity of sectoral projects, including many small loans to the arts and entertainment industries and small industrial sectors, reflecting the influence of private and semi-private firms acquiring BNDES funding.

The focus on energy-related spending is notable. Table 5.2 shows the largest loans during the study period. The largest credit lines went to Petrobras to support its development of recent oil discoveries off of the coast of Rio de Janeiro state. Five of the other loans finance the production, generation, or distribution of energy. About 27 percent of the loans (over R$73 billion) went to the energy sector, including ethanol production and cogeneration of electricity from processing wastes. The category of energy infrastructure projects also takes in many designed to increase the extent and efficiency of electricity transmission networks and large and small fuel pipelines. Major blackouts in 2001 brought attention to Brazil's energy deficit, making this a priority for BNDES lending, which follows the priorities of the Ministry of Mines and Energy (Ministério de Minas e Energia 2010; Hochstetler 2011). As growth slowed in 2012, Dilma turned even more to infrastructural outlays as a counter-cyclical strategy, keeping energy and utilities at the forefront.[12]

The continuity of sectoral priorities for BNDES lending maps onto the very same industries that dominated the ISI period and continue to dominate the Brazilian economy (Amann 2009; Schneider 2009). The bank instituted a new form of loan contract during this period that institutionalized special treatment for large and reliable firms with which it had done business in the past. Multiyear credit lines covered a diverse set of national and international investment plans rather than isolated projects. Steelmaker Gerdau signed the

Table 5.1 Top sectors receiving BNDES loans, 2002–2011

Year	Top sectors by value	Top sectors by number of loans
2002	Electricity and gas Other transportation (shipbuilding) Motor vehicles	Electricity and gas Arts and entertainment Motor vehicles
2003	Electricity and gas Telecommunications Retail trade	Electricity and gas Arts and entertainment Sugar-cane complex
2004	Electricity and gas Telecommunications Motor vehicles	Electricity and gas Food products Arts and entertainment
2005	Telecommunications Electricity and gas Food products	Food products Arts and entertainment Museums and archives
2006	Telecommunications Electricity and gas Motor vehicles	Movie and video production Electricity and gas Sugar-cane complex
2007	Electricity and gas Telecommunications Food products	Electricity and gas Arts and entertainment Sugar-cane complex
2008	Electricity and gas Food products Telecommunications	Electricity and gas Movie and video production Sugar-cane complex
2009	Electricity and gas Petroleum refining Petroleum production	Electricity and gas Food products Movie and video production
2010	Food products Sugar-cane complex Motor vehicles	Museums and archives Movie and video production Electricity and gas
2011	Electricity and gas Civil engineering Telecommunications	Electricity and gas Movie and video production Museums and archives

Note: Sectors are classified according to International Standard Industrial Classification (ISIC) codes from the United Nations. Loans in all years incorporate those in the BNDES's industry and infrastructure divisions, while those in 2009–11 also include those in the raw materials division.

Source: BNDES data, elaborated by Hochstetler and Montero (forthcoming).

first of these in 2005, a R$900 million credit line to modernize and update the technology in its factories and to increase its competitiveness. More than twenty other firms followed Gerdau's example. A few large firms also receive BNDES funds as winners of government construction contracts (e.g., Camargo

Table 5.2 Largest BNDES loans, 2002–2011

Largest loans: industry, infrastructure, and raw materials divisions, 2009–2011			
Firm identifier	R$million (US$)	Year	Purpose
Refinaria Abreu e Lima (Petrobras and PDVSA)	9,890 (5,235)	2009	Refining of Petrobras's oil production
Petrobras	9,410 (4,981)	2009	Exploration and production of petroleum
Eletronuclear	6,146 (3,680)	2011	Build Angra 3 nuclear energy plant
Transportadora Asociada de Gas (Petrobras)	5,700 (3,017)	2009	Build pipeline for Petrobras's production
Norte Energia	3,68 (2,238)	2011	Build Belo Monte hydroelectric plant (March tranche of 2)
Energia Sustentável do Brasil	3,635 (1,866)	2009	Build Jirau hydroelectric plant, localized transmission lines
JBS	3,480 (2,000)	2009	Internationalize meatpacking enterprise
Santo Antonio Energia	3,094 (1,267)	2009	Build Santo Antonio hydroelectric plant
Vivo	3,031 (1,715)	2011	Improve infrastructure for new telecommunications technologies
Marfrig Alimentos	2,500 (1,418)	2010	BNDES assistance with issue of debentures by food processor
Largest number of loans: infrastructure and industry divisions only, 2002–2011			
Firm or firm family	Total loans R$million	Number of loans	Primary sector of firm or firm family
Weg	1,281	15	Manufacture of electrical machinery
All America Latina Logistica	4,591	12	Civil engineering
Light	2,470	11	Electricity supply
Conspiração Filmes	16	9	Motion picture production
Fiat Automoveis	2,829	9	Manufacture of motor vehicles
LDC Bioenergia	434	9	Sugar-cane complex
Marfrig Alimentos	4,331	9	Food processing
Natura Cosmeticos	321	9	Manufacture of chemicals

Source: BNDES data, elaborated by Hochstetler and Montero (forthcoming).

Corrêa and Odebrecht) or through export supports (e.g., DaimlerChrysler's Brazilian subsidiary). The BNDES was sensitive to the claim that such large loans simply rewarded companies that were already strong, but bank executives claimed that support for such "leader firms" was crucial to deepening Brazilian global penetration (Coutinho 2010: 29; Além 2011).

A focus on the bank's large loans misses most of its innovation support, which goes to smaller and newer firms. Most firms that signed loan contracts with the BNDES during the study period received just one or two small loans. For example, in 2009 the *Cartão BNDES* (BNDES Credit Card), a line of financing for small and medium-sized enterprises that began in 2003, added coverage of services that teach the methodologies and regulations often required for foreign trade, including certification in global quality schemes such as the ISO 9001, 14001, and 15100 systems (PR 9/11/09).

The PITCE Directives focused on reducing external vulnerability and limits on growth, calling for increasing exports and paying down the debt (Presidência da República 2003: 1–2). Eventually, however, the BNDES underwrote a far more expansive version of internationalization, beginning mid-decade with the commodity boom. The first step was export promotion. Official trade finance in Brazil had modest beginnings in the 1960s, but was scaled back in the 1980s and had to be re-created from scratch (Sucupira and Moreira 2001: 92–3). In 1991, the BNDES began to provide supplier credits for capital goods sold to other Latin American countries in an agreement among Latin American central banks. The program was renamed BNDES-EXIM in 1997, when it began to function like a fully fledged export–import (exim) credit facility, offering both pre- and post-export credit lines to suppliers and foreign banks. Just two years later, disbursements had reached $2.1 billion annually and were 20 percent of total BNDES disbursements (ibid.: 93). Exim disbursements continued to grow rapidly through the 2000s, although they were eventually dwarfed by the rise in total disbursements. In 2011, the BNDES created the BNDES Automatic Exim program, which gave exporters the proceeds for their high value-added industrial sales in Latin America up front, while participating banks with international operations with credit lines from BNDES provided financing to the importers.

The idea that Brazilian firms should be helped towards even greater international involvement in the form of foreign direct investment (FDI) was first floated in 1994 in a new internal BNDES journal, the *Revista do BNDES*. The idea was sketched in a couple of pages before the author reports that the bank's legal team squashed it, saying that the BNDES could act only inside Brazil (Souza 1994). A 1997 rule change allowed indirect FDI finance; then a 2002 change allowed direct FDI support as well. This shift coincided with the real effect on industrial restructuring caused by increased FDI inflows into sectors such as steel, aircraft production, petrochemicals, and pulp and paper (Kingstone 1999). The BNDES's effort to provide financial support for these trends was focused on providing working capital related to construction and the acquisition or modernization of plants and branches abroad, as well as purchases of corporate interest (if complementary to exporting). The bank may provide 60 percent of the financing through loans or by raising capital through bonds and securities. The first loan for FDI was approved only in 2005, when the BNDES financed the meatpacker JBS-Friboi to buy a Swift meatpacking plant in Argentina. Loans for FDI trickled out during the 2000s, all bearing clauses that required the projects to include substantial percentages of Brazilian exported goods. In November 2009, for example, Lula reported that, between 2005 and 2009, the BNDES had given Argentina credit lines of $1.2 billion for infrastructure and industry and another $1.5 billion for gas pipelines, sanitation, and water. Brazil had offered Venezuela a $10 billion credit line earlier for projects that involve Brazilian businesses (*Folha de São Paulo*, 22 May 2009). These kinds of open credit lines to Brazil's neighbors are linked to Brazilian firms and the export of Brazilian goods and services, and conventional commercial viability is insisted upon.

Finally, in 2008, the Lula administration introduced another set of changes as part of the PDP. The BNDES now began to set up offices abroad, beginning in 2009 with an office in Uruguay for Mercosur activities and to support Brazilian interests in South America. The next step was an investment holding company in London. This is meant to increase Brazilian visibility in a major global financial center and to support Brazilian businesses abroad, as well as to facilitate the activities of foreign investors who want to invest in Brazil. The BNDES has also signed agreements to coordinate investments with the development banks of the BRICSA countries. An international area within the bank coordinates all these activities, and the BNDES is seeking to expand its framework of action further to include actual lending outside Brazil.

Technology Promotion: Finep

One of the defining characteristics of the developmentalist period has been the promotion of innovation, R&D, and the adoption of new technologies in production through the acquisition of machinery and equipment. During the ISI period, the BNDES's focus was on infrastructure and industry. This orientation diversified slightly when the military sought to expand industrial policy to promote research and development. In 1971 the generals developed a fund, the National Fund for Scientific and Technological Development (*Fundo Nacional para o Desenvolvimento Científico e Tecnológico*, FNDCT), to finance the creation of postgraduate programs in Brazilian universities and charged Finep with the task of managing it. During the 1970s, Finep expanded from financing postgraduate research to working with private firms and universities on joint projects. With the advent of the debt crisis and inflation during the 1980s, these resources dried up and, while the subject of productivity and innovation became a priority of programs such as the Collor-era PBQP, little was done to implement ideas in this area.

The Cardoso administration reconstituted Finep as a public firm under the direction of the Ministry of Science and Technology (Decree 1.808, *Estatuto da Finep*). After 2000, the FNDCT was expanded to include fourteen sectoral funds, and under the 2004 Technological Innovation Law it was to be infused with vastly greater resources. Figure 5.3 shows the evolution of the FNDCT, which matched the periodization I have described, with declining activity between 1985 and 1994 and then a notable upsurge, especially after 2004. The Lula government expanded Finep's credit lines to complement the BNDES's own focus on technology-intensive projects (see Hochstetler and Montero forthcoming). Finep's resources increased by more than 50 percent in 2011 alone, as the bank provided R$6 billion through the *Programa de Sustentação do Investimento*.

Finep's range of activities did not change very much after its creation. It remained the chief distributor of large grants to universities to support research and development, but it was allowed after 2006 to provide grants and loans to support the R&D operations of private firms and the acquisition of machinery (Finep 2007: 15). It also provides lines of credit at below market rates to private firms, drawing from the FNDCT but also from the development funds managed by other ministries, the BNDES, and the public pension fund, *Fundo de Amparo ao Trabalhador*, which is its second largest source of funding. Notably, Finep has expanded its venture capital operations in recent years as part of a concerted effort by the Lula and Dilma administrations to improve Brazil's paltry R&D spending, which stands at an average of 1.02 percent of GDP per annum (Fonseca 2011).

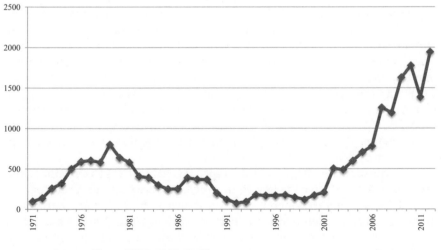

Source: Finep (*2007, 2012, 2013*).

Figure 5.3 *FNDCT financing, 1971–2012 (R$million, constant at 2005 rate)*

Finep and the FNDCT represent a significant, albeit heretofore insufficient, commitment to promoting innovation, with effects that are thus far encouraging. Negri, Negri, and Lemos (2008) have undertaken the most comprehensive study of the Finep's recent activities and its effects on the capacity of firms to innovate. Based on data taken from 80,000 firms employing at least ten people and covering the period 1996–2003, Negri and his colleagues studied seventy firms that had taken FNDCT monies and compared them with cohorts of firms that had not taken FNDCT funds but had notable R&D facilities or patents on file. The results are mixed, but they show on balance a more positive effect on R&D activities by firms receiving FNDCT monies compared with those firms that are non-beneficiaries (i.e., they rely on their own facilities). Such findings suggest that there is much unrealized potential in the innovation-promotion system, which is not as far along as the policy domains covered by the BNDES.

Overall Performance

The pursuit of continued developmentalism in Brazil was strategic and consistent with the finding that liberalization combined with supply-side state intervention in key sectors generates substantial improvements in growth (see Ferreira Filho and Horridge 2006; Rodrik 2007; Krugman 1995). In this section I turn to the question of whether Brazilian developmentalism since 1985 has promoted investment and growth overall.

The aggregate investment rate is much too unreliable and complex, since it relies on calculating multiplier effects of government spending on private resources. I prefer to use a more precise indicator that is commonly employed to measure the acquisition of fixed assets by the private and public sectors: gross fixed capital formation (GFCF).[13] The most relevant indicator is the annual variation in GFCF, since this represents new fixed capital asset value being added to the economy, excluding financial transactions, inventory movements, and other non-fixed capital items from balance sheets. Since GFCF is a more specific measure of investment by companies, it tells us more than the aggregate investment rate about the allocation of resources to future production. When compared to the aggregate growth rate of GDP, GFCF indicates whether the economy is adding or subtracting new capacity for future production.

GFCF measures investments of the type targeted by the BNDES, Finep, and other agents of industrial policy. In this regard, more work has been done on BNDES disbursements, which have been shown to be a reliable predictor of gross capital formation (see Rigolon 1996; Plattek 2001).[14] A comparison of Figures 5.1 and 5.4 demonstrates that disbursements and GFCF evolved similar patterns in the period 2002–8. GFCF grew higher than the aggregate GDP for most of that time. The volatility after 2008 was the result of the global recession and then the strong counter-cyclical effort by the Lula government

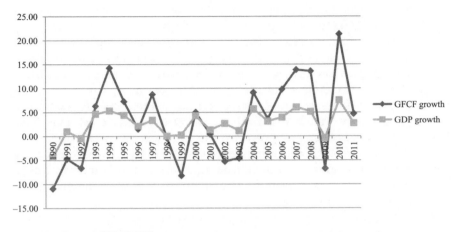

Source: IPEADATA.

Figure 5.4 *Gross fixed capital formation and GDP growth, 1990–2011*

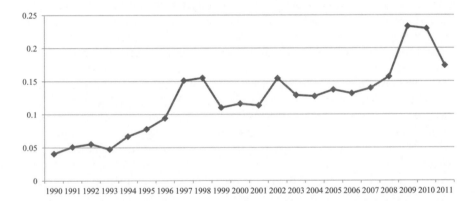

Sources: BNDES, Plattek (2001: 113), and IPEADATA for GFCF.

Figure 5.5 *BNDES disbursements as a percentage of GFCF, 1990–2011*

in areas outside of BNDES disbursements such as PAC-related infrastructure projects. Figure 5.5 demonstrates that BNDES disbursements as a percentage of GFCF increased sharply as Lula's industrial policy system expanded. This is consistent with studies published by the BNDES, which show disbursements are responsible for an average of 21 percent of gross capital formation (BNDES 2011: 9).

Gross fixed capital formation is not the only indicator for the timing and effect of public support. Figures on the adoption of new technologies to modernize production and the notable improvements in labor productivity in the industrial sector coincide with the periodization of industrial policy movements outlined above (see Suzigan, Negri, and Silva 2007: 36–7). Given that a growing portion of the industrial policy system aims to improve productivity, this provides further corroborating evidence of the enabling effects of developmentalism, especially in the post-2002 period.

Yet it should be remembered that Brazil has witnessed such good times before, only to see these fizzle out as macro-economic conditions have changed. Several indicators suggest that this time may very well be different. As chapter 2 demonstrated, international reserves have given the state a cushion to enact counter-cyclical policies for a period of time. Improved debt-to-GDP ratios and fiscal surpluses also reinforce the sustainability of the current development strategy.

One alternative view of industrial policies is that they had a small effect on transforming an economy that grew after 2002 due primarily to the exports of primary products and natural resource manufactures.[15] First, this position ignores the fact that most of Brazil's economic growth has come from the expansion of the domestic market. Increases in aggregate demand have coincided with the strongest growth rates of the last decade (Santana 2012: 218). Second, there is a clear relationship between public investment in research and development and the restructuring of natural resource-based manufactures during the 1990s and the subsequent competitiveness of these exports. So even the successes of the commodity boom can be traced to the activities of the BNDES, Embrapa, Finep, and other public agents of industrial policy. Third, Brazil's export performance is not exclusively the result of commodity demand; Brazilian industry's increasing integration into global markets through trade is another major source (ibid.: 220). The composition of trade from 1998 to 2011 shows an increasingly more diversified profile, inconsistent with a commodity boom explanation (Suzigan, Negri, and Silva 2007). In fact, the balance of empirical work on this question has shown no strong correlation between growth in commodity prices and demand for Brazilian exports (cf. Almeida 2011: 171). Fourth, the import side, which is neglected by commodity boom explanations, has become as important in Brazil's growth picture. The upsurge in imports, especially from China (see chapter 7, figure 7.1), is especially acute in medium- to high-technology industries that have used imported capital goods to increase productivity rapidly (Santana 2011: 145; Santana 2012: 221–2). Sectors such as electronic equipment, automobiles, telecommunications, and capital goods have become more import-intensive to support processing activities that result in strong export coefficients (Almeida 2011: 172). It should be recalled that these are the sectors that were the principal targets of industrial policy after 1988. Such findings militate against a hasty conclusion that it is primarily a commodity boom that sustains the Brazilian growth model. The relationship between imports, exports, and industrial growth is far more nuanced and consequential.

Another alternative argument is that the role played by public agencies, firms, and banks has been less than the role of the growing private financial market. Santana (2011) evaluates this claim and finds that private sources of medium- to long-term debt in the form of debentures have been significant only in the small market for venture capital for start-ups, an area in which Finep has been expanding its activities noticeably (Fonseca 2011). Although the annual average for private finance boomed to R$52.5 billion, that was still below mean annual disbursements by the BNDES *alone* (R$80.4 billion) between 2002 and 2011 (see figure 5.2; Santana 2011: 142), not to mention the far greater amounts available through the pension funds, the largest of which are public. The BNDES remains the chief source of long-term capital for investment in all major sectors and 20 percent of all finance by Brazilian banking to the private sector (Santana 2012: 222). In comparative perspective, the BNDES's average annual lending levels make it the most active development bank in the world (cf. Almeida 2011: 180).

The value of the strategic decisions made by the BNDES and other agents of industrial policy was verified after the global financial crisis of 2008. Exports fell between September 2008 and March 2009 more than expected, at 16 percent, but less than a fifth of the industrial sector was affected (Sant'Anna, Puga, and Nascimento 2009). The quick recovery of manufacturing on account of its focus on the expanding domestic market, a priority of developmentalist industrial policy, proved to make the sector more resilient when international markets froze (Almeida 2011: 176). The expansion of public credit in the aftermath of the crisis was a key factor. More than 83 percent of the growth of available credit to the private sector in Brazil in 2008 and 2009 came from the public banks, with the BNDES accounting for a third of that amount (Santana 2011: 145, fn 5; Almeida 2011: 177). This was one of the primary reasons Brazil came out of the recession after only a six-month slump. Since being elected in October 2010, Dilma Rousseff's government has expanded the PAC-2 and official finance, placing even more resources in favor of a Keynesian response to the downturn.

Strong economic performance since 2003 is the basis for many of the more optimistic views that there is a "new Brazil."[16] But understanding Brazil's economic development model since the democratic transition requires more than appreciating the role of commodity exports and the application of Washington Consensus macro-economic reforms. Brazil's economic turnaround did not coincide with trade liberalization or a purposeful reform of its highly regulated domestic markets. During the 2000s, when the country experienced a prolonged boom, the World Bank still ranked it fifty-second in terms of the competitiveness of its domestic market, given the extensive rules that govern the economy. Brazil did not adopt the full gamut of structural adjustments that other economies in Latin America such as Mexico and Argentina did, and it certainly did not embrace the same ideological fervor seen in those two countries when it did implement neoliberal reforms during the Cardoso administration. According to the Brazilian political scientist Maria Hermínia Tavares de Almeida (1996: 226), Brazil implemented "neoliberal reform without neoliberalism" (*"reformas neoliberais sem neoliberalismo"*). That is, it pursued structural reforms such as privatization and liberalization with an eye towards the needs for industrial restructuring.

Neoliberal and pessimistic views of the turnaround have ignored the way that the Brazilian development strategy pursued developmentalist policies and priorities after 1985. These policies differed fundamentally not only from neoliberalism but also in important ways from the statism pursued during the ISI era. Understanding these tendencies requires seeing the entire approach across time and through the interconnected strategies of state banks such as the BNDES, agencies such as Finep, the pension funds, current and former state firms, and the private sector, many of which were the beneficiaries of ISI policies in the past. The evolution and performance of developmentalism in Brazil also suggests that pessimistic views of the Brazilian state's capacity were overdone. The turnaround in this area has been real and lasting due to the sustained capacity of the economic bureaucracy and industrial policy to enable growth and investment.

CHAPTER SIX

Welfare and Class Mobility

Brazil's progress in improving its rates of poverty and decreasing inequality during the last decade underscores the country's turnaround like virtually no other set of indicators. According to the United Nations Development Programme's *Human Development Index* of 2011, Brazil ranks eighty-fourth out of 187 countries in the world, with a score of 0.718, though that is improved from 0.600 in 1990, 0.665 in 2000, and 0.692 in 2005.[1] Brazil posted one of the highest growth rates in the HDI for those countries listed in the second tier of the ranking ("high human development") (UNDP 2011). Much of this progress can be attributed to changes in social policy. Brazil spent an amount comparable to 3 percent of GDP in 1987 on social policy, but that had increased to 21 percent by 2005 (Haddad 2009: 187). Quality also improved, along with the amount of money spent on contributory and non-contributory social assistance, public healthcare, and education. All of these policy areas have seen notable innovations.

This chapter evaluates the extent to which Brazil has experienced a turnaround in its socio-economic indicators and the degree to which social policy has played a role in that process. Regarding structural change, there is little doubt that Brazilian society is developing and in ways that reinforce optimism that the country can continue to make progress on inequality. But social policy will need to adapt fundamentally to sustain these changes. Despite some important evolutions in social policy that have improved the lives of the poorest Brazilians, the welfare state continues to maintain privileges for a few. The net of social protection has expanded modestly in ways that cover the precarious lives of the indigent. Yet, by also providing undue protection for the relatively well-off, social policy preserves patterns of income and class inequality.

As with other policies examined in this book, there is a historical tendency in the democratic period. The Brazilian welfare state has reinforced social inequalities since Getúlio Vargas's *Estado Nôvo*, which granted pension and healthcare protection to formal-sector workers but failed to create processes to extend those benefits to other workers. Beneficiaries of these social policies were usually the ones who stood in the way of reform, as they refused to give up control of pension privileges (Madrid 2003: 140). Under the military regime, social policy reform unified formally disparate programs and extended coverage to rural workers and domestic employees, but the changes did not extend to public-sector workers and the military, preserving inequities that persist to this day. With the growth of informal labor, especially since the transition to democracy, fewer workers today enjoy these protections, making those who do an elite within the labor market.

A second claim made in this chapter that resonates with those put forward in previous chapters is that the implementation of modest, conservative, but still effective social reforms has coincided with the gradual de-polarization of Brazilian politics during the democratic period. Policies such as land reform once promised fundamental transformation of the class structure and were the shibboleths of leftist and populist politicians, but the issue also helped to cause the breakdown of democracy in 1964, when João Goulart became embroiled in the question. Leaders such as Cardoso and Lula have stuck to a far more moderate script. They have eschewed transformative policies such as ambitious land reform and income distribution, preferring instead significant resettlements of landless peasants without extensive expropriation of private land and targeted cash transfers that do not challenge primary fiscal surpluses or threaten the property rights or wealth of the top three income deciles of the population (Singer 2012).[2] Despite the intensity of the political competition between Lula and Cardoso and their parties, the PT and the PSDB, respectively, social policy became another area of continuity between the two governments, though Lula clearly increased the size of social welfare commitments. This provides further support to the argument that the last two decades of democracy have benefited from a mixture of political de-polarization and consensus around points of good policy governance, all the while favoring gradualism and the slow fine-tuning of institutions.

A third claim is that social policy-making is yet another area in which the more pessimistic approaches to Brazilian institutions have been inaccurate. Scholars of welfare institutions in Brazil have tended to bemoan the tendency of particularism, clientelism, and even corruption to undermine the universal objectives of promoting greater class equality and reducing poverty (Weyland 1996; Kaufman and Nelson 2004). Yet Cardoso and the PT presidencies embraced universalism to an unprecedented degree and achieved real changes that belie the sustained pessimism of some observers (Melo 2008). For their part, conservative critics in Brazil have reverted back to a well-known charge against social welfare as *assistencialista* (paternalistic), but little has come from these accusations, as the policies of Cardoso and the PT presidencies have remained popular and have become political assets to their advocates.

Of course, these points are co-dependent. It would be difficult to imagine the embrace of universalism in social policy to any degree without a previous emerging elite consensus favoring market orientation in economic policy and the consolidation of capitalist property rights. And, despite the persistence of unevenness in the administration of social policies such as pensions and healthcare, the formalization of the labor market and the focus on innovation in welfare policy in favor of universalism holds promise for correcting these imbalances. In the sections that follow, I examine the turnaround in major social indicators before delving into the progress seen in social policy areas, including anti-poverty programs, pensions, healthcare, and education.

Structures of Poverty and Inequality

Since the colonial period, Brazil has had a large population of poor people who earn a relatively small percentage of the national income. The historical origins of inequality and poverty can be traced to the system of large-scale agriculture based on repressed labor (some of it slave labor) and a small class of landowners that defined the economy during the seventeenth through the late nineteenth centuries. Industrialization did not eradicate most of these inequalities but made them worse, as labor-saving technologies and the demand for skilled workers put greater distance among the classes (Amann and Baer 2009). Poverty alleviation, while often promised by politicians, was not delivered in any sustained way. The result was that, between 1967 – the beginning of the high-growth Brazilian "miracle" – and 1980, the country enjoyed strong relative growth, but inequality grew as well (IPEA 2010). During the first decade of democracy, growth rates fell but inequality continued to rise. Only with the advent of several factors beginning in 1994 did these figures turn around. The change was led by the controlling of inflation under the Real Plan, declining income disparities across households with different education assets, and convergence of rural and urban standards of living during the 1990s. The advent of expanded and targeted social assistance to the poor under the Cardoso administration and especially during the PT presidencies also caused inequality to decline (Ferreira, Leite, and Litchfield 2007). After 2005, Brazil enjoyed *both* increasing growth and decreasing inequality and poverty in a sustained way for the first time in its democratic history.

The trajectories of poverty and inequality have proven to be non-linear, both of them rising during the structural crises of the 1980s and then turning downward following the Real Plan. Between 1994 and 2004, poverty rates, using the R$100 per capita per month standard, fell by a third. Inequality declined more slowly. Brazil is the seventh most unequal country in the world. More than two-thirds of the income is concentrated in the hands of the top two income deciles, while the bottom two deciles earn only 2.3 percent (Paes de Barros, Carvalho, Franco, and Mendonça 2007). Poverty and inequality, while different, are intertwined in Brazil. In judging the reduction of poverty rates over the last twenty years, Marcelo Neri (2009: 240) notes that the rate of this decline has been faster due to the decline in income inequality. For example, if inequality were to decline so that the average Gini coefficient for Brazil were more like the level of one of the more developed states such as Rio (0.561), then the poverty rate would fall 2.4 times faster than it has already.[3] Yet it should be noted that the decline that has occurred in poverty in tandem with inequality remains impressive. The fall in inequality between 1993 and 2004 explains almost half of the decline in poverty (Ferreira, Leite, and Litchfield 2007: 23).

Poverty and inequality are disempowering, as they undermine the efforts of the least well off to mobilize on their own behalf, making them more dependent and susceptible to having their votes bought by political machines and their economic and social rights ignored by the owners of capital (Scott 1969). Poverty and inequality produce other social ills, including violent crime, which has grown worse in the major cities. This is also one of the main dimensions of geographic unevenness, in that infant mortality, life expectancy, poverty rates, and literacy differ across the regions. Infant mortality declined overall from 88 deaths per 1,000 live births in 1980 to 28.6 in 2006, though, for the Northeast, ten more babies die on average. Although, as a whole, life expectancy improved from sixty years in 1980 to seventy-two in 2006, citizens in the poor Northeast live six fewer years on average (Baer 2008: 353). The population living in "extreme poverty" – that is, on less than $1 dollar per day – is five times greater in the Northeast than in the Southeast. Literacy in the Northeast stood at 81.3 in 2009 to the Southeast's 94.3 and the South's 94.6 (IPEA 2011: 151).[4]

Poverty

Improvements in household median incomes, inequality as measured by the Gini coefficient, and poverty rates (percentage of the population under the poverty line) are summarized in table 6.1. The data show notable gains across all three of these basic indicators after 1994, but the most acute progress occurred after 2004. Using the World Bank's international benchmark of poverty, about 14 million people claim to live on $1 per day. Based on conventional headcount data, 11.6 percent of the population lived on a $1 per day in 1992, but that proportion fell to 7.3 percent in 2003 and 4.2 in 2008. The shift at the $2 per day threshold was also significant: 26.5 percent in 1992 versus 20 percent in 2003 and 10.6 percent in 2008 (Neri 2010: 68).

Citizens who live at or below the $1 per day threshold can be said to be in "extreme poverty," and it is this group that experienced the most stunning improvement. During the democratic period, the population living in extreme poverty decreased by 60.5 percent (Neri 2009: 232–3; Silveira-Neto and Azzoni 2012). Although the stabilization of prices during the 1990s contributed to the trend, the decline during the 2000s was the fastest. The fall in extreme poverty of 8.6 percentage points between 2002 and 2006 is equivalent to the fall in poverty for all of Latin America for a fifteen-year period beginning in

Table 6.1 Mean income, Gini coefficients, and poverty rates, 1981–2009

Year	Mean household monthly income (in Oct. 2009 R$)	Gini coeff.	Poverty rate
1981	467.75	0.584	40.79
1982	480.02	0.591	41.00
1983	406.13	0.596	48.73
1984	404.59	0.589	48.30
1985	485.25	0.598	42.01
1986	709.89	0.588	26.41
1987	529.02	0.601	38.71
1988	490.77	0.616	43.57
1989	562.94	0.636	41.36
1990	510.97	0.614	41.92
1991	450.45	0.580	42.85
1992	443.80	0.583	42.09
1993	467.62	0.604	42.98
1994	484.75	0.600	42.10
1995	579.92	0.601	35.08
1996	591.28	0.602	34.73
1997	590.65	0.602	35.18
1998	596.81	0.600	33.97
1999	563.49	0.594	35.26
2000	583.65	0.600	34.73
2001	571.31	0.596	35.17
2002	571.62	0.589	34.93
2003	538.21	0.583	37.13
2004	550.84	0.572	37.17
2005	583.96	0.569	32.58
2006	638.29	0.563	31.61
2007	655.83	0.556	29.09
2008	689.61	0.548	25.16
2009	705.72	0.543	21.42

Source: IPEADATA (figures for 1991, 1994, and 2000 are imputed).

1990. The fall in poverty rates was most acute for the poorest, who receive less than a quarter of the monthly minimum wage.[5] Using this metric, between 2001 and 2008 this group was reduced from 21 percent of the population to 11 percent. The decline of poverty was most pronounced in the Northeast, where the rate fell from 40 percent to 22 percent during this time (Hall 2012: 29). That amounts to 8 million people emerging from extreme poverty in one region alone (Neri 2010: 70).

The turnaround in Brazil's social indicators has been so dramatic and focused on the last decade that observers have tended to claim that government policies are the cause of it. Most notably, Marcelo Neri has termed the triple approach of employing conditional cash transfer anti-poverty programs, raising the minimum wage more than 50 percent in real terms after 2003, and extending consumer credit as "Lula's Real Plan." The original Real Plan reduced the number of persons living under the poverty line by 18.5 percent, while "Lula's Real Plan" reduced that number by 19.2 percent (Singer 2009: 93–4). This has had implications for inequality as well, with one-third of the reduction in income inequality due to non-labor income such as social transfers from pensions and social assistance (Silveira-Neto and Azzoni 2012: 435; Neri 2011).

Class Structure and Inequality

A combination of targeted anti-poverty transfers, continued stable prices if not relatively low inflation, an expanding formal labor market, and greater educational access reduced the Gini coefficient after 2001 an average of 1.2 percent per year. The rate of the decline in inequality was as fast as the rate of its increase during the 1960s (Neri 2010: 59). For the period 2001–5 alone, that was a faster decline than for fifty-six of the seventy-four countries with comparable data on inequality (Paes de Barros, Carvalho, Franco, and Mendonça 2007). Within Latin America, Brazil was third, after Ecuador and Paraguay, during 2000–7 (Neri 2011: 58). Most of this improvement is due not to the modest fall in the share of national income held by the top 1 percent or the top 10 percent but to the upsurge in the share of the bottom 10 percent, by an average of 11 percent since 2000 (Neri 2009: 229–30). While inflation control and shrinking disparities in rural and urban households explain more modest decreases in inequality during the 1990s, more substantial and better-targeted social assistance help to account for the more rapid and recent reductions in inequality (Ferreira, Leite, and Litchfield 2007).

The Brazilian class structure can be divided into quintiles: a high-income group (1st quintile), a middle-income group (2nd quintile), a low-middle-income group (3rd quintile), a working-class group (4th quintile), and a poor working or simply "miserably" poor group (5th quintile) (Quadros 2007). The division of social classes according to occupation and income has been criticized for overlooking aspects of status such as race (Figueiredo 2004) or demographic groups with no labor income, such as the elderly and children, who are more likely to be poor and live in households in the lower income deciles (Neri 2009). An alternative measure that attends to these differences but still provides an aggregate metric is consumption. Since the 1970s, the Brazilian Association of Marketing Research Institutes (*Associação Brasileira de Institutos de Pesquisa de Mercado*) has used a quintile distribution based on consumption patterns with the following labels: A1, A2 (upper classes); B1, B2 (middle classes); C (lower-middle and working classes); and D and E (lower classes and the poor). Class C represents the largest proportion of the total population, at 30 percent (Souza and Lamounier 2010: 3).

Data from the National Household Sample Survey (*Pesquisa Nacional por Amostra de Domicílio*) of the Brazilian Institute of Geography and Statistics (*Instituto Brasileiro de Geografia e Estatística*) shows that the middle class, operationalized as the second and third quintiles, represents the intermediate categories in the distribution of wages by occupation and household income. The bottom two quintiles include rural workers, domestic workers, and poor self-employed labor. The dramatic rise of bottom quintile families into the next higher quintile is a change that marks a sharp contrast with the evident stability of the other three quintiles over time. This reflects the extraordinary improvement of the lives of the miserably poor in recent years. Neri (2010: 73; 2011: 151) shows that these shifts generated upward mobility in the AB and C classes, which expanded 37 and 31 percent, respectively, between 2003 and 2008.

Changes in the occupational structure reflect how the class structure has evolved in Brazil. The labor market since 1981 has become more flexible, with large increases in the ranks of the self-employed, particularly in the service sector (Pochmann 2012). As a corollary, during the 1980s and 1990s, industrial work declined, leaving urban workers with less of a share of national income at the end of the 1990s and facing higher unemployment rates than at the beginning of the democratic period (Quadros and Antunes 2001). The figures also show a marked weakening in small-scale farming, in terms of both self-employed farmers and employed farm labor, and its displacement by large-scale, corporate agriculture (Santos 2001; Quadros and Antunes 2001). The weakening of industrial employment, along with the fall in the industrial sector's share of GDP, underwrote the hasty conclusion that Brazil experienced "de-industrialization" during the democratic period. As chapter 5 showed, this view misreads how industry adjusted during the 1990s and became better able to expand during the 2000s, especially through exports and efforts to improve productivity. Services held their own in the employment picture and grew especially for those workers earning up to one and a half times the minimum salary per month. During the 2000s, 94.8 percent of the 21 million jobs created during the decade were in this income category, comprising millions of clerks, construction workers, transport and dockworkers, and general service positions (Pochmann 2012: 27–32). This underscores how the bottom quintiles did comparatively better than the middle quintiles of the income distribution.

The formalization of the labor force accelerated during the 2000s. Defining formal versus informal labor in Brazil is difficult, but one shortcut is to count the number of registered workers holding worker cards (*carteiras assinadas*). These individuals pay into the social security system and are covered by its benefits upon retirement. The number excludes formal-sector laborers, who do not pay into social security, but *carteiras assinadas* is accepted as a proxy for the approximate size of the formal labor market nonetheless (Telles 1993). Based on data taken from the National Household Sample Survey, aggregate measures of the labor market structure indicate that formal work has been increasing in the last decade. Based on current numbers, 57 percent of the workforce is active in the formal labor market, while 37 percent are in the informal market, are self-employed, or work for no remuneration (IPEA 2011: 198–9). Figure 6.1 shows increases in the percentage of formal-sector workers between 2001 and 2009. While the percentage shifts seem modest, each represents millions of workers brought into formal employment and under the protection of the social safety net in a relatively short period of time. Especially notable is that women have improved their positions substantially, which has strong implications for the welfare of children and households as a whole. An average of 240,600 jobs were created in the formal sector each month through 2010 (ibid.: 199). Between 2004 and 2007 alone, 6 million new formal-sector jobs were created, with an estimated 4 million more in the

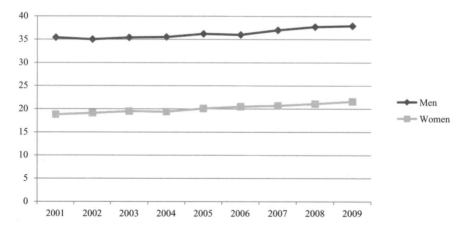

Source: Instituto Brasileiro de Geografia e Estatística, *Séries Estatísticas e Históricas*, Série PD352 (www.ibge.gov.br) (accessed October 1, 2012).

Figure 6.1 *Percentage of the economically active population with carteiras assinadas, 2001–2009*

informal sector (Neri 2009: 225). Data collected by IPEA (2011) show appreciably higher income growth rates for workers with *carteiras assinadas* than for those without. Given the social protection that accrues from formal-sector employment, there is little doubt that the expansion of the formal sector has been one of the chief means through which inequality and poverty have been alleviated in Brazil over the past decade.

The evolution of real wages is an important subplot in the story of declining poverty and inequality. The minimum wage experienced a real increase of 58 percent between 1998 and 2008 (100 percent since 1992), with most of that coming after 2003 under Lula's presidency (Neri 2010: 60). The minimum wage was set at R$425 per month by *medida provisória* no. 474 at the end of 2009 and approved as law no. 12.255 in June 2010. Wages in the formal sector increased during the 2000s, with the highest jump (7 percent) occurring in 2010 (IPEA 2011: 199).

Has wage expansion and broadened employment in the formal sector produced social turnarounds overall and have these shifts been complemented by the pattern of economic growth in Brazil? Assessing the effects of these complicated changes is difficult because not all good things go together. Increased wages have strengthened consumption, which has been a prime mover of economic growth through the domestic market. However, the increase in income and formalization of work has also enabled households to spend on credit, creating increasingly unsustainable levels of consumer debt.[6] Inequality in wage rates between urban and rural workers remains an additional challenge. Brazil's commodity boom, particularly in agriculture, has had a relatively weak effect on wage rates, since workers in the primary export sector are paid much less than industrial workers, and the sector has seen a marked decline in employment opportunities as it has moved to more capital-intensive means of production (Pochmann 2012: 37; Skidmore 2004: 135–6).

Social Policy

The Brazilian welfare system provides significant social protection to millions of citizens through substantial transfers to social security, education, healthcare, and public assistance. Total social spending averages 23 percent of GDP, higher than any other Latin American country except Cuba (29 percent) and close to the average of the OECD economies (25.5 percent) (Neri 2010: 62–4). These transfers have played a key role in reducing poverty and inequality during the turnaround, but they have also deepened inequality in precise ways. The problem is not that an insufficient amount is spent on poverty alleviation but that the amounts that go to relatively privileged classes are not reallocated more equitably on behalf of the poor (Hunter and Sugiyama 2009). The inequalities of the social welfare system have deep roots in Brazilian history, stretching back to the corporatist institutions created by Getúlio

Vargas's *Estado Nôvo* which linked pension and healthcare benefits to formal-sector employment, the civil service, and the armed forces, leaving the larger informal urban and rural labor force outside of the range of these protections. The next subsections analyze origins and changes in four key areas of social policy: poverty alleviation through social assistance – especially conditional cash transfers, pensions, healthcare, and education.

Poverty Alleviation through Conditional Cash Transfers

Conditional cash transfers (CCTs) are non-contributory programs that target income subsidies to poor mothers with the goal of creating positive social outcomes, such as keeping children in school and improving the health of families. CCTs are universal because they go to a large and geographically dispersed population of poor families, who can access the money by first meeting a set of entry-level qualifications, mostly low income. They continue to receive the transfer as long as they meet the conditions (Handa and Davis 2006).

Ideas for CCTs of some type entered political debates in Brazil just a couple of years after the transition to democracy. The earliest proposals at the federal level came from a PT political-technocrat, Eduardo Suplicy, but efforts in 1995 and 1996 by the Cardoso administration and PSDB officials intimated that they would develop their own ideas. In the meantime, the first notable conditional cash-transfer programs were implemented at the subnational level. Cristovam Buarque, the PT governor of the Federal District, initiated in 1995 the first cash-transfer program to achieve notoriety. His *Bolsa Escola* (School Grant Program) created an incentive for families to keep their children aged seven to fourteen in school. A concurrent program emerged in Campinas, São Paulo, under the leadership of the PSDB mayor José Roberto Magalhães Teixeira. Cardoso created a federal version of this program in 1997, hired several of the Campinas designers, and then expanded the initiative in 2001.[7] By 2000, midway through Cardoso's second term, as many as 1,115 cities were enacting *Bolsa Escola* programs of their own.[8] By 2002, 95 percent of all municipalities were participating in the federal version (Melo 2008: 169).[9] The format of the *Bolsa Escola* CCT was replicated by Cardoso's administration in other areas, including food and nutrition for children (*Bolsa Alimentação*) and cooking gas (*Auxílio Gás*). So, by the end of Cardoso's second term, total CCT expenditure composed a quarter of all spending on the poor (Hall 2008: 801).

Lula's presidency doubled social assistance to the poor, expanding the CCT programs in particular, which almost tripled in size as a percentage of the total social spending budget (from 1 percent in 2001 to 2.9 percent in 2006). Lula's campaign in 2001–2, *Fome Zero*, focused on hunger eradication. His idea for a *Cartão Alimentação* (food card) program fit the campaign theme but was roundly criticized as an *assistencialista* version of a food stamp program.[10] Once Lula was in power, criticism of the program mounted, combined with inter-bureaucratic squabbles regarding the other CCTs from the Cardoso era (Hall 2008, 2012). The need to bring order to an increasingly unwieldy system convinced Lula to dismantle the original *Fome Zero* and combine instead the Cardoso-era programs together with the *Cartão Alimentação* under one rubric, to be managed by the Ministry of Social Development. The result was the *Programa Bolsa Família* (PBF, Family Grant Program), which pooled four distinct cash-transfer programs (education, cooking gas, nutrition, and anti-hunger). By 2006, the PBF covered more than 11.1 million families (approximately 55 million citizens), and by March 2011 the number was well above 13 million, with 52.4 percent of these concentrated in the poorest states of the North and Northeast (see figure 6.2) (IPEA 2011: 70). At a total of $5.5 billion, the PBF represents 0.4 percent of GDP, less than 3 percent of total social spending and only 37 percent of the amount spent on social assistance (ibid.: 76; Hall 2012: 35). To put this in perspective, Brazil's creditors receive per annum more than six times the total budget for the PBF (Amann and Baer 2009: 37).

Application of the PBF is straightforward. Eligible families meet with local registers that collect their information and place them into the Unified Registry (*Cadastro Único*), which compares reported income and consumption patterns to verify the information provided. Once the means test is passed, cash is transferred electronically onto ATM cards issued by the *Caixa Econômica Federal*, the federal savings bank. The cards are sent to the female head (or the male head if the family has no female adults) of every household that has an aggregate monthly income of no more than R$140 ($88). The funds are disbursed at monthly increments of about R$58 to R$242 ($36 to $151), depending on the number of children in the household and provided that all children aged six to fifteen attend 85 percent of their classes (80 percent for those aged sixteen to seventeen), maintain the regular vaccine schedule (for children younger than seven), and, along with any pregnant or breast-feeding mothers in the household, are periodically seen by a healthcare professional.[11] Poor households may also qualify for additional subsidies from *Auxílio Gás* and *Cartão Alimentação* in the northeastern states of R$15 ($9) and R$50 ($31), respectively. Periodic follow-up visits of sample beneficiaries test whether the conditions are being met, though these studies have been more successful in verifying compliance with the educational requirements than with the healthcare requirements (Soares, Ribas, and Osório 2010).

The *Bolsa Família* represented less an overhaul of poverty-alleviation policy and more a targeted and much needed add-on that has proven effective though not transformative (Singer 2012). Several studies have shown that the PBF targets a sufficient number of poor households in the lowest two income quintiles and that it has had an appreciable effect on overall poverty and inequality. Poverty rates have fallen by an average of 12 percent as a result of the PBF, as cash transfers represent the second source of household income for the lowest income deciles (Soares, Ribas, and Osório 2010: 179). The PBF

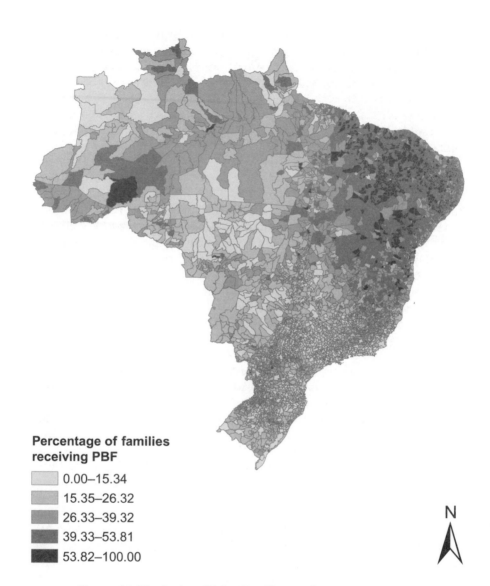

**Percentage of families
receiving PBF**

	0.00–15.34
	15.35–26.32
	26.33–39.32
	39.33–53.81
	53.82–100.00

N

Figure 6.2 *Distribution of* Bolsa Família *transfers, 2006*

has also had an appreciable effect on inequality, accounting for a reported
21 to 24 percent of the fall in the Gini coefficient during the 2000s (Soares,
Soares, Medeiros, and Osório 2006; Silveira-Neto and Azzoni 2012). Although
there are mixed empirical results on the secondary effects of the PBF, various
studies have found an impact on household consumption (particularly a
marked increase in consumption levels of food, children's clothing, and edu-

cational resources) that has contributed to regional growth patterns (Oliveira et al. 2007; Hall 2008: 808–9). The program has significantly affected school attendance (or hours in attendance) and increased the number of health consultations, though there is no significant impact on child immunization and an unclear effect on nutrition (Soares, Ribas, and Osório 2010; Neri 2009; MDS 2010). Finally, the PBF did not represent a large portion of the social budget, let alone the total budget, so the opportunity costs of enacting it were low for all stakeholders.

Given the universal criteria of the PBF for accession of households and the structure of disbursements from the Ministry of Social Development directly to recipients through the *Caixa Econômica Federal*, there is little opportunity for politicians or others to engage in malfeasance. Since funds are disbursed directly by the federal government, subnational politicians find it difficult to claim credit for the program, so they can expect to reap few political rewards from the attempt (Fenwick 2009). Municipal politicians cannot guarantee enrollment or threaten to reject participants once they are in the system, since these officials do not control disbursements (Fried 2011: 1044). If there is any politician who has received any credit for the PBF, it has been Lula (Hunter and Power 2007; Zucco 2008; Figueiredo and Hidalgo 2009; Marques, Leite, Mendes and Ferreira 2009).[12] Despite these restrictions and weak incentives, some evidence of poor oversight and conflict of interest at the municipal level has been reported (Hall 2008: 809–10), though statistical and spatial studies of disbursement patterns confirm that political criteria do not govern the distribution of PBF monies and that the program's targeting gets better results than similar programs in Mexico and elsewhere in Latin America (cf. Fried 2011; Haddad 2009; Soares, Ribas, and Osório 2010; Soares, Soares, Medeiros, and Osório 2006). Virtually three-quarters of all PBF funds go to the poorest income quintile.

The *Programa Bolsa Família* may be the most well-developed national, universalistic and programmatic social policy in Brazilian history. Its effects on reducing poverty and even inequality are debated, but it is unquestionable that the weight of the empirical evidence credits the program with having a positive effect (cf. Ferreira, Leite, and Litchfield 2007). Of course, the PBF is insufficient for eradicating poverty, since it is focused on boosting consumption and not income generation (Hall 2008). Despite that, its modest success is the exception in an array of social policies, most with long histories stretching back to the Vargas years, that have failed to provide a sufficient degree of social protection to the poor and that have even deepened structural inequalities.

Pensions

No other area of social policy preserves class inequality in Brazil more than the uneven application of social security. Pensions take up half of all social spending – an amount equivalent to 11 percent of GDP. In comparison with CCTs, pensions compose 82 percent of all cash transfers in Brazil. Yet, unlike CCTs, these payments are intensely regressive.[13] Brazilian social security is mostly a contributory pay-as-you-go system focused on offering a defined benefit after retirement, but only some formal private-sector employees earning enough to make regular contributions and civil servants and military personnel who do not already have access to their own pension systems are part of the General Social Security Regime (*Regime Geral de Previdência Social*, RGPS) managed by the National Social Security Institute (*Instituto Nacional da Seguridade Social*, INSS).[14] Civil servants at all levels of the federation are covered by a non-contributory system known as the Unified Juridical Regime (*Regime Jurídico Único*, RJU). Using data from 2006, Ansiliero and Paiva (2008) break down social assistance and social insurance more specifically and include the RJU to get a more accurate global figure of how many workers aged sixteen to fifty-nine have social protection. They find that 52 million Brazilian workers (64 percent of the economically active population) are covered by the public pension system, while 29 million (36 percent of the economically active population) are uncovered. The number of beneficiaries drawing a pension had reached 23.9 million by June 2010 (IPEA 2011: 21). The unevenness of the system has gender, racial, and geographic dimensions as well. Approximately 4 percent fewer women than men are covered; more than 12 percent fewer blacks are covered compared with whites; and coverage in the poor northeastern states averages about 14 percent less than in the developed southeastern states.

Until the system was reformed during the Cardoso and Lula administrations, the terms governing benefits were entirely unsustainable. Workers could retire with a minimum vestment period of five years, and disbursements, often larger than the past salary, were adjusted upward whenever workers were granted raises. Workers could retire early regardless of their age if they had been in employment for thirty years (for men) or twenty-five years (for women).[15] The benefits themselves were relatively generous, paying out 70 percent of a worker's salary based on the last three years worked, and even these payments were subject to periodic increases based on the minimum wage. Retired public-sector workers, if they had labored in more than one post, could claim multiple pensions, and all of these were subject to increases if current civil servants received raises. Notoriously, the unmarried daughters of military officers could claim a pension.[16] Given the non-contributory nature and generous terms of the RJU, these pensions consumed as much as 75 percent of what the RGPS did, though it covered one-seventh the number of workers (Kingstone 2003b: 225–6). The 1988 Constitution mandated that all pensions be adjusted for monthly inflation and that the minimum pension pay the full minimum wage rather than half, which was the previous standard. These adjustments explain why average benefits increased by 78 percent between 1988 and 1996 (Madrid 2003: 142).

As private pension spending equaled 5.5 percent of GDP and public-sector pensions reached 6 percent by 1996, the pressure to address the fiscal sustainability of the system became more evident. Beginning in 1997, the contributions of workers ceased to cover pension disbursements sufficiently.[17] The timing of this fiscal watershed threatened the creditworthiness of Brazil, which was still working to consolidate the gains of the Real Plan with fiscal adjustments. Due to the rise in the number of formal sector workers paying into the system, more recent years have seen a decline of the fiscal subsidy to maintain the RGPS in particular. In 2010, the subsidy amounted to the equivalent of 1.35 percent of GDP, which is down from the high of 1.78 percent in 2006. The financing burden for the RGPS has fallen on a per-beneficiary basis, from 26 percent of each individual transfer to about 17 percent (IPEA 2011: 25). Urban contributions into the system have been stronger and more consistent than rural contributions, which represent the larger part of the RGPS deficit.

Proposals for reform under the Cardoso and Lula administrations sought to correct the erstwhile fiscal problems of the pension system, though they did little to remedy its structural inequalities. Cardoso tried to enact comprehensive pension reform that included provisions to require a vestment period of thirty years for women and thirty-five for men, a minimum retirement age of sixty for women and sixty-five for men, a cap on pension payments, and the elimination of the multiple disbursements and special exceptions such as the one for military daughters. Yet these measures were defeated outright in 1996 and watered down in a second attempt in 1997–8 (Madrid 2003: 159–63; Kingstone 2003b). The attempt at reform failed, as the groups representing beneficiaries retaliated through intense lobbying of congress. Cardoso's own majority party coalition also failed him, as members did not show up for the critical votes. Lula's attempt proved more successful than Cardoso's, but his reform was also watered down under the intense opposition of organized groups of beneficiaries. Still, he was able to secure passage in 2003 of a reform that increased the retirement age and both limited and taxed benefits going to the wealthy. These changes happened just as the fiscal pressures on the social security system ratcheted up after 2002. Pension benefits payments increased after this point due to the extension of benefits to domestic workers and an overall expansion in the formal labor force, as noted above (Ansiliero and Paiva 2008).

The current state of both contributory and non-contributory pensions, public and private, amounts to a social assistance system that is somewhat improved from the pre-reform period. More than two-thirds of all of the money INSS distributes goes out in a form equivalent to one minimum salary per month per household (Ramos and Querino 2003: 147). Even so, this income amounts to as much as 80 to 100 percent of the household income of the poorest 20 percent of the population, making it Brazil's most powerful poverty-alleviation policy (Lloyd-Sherlock 2006; Lloyd, Barrientos, Moller, and

Saboia 2012). Despite the unevenness of coverage, it provides a substantial minimum level of household income. Second, the system is on a sound demographic footing going forward. Presently, there are 5.6 workers per pensioner, and there will be 3.1 by 2030, a level that suggests the long-term sustainability of the pension system (IPEA 2011: 43). Brazil also has a high domestic savings rate compared with other Latin American countries, so there is potentially less pressure on the pension system to support the retiring population (Madrid 2003: 146).

Healthcare

Brazil's Constitution of 1988 declares that each citizen has a right to healthcare. This provision, which was a product of the efforts of activist and leftist healthcare workers who formed the *Movimento Sanitário* (Public Health Movement) during the 1980s, led to the provision of universal healthcare services. The *sanitaristas* were opposed to the existing Bismarckian system that protected only formal-sector workers and public employees and was run by a highly centralized federal agency, the National Institute of Medical Assistance and Social Security (*Instituto Nacional de Assistência Médica da Previdência Social*, INAMPS). The movement saw the growth of private insurers as a threat to the universality of access. The result of their pressure was the Unified Health System (*Sistema Único de Saúde*, SUS), which produced dramatic improvements in the coverage and quality of public health services. The management of healthcare was decentralized, with each municipality becoming an integrated service point for standard services, but for many towns their responsibilities became too much for their resources to bear. The *sanitaristas* were successful in having the constitution recognize local health councils as power-sharing and participatory institutions allowing the public to weigh in on health issues before municipal officials. More than 98 percent of all municipalities now have them (Avritzer 2009: 116). Yet, even with their success in establishing a universal right to healthcare and a participatory health system, the *sanitaristas* failed in their effort to create a single, public system of healthcare, though they won on the principle of decentralization and the eventual replacement of the INAMPS by the Ministry of Health. For-profit providers were able to fend off the *sanitaristas* to retain their position in the healthcare market, particularly in the ownership of hospitals (eight out of ten are in private hands). Since the well-off can avail themselves of both private and public insurance, households in the top three income deciles have more comprehensive and higher quality coverage than the rest of the population. Moreover, Brazilian tax law subsidizes private insurance by allowing deductions for their clients, who will also use the public system for the more expensive treatments.

The provision of universal coverage with the preservation of private insurance is a combination that produces inherent inequities in the system.

Approximately 22 percent of the population has access to private health insurance, which is subsidized by tax deductions. Since private insurance companies can avoid paying for the costliest and less common surgeries such as transplants, knowing that the public sector will cover these operations, the well-off tend to use a disproportionately costly area of the system and still avail themselves of private insurance protection. The privately insured are 34 percent more likely than those who depend on the SUS system to use health-care services (IPEA 2011: 122). Almost a fifth of SUS spending is concentrated on patients in the top three income deciles (World Bank 2004). Geographic inequalities make these other inequities more acute. The most highly trained doctors and the most advanced imaging and other diagnostic technologies are concentrated in the clinics and hospitals in the developed South and Southeast, leaving poor states in the Northeast, especially, with substantial shortages (Arretche 2004). Service patterns verify these inequities, as residents of the developed states in the South and Southeast receive medical care twice as much as citizens in the Northeast (Baer 2008: 356). The sum of these inequities is reflected in a little known anomaly: Brazil is the only country in the world with a universal healthcare system, legally defined, that spends more private than public money on healthcare. The aggregate commitment amounts to 8.4 percent of GDP, which is commensurate with some European countries, but, unlike those countries, public healthcare accounts for less than 50 percent of the total (WHO 2010).

The constitutional effort to create a common social safety net also made the financing of public healthcare more fragile than it would otherwise be. Public health expenditures amount to 3.3 percent of GDP, with 65 percent coming from the federal government, 20 percent from the states, and 15 percent from municipalities. The constitution linked the tax revenues from social contributions to both the public health system and pensions. As pension obligations grew during the 1990s, the money available to finance healthcare was squeezed (Melo 2005: 869). Once healthcare policy-making was transferred completely to the Ministry of Health in 1993, the Ministry of Social Security ended its mandatory 30 percent transfer of social contributions to this ministry, making it wholly dependent on the annual budget (Weyland 1996). As more healthcare was provided by the social security system, the focus of service became curative care as opposed to preventive care. This fostered stronger growth in costs and exacerbated the inequities in the system. After 1998, Cardoso's health minister, José Serra, produced more robust reforms. The Ministry of Health introduced new public health measures promoting preventive care, unprecedented regulation of private insurers, and increased transfers to fund municipal services, uniting all local systems within the SUS. The reforms linked federal transfers to the level of service states and municipalities were willing to provide, thus keeping transfers in line with costs while preserving the autonomy of subnational governments to pursue their own healthcare policies (Arretche 2004).

The SUS has its strong points. First, the healthcare infrastructure serves much of the population. The core of the system is the network of local clinics (*Unidades Básicas de Saúde*, UBS) that attend to 80 percent of the health problems of the country by focusing on vaccines, basic curative medicine, ordinary office visits, and simple lab work. By late 2011, Brazil had 38,000 UBSs, with another 25,000 in the planning stages through 2014, most of them slated for the poorest cities under Dilma Rousseff's anti-poverty program, *Programa Brasil sem Miséria* (Brazil Program without Misery). The UBS system grew rapidly during the 2000s, and by 2008 each clinic had a core family health team (*Equipe de Saúde da Família*) composed of at least one doctor, one nurse, and a community health official. Second, as a consequence both of the wide availability of the UBSs and of official efforts to contain costs, hospitals specialize in emergency medicine and more serious health problems. The creation of pre-hospital Units of Quick Assistance (*Unidades de Pronto Atendimento*) and a network of mobile paramedic services (*Sistema de Atendimento Móvel de Urgência*) take pressure off of the hospital system.

Community-based health programs have sprouted up to attend to local populations in some of the more rural and remote areas of the poor states of the Northeast that do not receive SUS resources. The *Programa Saúde da Família* (PSF), which was created in 1994, is the most notable of these, as it targets health services to the poorest communities and dispatches healthcare teams (*Equipes de Saúde da Família*) to make home visits. The experience of the PSFs was so influential that they were copied throughout Brazil. By 2003, there were PSFs in 4,944 of Brazil's 5,564 municipalities (Sugiyama 2008: 84–5).

Health outcomes reflect the improvements in the healthcare system as well as increasing household incomes. Although not all poor Brazilians use the SUS, an estimated 80 to 85 percent do. Because of this near universal access, the decline in infant mortality is particularly notable, as it is linked to provision of better and more pervasive prenatal care and the fact that almost all deliveries take place in the presence of a healthcare professional. Still, inequalities persist even here, as babies born to families in the lowest quintile income group are three times more likely to perish early than babies born to families in the top quintile (UNDP 2006). Access to safe water, sanitation, and more effective treatments for chronic diseases such as dengue and malaria, as well as more typical symptoms such as diarrhea, explain much of the improved health profile of Brazilians (Baer 2008: 353–5).

Education

Perhaps no other social policy affects long-term inequality more than education, given that the number of years of schooling remains the most powerful determinant of income. While significant spending on primary and secondary public education is most likely to make the biggest difference for the poor, Brazilian governments have tended to spend more on higher education and less than they should on earlier levels. Although the universities serve only 2 percent of all students, they receive more than 56 percent of the federal education budget (IPEA 2011: 132).[18] Spending increased for primary and secondary schooling during the democratic period so that it now composes 38.4 percent of the education budget. Both public and private sectors play key roles in Brazilian education. More than 85 percent of all primary and secondary schools are public but more than 65 percent of higher education is private (Draibe 2004: 377). As in healthcare, education policy is made, and funding is shared and implemented, at both the federal and the subnational level. The law allocates 18 percent of federal taxes and 25 percent of all subnational revenues to primary and secondary education.

The problems of Brazilian education are varied, but they hinge on two dimensions – access and retention on the one hand and quality on the other. The increase in spending on primary and secondary education accompanied real gains in access by the poor to public schooling even as the middle and upper classes continued to send their children to private school. In the critical "middle school" ages of seven to fourteen, school attendance went from 83 percent in 1994 to 97 percent in 2007. High-school-aged students (fifteen to seventeen years), who normally have lower retention rates than younger children due to the tendency to venture into the labor market early, saw attendance improve as well, from 65 percent in 1994 to 82 percent in 2007. However, the quality of public education at primary and secondary schools has remained poor, short-changing the less well-off. According to UNESCO data, Brazil ranks 114th in educational quality out of 125 countries surveyed. It underperforms terribly considering what its income per capita would predict (Amann and Baer 2009: 39–40). During the early 1990s, teacher qualifications and salaries at both the primary and the secondary level trailed behind expectations (Draibe 2004: 383). The decentralization of education policy during the 1980s and 1990s exacerbated differences across the regions while undermining any effort by the federal government to exert control over subnational education policies (Borges 2008: 238). As with other areas of social policy, educational access and quality vary geographically, with fewer enrollments per capita and lower quality education as shown by student performance on national exams in the poor states of the Northeast in comparison with the South and Southeast. Before reform of the system in 1998, average spending per pupil was twice or even three times greater in the richer states than in the poor states (Gordon and Vegas 2005: 154). Regional inequalities extend to the postgraduate level, as only 15 percent of publicly funded postgraduate fellows come from the Northeast, compared with 57.5 percent from the Southeast (IPEA 2011: 161).

Unlike the case of healthcare, where the initiative for reform came from a movement (the *sanitaristas*), or the case of conditional cash transfers, where municipal innovators played a leading role, educational interest groups such as teachers' unions, communities, and local governments have not been very influential in sparking reform. Change has come from the federal government, initially in halting steps under José Sarney and Itamar Franco in terms of decentralizing some federal programs such as the one governing school lunches. The Cardoso administration engaged in far more consequential reform. A scholar and former educator himself, Cardoso sought to change the structure of primary and secondary education radically by decentralizing it further and funding subnational governments according to set criteria. The most important changes came in the form of the Fund for Primary Education Administration and Development and for the Enhancement of Teachers (*Fundo de Manutenção e Desenvolvimento do Ensino Fundamental e de Valorização do Magistério*, FUNDEF), which was approved in December 1996 and fully implemented in 1998. The FUNDEF represented the most effective effort up to that point in reducing educational inequalities at the primary level (Hunter and Sugiyama 2009: 39; Draibe 2004). It targeted additional spending on the poorer states and municipalities that fulfilled their obligations to spend up to 25 percent of all their tax revenues on primary and secondary education. The program mandated that at least 60 percent of this amount was to be spent on teacher salaries and training. FUNDEF also required that the federal government top up expenditures in any states that fell under the per capita floor for spending. The law standardized teacher career management systems by adopting salary scales and terms for promotion. Since the monies were distributed based on enrollments, teachers, principals, and even mayors had incentives to promote more access and greater retention (Melo 2005: 874; Draibe 2004: 397). This served to decentralize education policy-making to municipalities, which could now count on a more reliable source of funding (Melo 2008: 165).

The program's decentralization of spending, accompanied by clear federal guidelines and additional fiscal resources for laggards, proved significant in addressing inequalities. An annual sum equivalent to 1.5 percent of GDP was transferred to states and municipalities (61 percent to states and 38 percent to municipalities), and the effects on access in particular were notable. Although the FUNDEF failed to guarantee in practice the federally mandated minimum per student, its incentives for states and cities to increase their spending were sufficient to begin to even out previous regional disparities in per-student spending at the primary level (Soares 1998).[19] Average spending per student increased by 22.7 percent across Brazil and an astonishing 90 percent in the Northeast (Draibe 2004: 401). Enrollments increased at their highest rates in the poor states of the Northeast (ibid.: 400; World Bank 2002). The effects of the FUNDEF on retention, class sizes, and student performance on standardized examinations have been positive as well, though more modest (Gordon and Vegas 2005). As with other Cardoso-era social policies, the Lula government kept the FUNDEF and expanded it, launching in January 2007 the Fund for Basic Education Administration and Development and the

Enhancement of the Status of Education Professionals (*Fundo de Manutenção e Desenvolvimento da Educação Básica e de Valorização do Magistério*), which replaced the FUNDEF. Access improved under the PT presidencies across all age groups (Soares and Nascimento 2011: 10). Bolstered by the PBF, the federal government has more mechanisms at its disposal to create incentives for the families of poor children to go to and stay in school.

Although the Cardoso government rhetorically made reform of unequal access to higher education a priority, it was only under the Lula presidency that action was finally taken. There is a contradiction in the relationship between public and private in the Brazilian education system that parallels the contradiction between these two spheres in healthcare. Given the poor quality of primary and secondary public schooling, it is ironic that the most prestigious institutions of higher education are public, funded by the federal and the state governments.[20] This irony is at the heart of the chief inequality across the education system: students from the private primary and secondary schools are much better prepared to pass the competitive entrance exam (the *vestibular*) to receive a free education at one of the top public universities (McCowan 2007). Inequality in education access has a strong racial dimension, as only 20 percent of all university students are of Afro-Brazilian or mixed race, despite a total population that is almost 50 percent of African ancestry (Johnson 2008).

To address the problem, the Lula administration in 2005 launched the University Program for All (PROUNI, *Programa Universidade para Todos*), which granted tax exemptions to private universities providing scholarships to students of modest means. The program included quotas for Afro-Brazilians, mulattos (*pardos*), and indigenous people. Of the 748,000 students to benefit between 2005 and 2011, half were students of color, making PROUNI the most extensive affirmative action program in the country (Feres, Daflon, and Campos 2011). The federal government established a second program to guide the public universities to adopt similar affirmative action policies, but it has failed to implement a similar set of incentives to those contained in the more robust PROUNI measure (ibid.). Nevertheless, over 70 percent of all public universities have affirmative action policies in place, two-thirds of which initiated these policies not by state mandate, but of their own accord through internal deliberations and processes. This is reflective of the growing vitality and influence of Afro-Brazilian social movements and professional groups, who have pressed institutions of higher education and enabled black students to prepare for the *vestibular* (Johnson 2008: 223–4).

To address quality issues, the Lula government developed a standardized testing regime to culminate in a Census of Basic Education (*Censo da Educação Básica*).[21] In March 2007, the federal government launched a diagnostic measure of education quality, the Basic Education Development Index (*Índice de Desenvolvimento da Educação Básica*, Ideb), which formed the main part of the

Education Development Plan.[22] According to the Ideb, virtually all of the Brazilian states have made steady progress in improving the quality of primary and secondary education, though the country as a whole is still short of reaching standards set by the Organization of Economic Cooperation and Development (OECD), which maintains the most comprehensive cross-national education quality testing regime focused on reading, mathematics, and science (IPEA 2011: 145). Yet, even here, there are signs of improvement. Between 2000 and 2009, average scores on the OECD's Pisa test of fifteen- and sixteen-year-olds increased in linear fashion, and the same has been true on Brazilian standardized tests for younger students (Soares and Nascimento 2011).

Although they represent about 7 percent of total education spending, public technical training academies have received in the last ten years an unprecedented number of students seeking post-secondary education. Enrollments in the network of technical academies grew by 39 percent between 2006 and 2009 alone. With 1 million students enrolled, the Lula government expanded space in these schools to create another 630,000 places (IPEA 2011: 147). This will require the rapid expansion of state technical academies and vocational schools within the so-called S system (the *Serviço Nacional de Apredizagem Industrial* and the *Serviço Nacional de Aprendizagem Comercial*), but the infrastructure is in place to serve increased need and demand.

The Dilma administration preserved and extended the Lula government's programs in education. Some notable contributions include the "Science without Borders" program, which is intended to send up to 100,000 Brazilian university students abroad, more than half of whom will likely go to study in the United States.

Across all of the major social indicators – income distribution, wealth, health-care, social security, and education – Brazil's turnaround has been very real. Most prominently, with the *Programa Bolsa Família*, the country may well have created a *de facto* minimum income that, along with the FUNRURAL non-contributory pension and the minimum wage, provide a floor for household earnings that may be adjusted higher in future years as resources permit. Along with the expansion of healthcare services to the poor in urban and rural areas and the participatory power-sharing enjoyed by health councils, improvements in access to primary and secondary education, and even modest openings of higher education, this combination of policy mechanisms form an effective poverty-alleviation and even poverty-prevention repertoire.

Cutting further into the country's extreme income inequality, however, will require transferring resources from the top income quartile downward. The lopsided benefits of the pension system should be a priority for all future reforms in this area. Brazil needs policies that go beyond poverty alleviation to address the precarious nature of work for millions in the poor working class who do not qualify for the PBF, especially in urban areas. Blacks and women in the informal sector and those working in the formal sector without social security protection are most vulnerable to falling through the cracks. These groups are in danger of not seeing their life chances improve, even as families much poorer than they enjoy greater assistance.

CHAPTER SEVEN

Brazilian Foreign Policy

Brazil's role in the world is difficult to categorize. The evolution of the country's international relations remains subject to shifts that cause it to have a kind of identity crisis. Its large domestic market, its environmental and natural resources, its advanced technology, and its considerable capital should make Brazil at least a regional power, but the governments of the democratic period have not pursued the clear or consistent foreign policy of a regional power. Despite its abundant economic and security resources, it lacks the will to throw its weight around. This contradiction has been reflected historically in the way that the Foreign Ministry, also known as Itamaraty, has assiduously worked to enhance the credibility of Brazil in the world and within Latin America but has been reluctant to pursue stronger ambitions to acquire dominance or manifest imperialist temptations (Burges 2009). Even though the turnaround produced notable improvements in Brazil's economic performance and political governability, it did not make the country a global power. Brazil lacks the military and financial capabilities to influence international institutions and other regions of the world on its own. Even its status as a regional power in South America is still emerging, though this is tempered by the fact that its neighbors are not ready to be led or represented by Brazil (Almeida 2010). The result is a foreign policy that remains fluid and has been perpetually evolving, with differences evident between the democratic and non-democratic periods, over the duration of the democratic period and between particular presidents.[1] This chapter demonstrates that no clear consensus has shaped Brazilian foreign policy during the democratic period, which has led to a contradictory pattern of occasionally demanding the transformation of global processes without the demonstrated will to make sacrifices and show leadership either at the regional or the global level. Consequently, it is precisely in this area that the implications of the turnaround are most ambiguous and subject to change. Brazil is a middle power without a clear mission that consistently links its ambitions and interests with concerted actions.

Brazilian foreign policy during the last twenty years has followed several trends, but none of these have clearly enhanced its international relations or positioned it to take advantage of the country's reversal of fortune. The first and most noticeable in the democratic period is that Cardoso and the PT presidencies became diplomats-in-chief, crafting the international relations of Brazil far more directly than was the case with their predecessors, who delegated that responsibility to the professional diplomats of Itamaraty (Cason and Power 2009; Malamud 2005; Souza 2009; Vilela and Neiva 2011). "Presidential diplomacy" involves more foreign travel, the hosting of international summits, and generally more robust forms of personal engagement by the president in the framing and conduct of foreign policy. Burges (2009) traces the beginning of the most recent trend of presidential diplomacy to the time that Cardoso served as Itamar Franco's foreign minister, months before he became the finance minister. Yet it is the link to economic policy that is most relevant for understanding sustained presidential diplomacy. The internationalization of the Brazilian economy, and particularly the growing importance of trade and transnational investment, made foreign economic policy an extension of domestic economic policy, a priority of presidents. The focus on promoting Brazil's economic development remains the centerpiece of the way that the presidency defines the country's interests in the conduct of foreign policy – yet that underscores its inward-looking nature.

Regardless of the administration guiding foreign policy, Brazilian international relations during the democratic period have consistently embraced multilateralism as a means for dealing with issues ranging from security to trade to the environment (Lima and Hirst 2006; Amorim 2010). But support for multilateralism is acutely sensitive to the obligations of reciprocity. "Reciprocal multilateralism" means that collective responsibility prevents any one power from imposing its will on others, while all states have duties to treat others the way they have been treated (Cervo 2010). This underscores the value of non-discrimination in trade, collective responsibility in international environmental regimes, and collective international security through multilateral bodies such as the United Nations Security Council. This principle leaves little room for the exercise of leadership by any one country.

The belief in multilateralism resides, sometimes inelegantly, alongside a more nationalist and aggrandized self-image that Brazilian elites espouse of their country as *primus inter pares* in South America. Since 1993 especially, Itamaraty has embraced the notion of South America as a geopolitical and economic unit in which, naturally, the largest country, Brazil, has an outsize role as the hub of the continent (Vigevani and Ramanzini Júnior 2011). The most robust articulation of this concept of South America came from Celso Lafer, Cardoso's foreign minister in 2001–2, who brushed aside the obvious cultural and linguistic differences between Brazil and its Hispanic neighbors to argue that the countries of South America had elective affinities based on similar levels of economic and political development that required that they act collectively (Burges 2009: 72–3). The ostensible purpose of this formulation was to provide a modified version of the economic policies advocated by Washington (i.e., the Washington Consensus), but the shift from "Latin

America" to "South America" also served to bolster Brazil's leverage in the wider world as the leader of a continent. By focusing on South America as its power base, it excluded Mexico, the second largest Latin American economy, and all of the countries of Central America and the Caribbean that, like Mexico, orient their economic and security interests to the United States. This affords Brazil a range of regional partners who share a broad view of foreign affairs. After Lafer's tenure ended, and under the Lula administration, Itamaraty dramatically increased its diplomatic corps in South America and reduced its role in Europe (Lima and Hirst 2006: 30). The move, of course, delimited Brazil's ambitions to arrive at global power status by depending on its regional positioning.

Another recurring theme in Brazilian foreign affairs has been the maintenance of a historic balance between cooperation and competition in relations with the United States. Under the founder of modern foreign policy in Brazil, the Baron of Rio Branco, who served as foreign minister from 1902 until his death in 1912, close relations with the US provided protection from foreign incursions by European powers. Soon after Brazil began to advance its own industrialization under Getúlio Vargas, it became a more reliable partner of the US, and it was the only South American country to join the Allied effort in 1942 against the Axis powers. It supported the US during the Cold War in international forums such as the Organization of American States and the United Nations, even though it failed to receive a coveted permanent seat on the UN Security Council. The 1960s began a process that scholars call the "independent foreign policy" (*política externa independente*) in which Brazil separated itself from the American sphere of influence and re-established relations with the Soviet bloc. After the brief antagonism towards the US under the ill-fated presidencies of Jânio Quadros and João Goulart, the military governments reinstated a foreign policy that toed Washington's line on the Cold War. Yet the generals were willing to provoke the US again in 1977, when they cancelled an extant agreement with the Americans proscribing Brazil from developing its own nuclear technology. Given a strong current of nationalism in Brazil's domestic and foreign policy, it is not surprising that it has diverged at times from US interests to pursue an independent tack (Guilhon Albuquerque 2003). More recently, balancing US influence became an explicit dimension of foreign policy under Celso Amorim, Lula's foreign minister. Amorim practiced a policy of "benign restraint," in which Brazil challenged the US on specific issues such as the war in Iraq and discriminatory trade practices, but cooperated on the drug war, the war against terrorism, and the strengthening of international economic institutions meant to forestall crises (e.g., the IMF) and aid economic development (e.g., the World Bank) (cf. Amorim 2010).

Regionalism plays a central role in Brazil's international relations. The origins of regionalism in the country's foreign policy date back to Rio Branco's efforts to create a permanent alliance with Argentina and Chile – the so-called

ABC pact. From this point, and during the Cold War, Brazil sought to be the interlocutor for South America, a position that often led to rivalry with its old ABC partners. During the democratic period, Brazil continued to invest in regionalism, most notably through the common market group Mercosul (*Mercado Comum do Sul*), composed of Argentina, Brazil, Paraguay, Uruguay, and Venezuela.[2]

These associations have proven to be a double-edged sword, with smaller economies wary of being overrun by their larger neighbor. Brazil's actions have often justified this wariness, as it has periodically abandoned the principles of organizations such as Mercosul by adopting tariff and non-tariff barriers such as environmental regulations when domestic industries called for protection (Hochstetler 2003: 14; Cason 2000; Malamud 2011). In response, its regional partners have exacted concessions. Paraguay and Uruguay, as signatories of Mercosul, have been able to exclude more of their nationally produced goods from the common external tariff of 35 percent, and Paraguay, which shares the hydroelectric resources of Itaipú, has received additional payments for its share of electricity generated by the plant (Almeida 2010: 166). Bolivia, an associate member of Mercosul, challenged Brazil most directly when it nationalized by presidential decree on May Day 2006 oil and gas facilities managed by Petrobras, leaving the company after a negotiated settlement with only 18 percent of the profits. And although Latin America as a whole might gain from seeing Brazil join the UN Security Council, Mexico and Argentina have strongly opposed such a move.

Relations with Argentina have always been the most important among Brazil's South American neighbors, but they have also entertained the greatest extremes, swinging between periods of sustained cooperation and bellicose saber-rattling. The military governments in both countries during the 1970s pushed affairs to the limit by initiating a rivalry over nuclear technology and a competition over who would exert the most influence over the River Plate basin. These tensions eased following democratic transitions in both countries and the signing of various agreements, including in November 1990 a non-proliferation accord, the Declaration on Nuclear Policy of Foz do Iguaçu, which set the stage for deeper economic union the following year through the creation of Mercosul. And, despite the spasmodic evolution of the customs union and the intermittent trade disputes that renew Argentine–Brazilian rivalry, closer economic cooperation has ushered in the most stable period of bilateral relations in the Southern Cone (Cason 2000: 207; Remmer 1998). But the tensions between the two countries remain real, capable of flaring up during periods of acute economic crisis.

The trends and themes profiled above form only the most general guidelines for understanding the evolution of Brazilian foreign policy during the democratic period. As much as scholars of the country's foreign affairs would like to incorporate this trajectory into a coherent school of thought or imbed it in an understanding of just one organization such as Itamaraty, shifts in international relations defy such efforts. At times Brazilian foreign policy has been reactive to external forces and domestic demands, while at others it has been proactive and forward-looking, but these trends have not been sustained long enough to allow observers to pigeonhole them. All too often, changes in presidential administration, especially since 1993, have led to a debate about whether progressive policy consistency or wholesale paradigmatic shifts characterize Brazilian international relations. The next section deals with the particular debate concerning the differences between the foreign policies of the Cardoso administration and the PT presidencies. This subject has become the focus of much recent scholarship on foreign affairs, but, alas, it has produced few sustainable insights that serve to help observers understand how Brazilian foreign policy evolves. The subsequent sections are thematic, focusing analysis on foreign economic policy, international security policy, and environmental policy during the democratic period. In each of these areas, Brazil's foreign policy exerts a form of two-mindedness – an identity crisis that belies what should be the country's undisputed status as a regional power with up-and-coming global influence. Instead, it seems trapped in a middle power dilemma, of knowing that it ought to be a bigger player in international relations but seemingly unwilling or unable to play the leadership role, either in the region or in the world, to which the ambitions of many foreign policy-makers aspire.

Foreign Policy between the Cardoso and PT Presidencies

Unlike his successors, Cardoso had ten years to imprint his preferences on Brazilian foreign policy, beginning during the time that he served as Itamar Franco's foreign minister between October 1992 and May 1993 and then later as president from 1995 to 2003. As was the case in economic and social policy, Cardoso established a set of trajectories in foreign policy that found congruence with the international relations pursued by the PT presidencies. It should be recalled that Lula's "Letter to the Brazilian People" pledged to keep Brazil's commitments to the IMF, effectively consolidating in foreign economic policy the existing dedication to fiscal surpluses, stable currency, and low inflation. Although the Lula administration pursued a foreign policy with strong South–South inflections, the main emphases on enhancing Brazil's position in global trade and multilaterialism were carried over from the Cardoso era.

The consistency of foreign economic policy between the Cardoso and PT administrations was not pursued in all other areas, and, indeed, there is a debate among former foreign ministers and scholars about the degree of continuity.[3] Cardoso's foreign policy consolidated a trend in Brazilian international affairs following the democratic transition by reversing the military's reluctance to engage international regimes and so returning the country to international credibility. Itamaraty reverted to its long-held embrace of reciprocal multilateralism and away from nationalism. For some scholars, Lula's foreign policy represented more of a resumption of the pursuit of autonomy, particularly in terms of economic development (Lima and Hirst 2006: 25; Pecequilo 2008). If Cardoso's foreign policy was somewhat wedded to the institutions and interests of OECD economies, Lula's foreign policy pursued a more genuine South–South strategy, emphasizing aid and cooperation with poor countries in Africa and Latin America (Vigevani and Cepaluni 2007; Pecequilo 2008). Over 70 percent of his foreign trips were to Latin American, Asian, or African capitals, and these regions represented the destination of virtually all of Brazil's foreign technical missions and financial assistance (Ayllón Pino 2012: 191, 199). This "diplomacy of generosity," as Lula called it, emanated from the most leftist elements within the PT, whom Lula installed in positions of authority over foreign policy, if only to allay the worries of progressive factions within the party that they would not gain significant posts in the president's first cabinet (Hunter 2010; Burges 2009: 160–1). Lula's foreign minister, Celso Amorim, the secretary-general of Itamaraty, Samuel Pinheiro Guimarães, and Marco Aurélio Garcia, as Lula's advisor on foreign relations, often issued more nationalistic recommendations that conflicted with the preferences of the policy establishment in Itamaraty and elsewhere in Brasília. Almeida (2010) sees less of an exchange with leftist factions within the party and more of a direct imposition of a mixed bag of ideas ranging from nationalism and anti-imperialism emanating from the PT and dominating foreign policy. Lula's close relations with the Castro brothers in Cuba and Hugo Chávez in Venezuela, and his provocative association with Iran, attest to the capacity of his foreign policy to depart from Cardoso's positions. The same was true of Lula's pursuit of the India–Brazil–South Africa Dialogue (IBSA) as a means to forge closer trade and technological cooperation with other developing countries beyond Latin America. One fundamental distinction from the Cardoso years was that, given these new directions, Lula's foreign policy elites were much more inclined to talk about Brazilian leadership (Burges 2009: 183–4). Yet, at the same time, this South–South orientation broadened the range of developing countries Brazil considered its allies, thereby reducing the importance of retaining uncompromised support within South America (Lima and Hirst 2006).

How important are these differences across administrations when compared to the overall tendency to embrace continuity on principles of foreign economic policy? What there is of systematic empirical evidence for the differences among the foreign policies of the presidents focuses on indicators such as public statements and the records of presidential visits. Vilela and Neiva (2011) have conducted the most extensive quantitative study of foreign policy speeches to date, covering the Cardoso and Lula administrations. Their findings show that Lula's administration was oriented more towards Africa, Asia, and the Middle East and away from Europe, Cardoso's priority; but both governments gave South America precedence and both pursued reciprocal multilateralism.[4] It should be recalled that Lula's leadership in creating the South American Community in December 2004, and transforming it into the Union of South American Nations in May 2008, was a process that emerged originally from the summit of South American presidents in Brasília organized by Cardoso in September 2000. Saraiva (2007) shows that the South–South axis in Brazilian foreign policy dates back to Cardoso's time as Itamar Franco's foreign minister, so it is hardly a component that clearly separates the two presidents. Cardoso emphasized democracy more than social inequality, and Lula reversed the order of these priorities, but he kept both at the top of the list. Lula seemed to emphasize more a rhetorical call for an autonomous Brazilian foreign policy, but not one that went beyond the traditional parameters of preserving generally cooperative relations with the US and Europe. Beyond these themes, on virtually all other major issues ranging from international security to the environment, the two administrations tended to embrace similar principles of foreign policy, giving different inflections to some aspects.

Dilma's foreign policy through 2012 eschewed the more provocative international associations of her predecessor. Early in her term, she distanced herself from Lula's support for Iran by backing a US request for human rights monitoring of that country by the United Nations (Engstrom 2012: 839). Unlike her mentor, she has been less keen to placate far-left interests within the PT by giving them access to foreign policy-making. Nor does she have an international reputation to burnish as Lula did. Lula was viewed widely as an icon of the Latin American left and a global advocate for social justice issues, but Dilma has none of those expectations surrounding her, so the personal quality of her foreign policy is notably subdued by comparison. Dilma has traveled far less than Lula and focused much more on domestic issues, many of which, though, encompass an international dimension. For example, the priority Dilma has given the development of Brazil's energy resources will affect relations with Bolivia, Venezuela, Paraguay, and Argentina, all of which have strong ties to Brazil as markets for energy. Dilma has sought better relations with the US following the distance with Washington created by Lula, but this is unlikely to get Brazil much further on some key issues. One indication of this is that Barack Obama was eager to shower Dilma with accolades during his visit to Brazil in March 2011 but, unlike his promise to India, was disinclined to endorse Brazil's effort to secure a permanent seat on the UN Security Council. Dilma did not even warrant a state dinner when she visited Washington a year later, which is an honor routinely given to visiting heads of state from the other BRICSA countries.

A strong reason for the general continuity in the framing of Brazilian foreign policy is the importance that Cardoso and the PT presidents have given domestic policy priorities. Brasília's approach to trade, regional integration, capital account openness, and both inward and outward foreign investment has been shaped by domestic policy goals of price stabilization, growth of the domestic market, access to foreign markets, and the protection of Brazilian assets abroad. As developmentalist priorities have become a bigger driver of economic policy, rhetorical commitments to multilateral goals have become secondary. In foreign security policy, a similar tendency to defend national interests, sometimes at the cost of addressing transnational problems such as the drug war more efficiently through international cooperation, has taken hold. Environmental policy has challenged the growth-oriented administrations of Lula and Dilma to exploit energy and build infrastructure while preserving improvements such as declining deforestation rates. In these policy areas, all good things have not gone together, and Brazilian foreign policy-makers have often had to choose in favor of short-term national interests versus longer-term interests in carving out a global or regional leadership role for the country.

Foreign Economic Policy

Brazil's foreign economic policy is best described as being of two minds. During the 1990s Brasília generally followed an application of reciprocal multilateralism to international trade and investment regimes. It thus sought to extend its influence (and obligations) to blocs of trading partners such as the Mercosul countries and the European Union and to expand its network of bilateral ties to advanced capitalist and developing countries. But Brazilian elites do not see the rules governing international trade and investment as disinterested. Rather, according to Itamaraty, international markets are governed in an asymmetric manner, where the rules favor the interests of the advanced capitalist countries. This is a primary reason why Brazil has not accepted the more orthodox variations of the Washington Consensus of some other Latin American countries, and it is why the policy agenda gradually shifted during the 1990s to a mixed approach that melded liberalism and developmentalism (Burges 2009: 83–7). Even during the more neoliberal administrations of Sarney and Collor, business and government elites championed a policy of "competitive integration" that favored using export promotion and industrial policies to enable firms to compete with imports and foreign firms (Kingstone 2004: 164–5). Under Cardoso, these policies became more intentional, as chapter 5 showed. The advent of more expansive industrial policy under the PT presidencies coincided with the fragmentation of multilateral trade accords following the decline and eventual demise of the Doha trade round. This made the pursuit of competitive integration more difficult, as Brazil lost with the end of Doha a multilateral channel for shaping the international rules governing trade and investment. Its attempts to reconstruct a forum for significant developing countries, through either the G-20 or the IBSA/BRICSA countries, have thus far produced few notable successes.

The evolution of Brazil's foreign economic policy is first and foremost imbedded in the process of regional integration. From the early 1990s, Brazilian foreign policy elites realized the multiple benefits of speaking of "South America" as opposed to "Latin America" or the entire hemisphere. As mentioned before, the concept opened the door to integration but also to accentuating Brazil's standing in the region and in the world (Burges 2009: 71–4). Soon after the transition to democracy, the pursuit of greater economic cooperation with Argentina became the first path towards deeper regional collaboration. Following his inauguration, José Sarney signed the Program of Economic Integration and Cooperation (*Programa de Integração e Cooperação Econômica*) with his Argentine counterpart, President Raúl Alfonsín. Although this was meant to assuage tensions along Brazil's southern border, it broached the possibility of deeper economic cooperation between these erstwhile rivals. It revived trade between the two countries, laying the groundwork for a marked improvement in bilateral and regional commerce that would last until the crisis of the *real* in Brazil in 1999 and the Argentine financial meltdown of late 2001. In the meantime, Brazil's importance as Argentina's chief market for exports of manufactured products solidified their mutual interests, allaying erstwhile tensions.

Regional integration involving Argentina also made sense as part of a phased process of integrating the Brazilian market into global trade. By signing in March 1991 the Treaty of Asunción, which created the Common Market of the South (Mercosul), Brazil entered into its first customs union. Yet motivations were mixed, as the Brazilian government and domestic business groups preferred rules that were less binding than those of other customs unions, such as the earliest incarnations of the European Economic Community (Gómez Mera 2005: 127).[5] At the same time, the common external tariff of 35 percent during the 1990s satisfied the ambitions of some Itamaraty technocrats, who saw in the customs union a means to attract foreign direct investment to Brazil. In this vision, Mercosul would allow investors to use Brazil as a production hub with guaranteed access to neighboring markets but protect the area from extra-regional imports (Burges 2009: 37–8).

The actual deepening of regional integration through Mercosul proved tortuous due to its dependence on the relations among the various presidents. Shifts in incentives would cause presidents to reverse previous positions on the customs union (Malamud 2005; Gómez Mera 2008). Consequently, Mercosul proved vulnerable to sudden changes in macro-economic policy such as the maxi-devaluations of national currency that coincided with the *real* crisis in January 1999 and the Argentine financial meltdown of 2001 (Carranza 2003; Gómez Mera 2005). Equally sudden shifts in trade policy, such as Cardoso's decision to protect domestic producers by imposing much higher duties on automobile and auto parts imports in 1995, directly threatened the customs union (Cason 2000; Malamud 2005: 143–6; Gómez Mera 2009). Cardoso proved more restrained by comparison following a bout of

Argentine protectionism in response to the *real* crisis. Preserving Mercosul remained more important than tit-for-tat strategic trade interests (Burges 2009: 106–7).[6] This priority proved to be short-lived. Soon after Lula was elected, he traveled to Argentina on his first official visit. His promises of renewing the Program of Economic Integration and Cooperation and strengthening Mercosul were forgotten afterwards, as Brazil's growing trade surpluses with Argentina after 2003 increased trade tensions, setting the stage for a litany of disputes between the two partners in a diverse array of sectors, among them frozen poultry, textiles, shoes, appliances, autos, steel, dairy products, and machine parts (Gómez Mera 2009; Montero 2005: 125). Most fundamentally, during the 2000s, the Brazilian government turned to making the most of its position in global markets, moving regional integration onto the back burner in foreign economic policy (Vigevani and Ramanzini Júnior 2011).

Forging closer links with Brazil's Mercosul partners has often been a process in opposition to creating stronger links with the United States. In this regard, Itamaraty and the Ministry of Development, Industry and Trade (*Ministério de Desenvolvimento, Indústria e Comércio Exterior*), which manages much of Brazil's trade policy, have recognized the advantages of gaining more access to the American domestic market, but this has been tempered by skepticism as to whether Washington will follow through on its commitments to liberalize access (Burges 2009: 33). Trade rows, some involving the WTO, emerged during the 2000s over soy, orange juice, cotton, steel, and sugar, complicating the bilateral relationship. These and other differences in interest have kept consistently anemic ideas such as the Free Trade Area of the Americas (FTAA), which began as the hemispheric-wide Enterprise for the Americas Initiative of George H. W. Bush (1989–93). After more than twenty years of talk and occasional hemispheric summits, the initial visions of creating a free trade zone throughout the Americas now seems entirely fanciful. Part of the problem is that Brazil has stronger loyalty to a South American free trade area as a counterweight to the US (Gómez-Mera 2005). The BNDES has spent over $382 million on assistance to cross-border infrastructure and utility projects in Argentina, Venezuela, and Bolivia to bolster the prospects of greater integration without US involvement. So, when Brazil and the US co-chaired the FTAA process in 2003–4, negotiations broke down into squabbles between Mercosul and the US (Lima and Hirst 2006: 34). Yet the failure of the FTAA has resulted in costs for Brazil. The weakness of the initiative persuaded Washington to pursue bilateral trade ties with Chile, Peru, and Colombia, thereby undercutting Brazil's efforts at South American trade bloc unity (Souza 2009: 7).

Brazil was free to deviate from the principles imbedded in the FTAA because Lula had a broader range of maneuver in his foreign economic policy than in his domestic economic policy. In this regard he espoused heterodoxy even as his domestic economic policies embraced his predecessor's orthodoxy

(Vilela and Neiva 2011: 76). This deviation from Cardoso's approach is largely due to the PT's own equivocal stance on globalization, but it must not be interpreted as a break with the political economic principles of the preceding administration. Although the PT's critics charge that the president and his party are opposed to globalization, the Lula and Dilma administrations proved to be quite adept at promoting the internationalization of the Brazilian economy using public agents such as the BNDES and Petrobras, as chapter 5 showed. If they have enacted more fundamental changes, it has been in the emphasis given to trade and investment in other developing areas. Lula's trade strategy redirected Brazilian exports away from the Mercosul partners towards other developing areas such as China, Africa, and the Pacific Rim (Almeida 2011).

The renewal of developmentalist policy since the democratic transition became fully consolidated under the PT presidencies, fundamentally reorienting Brazil's approach to the global trading regime and the WTO. Under the General Agreement on Trade and Tariffs regime and the Uruguay round during the 1990s, Brazil took to opposing environmental regulations and information technology accords on the grounds that these impinged unfairly on the capacity of developing countries to scale up their own industries (Guilhon Albuquerque 2003). In the Doha trade rounds during the 2000s, Brazil joined other agricultural exporters in the developing world to push for more access to the markets of the developed countries. This position brought it into greater contention with these countries (Cervo 2010: 16). Not surprisingly, Brazil's activities at the WTO are dominated by actions brought by Brasília to liberalize agricultural markets and end subsidies in the more developed economies. These conflicts came to a head at the 2003 WTO ministerial meeting in Cancún, Mexico, where Brazil and other significant developing countries led a walkout, leading to the meeting breaking down in acrimony. Brazil stuck to its divisive position even as its trade surplus grew after Cancún and the Doha trade rounds faltered. Its actions helped motivate the expansion of the G-7 to the G-20, the primary forum for the most significant economies in the world.

While not rejecting the WTO process and, in fact, arguing on behalf of expanding it to include agriculture more formally, several tendencies prompted Brazil to cease accommodating the agenda of OECD economies at the trade meetings. First, the rise of South–South trade created avenues to gain access to foreign markets that are not heavily protected either by tariffs or by subsidies. Given the rising importance of agricultural and other commodity exports in Brazil's export bundle after 2002, Brasília developed a more acute interest in addressing the matter of OECD subsidies at WTO meetings (Souza 2009). Second, Brazil's commitment to developmentalism is an influential counterweight to the dominant discourse in international development institutions, which tend to embrace the importance of market efficiency and discount the need to transform productive structures (Chang 2011; Wade

2011). Brazil has sought to engage the WTO and change it rather than retreat from it. Lula floated like-minded leftists to head the WTO such as Roberto Amaral. Dilma's ambassador to the WTO, Roberto Azevedo, received the support of eighty-nine countries, mostly in the developing world, to become the next director-general in September 2013, though he was not the candidate favored by the United States.

A look at the evolution of Brazil's trade underscores some of the reasons for the new emphases given by the PT presidencies. Figures 7.1 and 7.2 detail the direction and origins of exports and imports, respectively. Trade with the European Union and the United States, which represented almost 60 percent of Brazil's exports and 44 percent of all imports in 1990, fell to less than 31 percent of all exports and 36 percent of all imports by 2011. There are two clear periods in the shift of direction. During the 1990s, there was a marked increase in exports to the Mercosul countries that were the original signatories of the Treaty of Asunción. Trade fell with these countries during the financial crises of the late 1990s and early 2000s but picked up again during the commodity boom following 2002. Trade with the bloc was notably affected by the addition of Venezuela (the line for Mercosul (b)). Between 2002 and 2011, Venezuela accounted for an annual average of $3 billion more in Brazilian exports to Mercosul. The 1990s saw the slow rise of Brazilian trade with China, but only after Beijing's accession to the WTO in October 2001 did

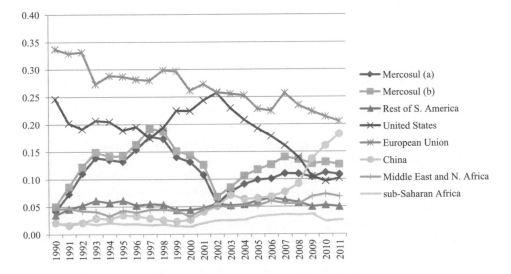

Note: Mercosul (a) excludes Venezuela; Mercosul (b) includes Venezuela.

Source: IMF, *Direction of Trade Statistics.*

Figure 7.1 *The direction of Brazilian exports as a percentage of total exports, 1990–2011*

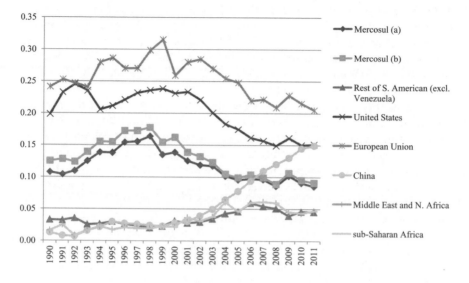

Note: Mercosul (a) excludes Venezuela; Mercosul (b) includes Venezuela.

Source: IMF, *Direction of Trade Statistics.*

Figure 7.2 *The origin of Brazilian imports as a percentage of total imports, 1990–2011*

trade increase and more rapidly than with any other major market. Total exports to China stood at $1.6 billion in 1995, $7.7 billion in 2005, and $46.5 billion in 2011, a stunning rise of twenty-nine times the 1995 baseline. Whereas exports to China were only 3 percent of total Brazilian exports in 1995, that figure had climbed to 18 percent by 2011. In 2009, China surpassed the United States as Brazil's top trade partner. By comparison, trade with the rest of Latin America, the Middle East and North Africa, and sub-Saharan Africa, despite Lula's South–South push, remained much the same during the 2000s. More notable is the shift of trade *within* the South–South dimension. Brazilian exports and imports with Mercosul countries have declined since 2006, while trade with China continues its upward trajectory.

To the extent that Brazil's evolving policy direction favors internationalization, new pressures to return to the principles of non-discrimination will emerge even as support for hemispheric alternatives such as the Free Trade Area of the Americas wane. The developmentalist push to expand exports produces a stronger link between Brazil and globalization, not a weaker one. It should be recalled that the industrial policies of the PT presidencies in particular envisioned goals that assumed a more profound deepening of the Brazilian economy's insertion into global markets. For example, the PDP targeted an increase of Brazil's share of global exports from 1.24 percent in 2008 to 1.5 percent (Cano and Silva 2010: 198).

There is an evident two-mindedness in Brazil's foreign economic policy. As regards Mercosul, Brazil has sought to make regional integration a counterweight to the United States and to enlarge its influence in the world. But these ambitions have been curtailed by Brazil's own apprehensions about sacrificing its national economic autonomy to regional formats that limit its strategic trade and industrial policies (Vigevani and Ramanzini Júnior 2011). A similar indecision affects Brazil's approach to the rules governing international trade and investment. The country remains committed to non-discrimination, and it defends its interests with this in mind at WTO trade and G-20 meetings. But it remains deeply sensitive to the efforts of advanced capitalist countries to limit "beyond the border" policies by developing countries that are defended by these same countries as protection of infant industries and market-oriented developmentalism.

The Internationalization of Economic Influence

As Brazil's foreign economic policy has concentrated most visibly on trade and regional integration, foreign direct investment (FDI) has played a subtler but no less important role in the strategic internationalization of the economy. During the turnaround, Brazil became one of the largest recipients of FDI among developing countries, accounting for more than 40 percent of Latin America's total of $154 billion in 2011 (ECLAC 2012). Large Brazilian firms have also become more significant investors in Latin America and beyond. State-controlled institutions such as the BNDES and Petrobras have also become major players, often linking their actions to the strategies of private firms.

Figure 7.3 shows outward and inward flows of FDI from 1990 to 2011. Once again, the period 2003–11 is distinctive. Although inward FDI recovered strongly after the Real Plan, the financial crises of the later part of the decade and the slowdown at the end of Cardoso's second term led to a noticeable decline. As the growth trajectory improved after 2003, inward FDI boomed, increasing from $10 billion in 2003 to $67 billion in 2011.[7] The use of third countries and investments coming from multiple subsidiaries across different countries makes attribution of the national origins of inward FDI tricky. But, based on official sources, European multinationals have remained the top investors, with 64 percent, followed by Japan at 13.6 percent and North American companies at 10.4 percent (ECLAC 2012: 28). A plurality of these investments (46 percent) was focused on the manufacturing sector, but services (44 percent), especially in telecommunications and commerce, are a close second. Energy represents a strategic sector, particularly in oil, though these investments are subject to strict local-content regulations. Nonetheless, foreign companies have invested heavily in the sector, including in biofuels,

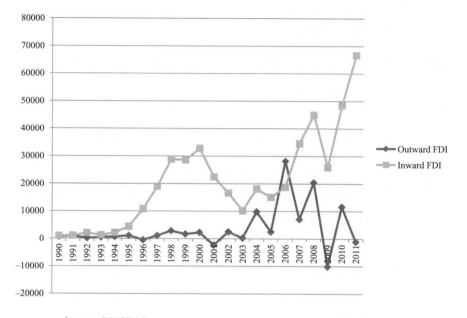

Source: UNCTAD.

Figure 7.3 *Foreign direct investment flows, 1990–2011 (US$million at current exchange rate)*

wind, solar, and petroleum exploration and refining. Multinationals now account for more than half of all electricity generation capacity, whereas in 2003 they represented less than one-third (ibid.: 17).

The economic turnaround contributed to a substantial increase in outward FDI. In terms of sales, size, and number, Brazilian firms led the rest of Latin America in the so-called *multilatinas* trend that captured the attention of the international financial press.[8] Figure 7.3 shows an irregular pattern for outward FDI as it peaks in 2006 at $28.8 billion. Yet these figures can be deceptive, since the dips reflect not disinvestment abroad but loans made by foreign subsidiaries of Brazilian firms in the home economy (ECLAC 2012: 8). The overall pattern of outward FDI is towards greater and more diversified forms of investment by Brazilian firms (Fleury and Fleury 2011). Table 7.1 lists the twelve largest multinational Brazilian firms by sales in 2011. The first five are among the ten largest *multilatinas*, with Petrobras being the biggest non-financial firm from the region in 2012. The sectoral composition as well as the investment and payroll distribution reflect a diversity in structure that suggests multiple strategies of internationalization. Excluding investments to the Cayman Islands and other tax shelters, these firms have invested heavily in South America, but also in the United States and Europe. Brazilian

Table 7.1 The largest multinational Brazilian companies, by total sales, 2011

Company	Sales (US$million)	Percentage invested abroad	Percentage of employees abroad	Sector
Petrobras	130,171	32	18	Oil/gas
Vale	55,014	51	27	Mining
JBS Friboi	32,944	67	62	Food
Odebrecht	32,325	57	49	Construction
Gerdau	18,876	61	48	Metallurgy
Brazil Foods	13,486	16	16	Food
Marfig	11,548	32	42	Food
Camargo Corrêa	9,610	15	17	Construction
Andrade Gutierrez	8,400	8	10	Construction
TAM	6,927	9	8	Airlines
Votorantim	5,680	50	36	Cement
Embraer	5,141	27	12	Aerospace

Source: ECLAC (2012: 49).

multinationals prefer greenfield projects as their chief mode of operation, shying away from mergers and acquisitions. The largest greenfield projects remain in the energy, construction, and food sectors (UNCTAD 2004, 2012).

The BNDES has increasingly been involved in the strategic internationalization of the Brazilian *multilatinas*, complementing Brazil's foreign economic policy in the area of trade. The bank became a chief financier of outward FDI during the Lula administration, and it even set up offices abroad in London and Montevideo to help the bank raise capital in international markets to finance Brazilian firms wishing to invest abroad. Federal laws restrict the BNDES's use of its core capital resources to finance outward FDI or exports from trade partners, though projects satisfying regulations that guarantee a return to the Brazilian economy commensurate with the amount of loans provided and capital raised for foreign ventures have been supported since 2002. The Dilma Rousseff government is considering loosening even these restrictions.

Foreign Security Policy

The foreign policy elites view international security policy as an area in which erstwhile principles of foreign policy are married with pragmatic ideas concerning relations with the US. In this area, Brazil has been most consistent in embracing the principle of reciprocal multilateralism, particularly when it comes to collective security in the world and in the region. At the same time, based on pragmatism, it seeks closer cooperation with the US than is the case in the bilateral relationship in economic affairs. This tendency is reflected positively in the Brazilian realization dating back to Rio Branco that the Americans share Brazil's interest in keeping European and other powers out of the hemisphere's affairs. In more recent years, it includes a shared principle in fighting common "internal" threats such as narco-terrorism. But cooperation with the US is also tempered by the wariness of becoming too dependent on American security resources. A more elaborate extension of this wariness is the proactive policy reflected in Celso Amorim's commitment to "benign restraint" of the United States. According to the doctrine practiced most under Lula's presidency, Brazil sought to balance against efforts by Washington to impose its will in the region while supporting the Americans in multilateral efforts that were consistent with building democracy and promoting stability in South America. One prominent example of balancing against the Americans involves the priority given to Amazonian defense, an area that is most sensitive to riling the nationalist sentiments of Brazilians. One consequence of this perspective is that Brazilian foreign policy elites have sometimes missed the way that security problems are transnational. Neither Cardoso nor Lula, for example, developed a coherent policy to address narco-trafficking, terrorism, or insurgency in neighboring countries (Burges 2009: 189).

Although Brazil has a larger defense budget than all other Latin American countries combined, it sees itself as a peaceful country committed to international law.[9] Brazil's commitment to these principles is reflected in word and deed, as the country has signed up to every major treaty that regulates the behavior of states towards one another and with respect to their own people. It is a signatory to the UN Declaration of Human Rights, the International Covenant on Civil and Political Rights, the International Covenant on Economic, Social and Cultural Rights, the Inter-American Convention on Human Rights, the Convention on the Rights of the Child, the Conventional Against Torture and Other Cruel, Inhuman, or Degrading Treatment or Punishment, and the Inter-American Convention to Prevent and Punish Torture. Brazil recognizes the authority of the Inter-American Court on Human Rights and the International Criminal Court in The Hague. Its penchant for reciprocal multilateralism has made it highly critical of US unilateralism and pre-emption, especially in the run-up to the war in Iraq and in the treatment of prisoners at the US base in Guantánamo, Cuba. Brazil supports collective security and multilateral approaches to resolving armed conflicts. For example, it has worked through the Organization of American States, Latin America's chief multilateral forum, as well as through Mercosul and the UN, to strengthen peace and democracy elsewhere. Brazil committed its own soldiers to UN peacekeeping operations in Haiti and East Timor. And

Brasília has used these experiences to argue on behalf of a larger role for the country in the UN, notably in a call to "democratize" the Security Council by creating additional chairs, including a permanent one for itself.

Brazil's embrace of collective security as a principle was reflected in a significant downscaling of its military rivalry with Argentina. Both countries ended their nuclear weapons programs during the 1980s, leading to a signed agreement in 1990 that renounced the development of nuclear weapons in South America (Resende-Santos 2002). Argentina and Brazil also agreed, at a critical time following transitions to democracy in both countries, to shift security policy from the armed forces to their foreign ministries, strengthening civilian ministerial control over security policy-making (Sotomayor Velázquez 2004). This move made possible the development of a strong and secure relationship with Argentina as a pillar of Brazil's National Military Defense Strategy (Ministério da Defesa 2008). The new strategic vision allowed a shifting of military assets from the southern border to Amazonian defense, which has become the priority in the national security profile (Pion-Berlin 2000: 52–3). Commensurate with these emphases, the National Military Defense Strategy commits the country to a major upgrading of its armed forces, including acquisitions of nuclear submarines from the French and new fighter jets.

Basing security concerns on improved relations with other neighbors in South America has proven a trickier proposition. Relations with Hugo Chávez's Venezuela and Evo Morales's Bolivia reflect a tendency to maintain cordial relations at an executive level while pursuing a more cautious approach to defend Brazilian interests through intermediaries. Even as Lula sustained close, personal contact with the late Chávez, the Brazilian military and Itamaraty remained vigilant about the Venezuelan president's interests in applying his Bolivarian revolution elsewhere in South America. Not having the benefit of Lula's close ties to Chávez, Dilma will have to remain vigilant as Chávez's successor, Nicolás Maduro, assumes responsibility for the relationship. Relations with the government of Evo Morales deteriorated in 2006 when the latter nationalized Petrobras's natural gas facilities, taking the provocative step of moving troops to guard the plants. In a similar act of effrontery in late 2008, Ecuador's president, Rafael Correa, refused to pay back a $200 million BNDES loan for a power plant to be built by the Brazilian engineering company Odebrecht. Before the dispute was settled, Lula's government recalled the Brazilian ambassador. As Brazilian economic ties have expanded in South America through trade and outward FDI, conflicts and rivalries have arisen, undercutting efforts to forge closer collaboration (Malamud 2011).

Brazil has also created problems for itself in its relations with the United States. Brazilian foreign policy has tended to favor a diplomatic approach to the use of sticks such as sanctions or military threats, but this orientation is based on several revisionist premises that tend to challenge the US more fundamentally. The cordial relationship with Iran during Lula's presidency is an example. Brazil was one of the few countries to endorse the results of Iran's disputed 2009 presidential election. Celso Amorim, Lula's foreign minister, visited the Middle East twenty-four times to establish that Brazil could be a partner in the region's peace process and that the US was no longer "the indispensable nation" in that area of the world. Brasília's insistence that Iran had as much of a right as India, a non-signatory to the Nuclear Non-Proliferation Treaty, to develop a civilian nuclear program challenged US policy fundamentally (Schweller 2011; Amorim 2010: 222–3). For Washington, this represented a major crack in Western opposition to Iranian proliferation. In its own view, however, Brazil was exerting its right to advocate for a completely different perspective of the dynamics in the Middle East.

Brazil's policy on Iran comes not from some ambitious motivation to shift the parameters of the debate in the Middle East but from its own view of its relationship with the United States, Europe, and other advanced capitalist countries. Amorim's foreign policy was an updating of the *política externa independente*. It maintained at its core a deep resentment against a past in which the Americans influenced Brazil's international relations but provided few rewards even when Brazil heeded American interests. So, if Brazil was to resist, it would have to do so in areas of immense importance to the US, including the nuclear non-proliferation issue. Brazil's position on its own nuclear industry reflected this shift, as it resisted inspections in 2004 by the International Atomic Energy Agency (IAEA) of its major nuclear plants (Angra I, II, and III) and stood against the IAEA's attempts to get it to implement additional protocols on the transfer of enrichment and reprocessing technology.[10] Brazil's motivations on this issue are complicated and involve resistance both by the navy, which still aspires to use nuclear technology in a new generation of ships, and by political leaders, who see further deepening of a commitment to the Non-Proliferation Regime as weakening the country before the great powers of the world.

As indicated above, when Brazil and Argentina agreed formally in 1990 to end their arms race, the armed forces were able to move resources from the southern border and concentrate on the Amazon. Strategic cooperation over the course of the last two decades has removed the La Plata region as the area of greatest concern for potential conflict. That has been replaced by the Andean–Amazon axis. Amazonian defense became during the 1990s the country's chief security concern, overlapping the challenge of the drug war, illegal incursions onto Brazilian soil, and dealing with guerrilla war on its borders with Colombia and Peru. The armed forces gained their most elaborate new defensive system in 1995, when the government contracted Raytheon, an American company, to build the satellite-based Amazon Surveillance System (*Sistema de Vigilância da Amazônia*, SIVAM). Although the armed forces have resisted taking primary responsibility for drug interdiction, SIVAM became a central part of Brazil's strategy to impede the illicit narcotics trade on its national territory. At the same time, the radar network became a bargaining chip in relations with the US, which remained heavily involved in drug interdiction and crop eradication in Colombia and the Andean countries. Beginning in 2011, Dilma's government expanded joint operations with neighboring countries and cooperative, inter-agency monitoring of the borders in the effort to interdict drug shipments (Meyer 2013). Closer cooperation with the United States, Andean countries and Colombia may soon expand to involve more use of unmanned aerial vehicles ("drones") and SIVAM.[11]

As much as Brazilian foreign policy is invested in reciprocal multilateralism, the country's security elites are reticent about engaging in tighter forms of collaboration with the security bureaucracies of neighboring states. Even though Brazil and its neighbors have been generally consistent in fighting terrorism, opposing armed insurgency, and cracking down on the narcotics trade, the armed forces of even the partner states of Mercosul have failed to cooperate more closely by forming any kind of common force based on the sharing of intelligence and joint actions (Burges 2009: 155–6). But, until Dilma's government, such matters were too often treated within the ambit of national polities, largely ignoring the transborder character of these problems. Partly this is due to the view in Itamaraty that foreign policy should address important questions but be sensitive to infringing the sovereignty of other states – a position that achieved a higher priority under the Lula administration (Vigevani and Cepaluni 2007). This norm has been tested most apparently in Brazil's support for democracy in South America.

Brazil has made the embrace of constitutional democracy a key organizing principle of its foreign security policy. Whether through the Rio Group, Mercosul, or the Organization of American States, Brazil during the democratic period has consistently argued on behalf of preserving constitutionality. This position was tested in the case of the 2002 coup attempt against Venezuelan President Hugo Chávez, which saw the Brazilians oppose tacit US support for the illegal action. Brasília reinforced the position it took earlier in opposing extra-constitutional action against presidents in Paraguay and Ecuador. Brazil moved to institutionalize this commitment to constitutionalism in the Treaty of Ushuaia, which added the condition that all Mercosul countries must remain democracies. Yet, even here, the logic of "benign restraint" as it applies to US action in the region is a guiding co-principle. Brazil supported constitutional democracy but simultaneously opposed the imposition of either authoritarian or democratic processes by external powers. So, in the case of Peruvian President Alberto Fujimori's attempt to rig the 2000 presidential vote, Brazil supported domestic efforts to resolve the dispute but stood in the way of American attempts to prescribe institutional solutions (Burges 2009: 136–7). Although this defense of the sovereignty of states is easily applied to the US, the principle limits the degree to which Brazil may itself be proactive in defending constitutional democracy elsewhere. Itamaraty has been sensitive to the potential for anti-democratic actions to prosper under the aegis of sovereignty, but Brazilian foreign policy has not evolved criteria for deciding consistently under what conditions more proactive and even prescriptive action is necessary.

Despite Brazil's expanding economic and diplomatic interests in the region and beyond, its foreign security policy suffers from a two-mindedness similar to the one that afflicts its foreign economic policy. A kind reading of its positions on sovereignty, democracy, and collective security is that these form the basis for the country's claim to be ready for a more robust international role by gaining a permanent seat on the UN Security Council. Cardoso's administration pursued this goal with less fervor than Lula did. The PT president's decision to commit Brazilian peacekeeping troops to Haiti reflects a clear attempt by Brasília to prove that the country is ready for a role in the Security Council (Vigevani and Cepaluni 2007; Burges 2009: 162). But these interests sit beside inward-regarding strategies such as "benign restraint" and an almost inexplicable unwillingness to become more involved in transborder problems that afflict both Brazil and its South American neighbors. Now that Dilma Rousseff has clearly backed off from her predecessor's ambiguous and dangerous approach to Iran and has embraced more transborder cooperation, Brazil may stand ready to soften the *política externa independente*. This effort may get the boost it needs from the security preparations the country must undergo to host the 2014 World Cup and the 2016 Olympic Summer Games.

Environmental Politics and Foreign Policy

Environmental politics is one dimension of the political system that can no longer be analyzed as exclusively domestic or international.[12] Both the subject and the major actors involved traverse the international boundaries of Brazil. More than any other environmental issue, Amazonian deforestation galvanized international attention in the late 1980s and, more than a decade later, as the implications for global climate change became more widely known, the 2000s. The annual rate of deforestation during the 1990s approached alarming levels, with 29,059 km² lost in 1995 alone. After a decline in the late 1990s, the rate shot up again, to 27,423 km² in 2004. The average annual rate over the 1990s and the 2000s has been around 16,489 km², with some encouraging signs of slowing from 2009 to 2011, when the annual rate fell to 6,900 km², the lowest levels recorded since 1970.[13] In generating these improvements, environmental activists within and outside of Brazil have had to engineer vibrant advocacy networks to bring pressure on the government and sometimes block energy development projects with high ecological costs.

Environmental activists in Brazil maintain strong connections with transnational networks, both governmental and non-governmental. The national environmental movement gained its strongest initial attention as ecological groups mobilized at the United Nations Earth Summit, hosted in Rio de Janeiro in 1992. In preparation for the meeting, environmental groups throughout Brazil planned summits of their own, involving other organizations in areas such as urban social issues and gender- and race-based concerns (Hochstetler 1997). Several years previously, in December 1988, the environmental movement gained international notoriety through the assassination by a local rancher of the rubber tapper union leader and environmental activist Chico Mendes. This revealed the contradictions between industrial development in the Amazon, which had been a priority of the military regime, and the sustainability of Brazil's largest ecosystem. The martyrdom of Mendes also suggested to Brazilians, who for decades had been inclined to embrace the dictum that "*Amazônia é nossa!*" ("the Amazon is ours!"), that international activists were not co-conspirators of foreign governments with imperialist designs (Keck 1995). Contact with international environmental organizations expanded rapidly after the 1992 Earth Summit, leading to the establishment of permanent branch offices for organizations such as Greenpeace and the World Wildlife Fund (Hochstetler and Keck 2007: 99). These contacts helped to project the influence of domestic environmental activists abroad by linking them to networks that mobilized at major meetings following Rio 1992, at UN environment and climate conferences as well as the annual gatherings of the World Social Forum in Porto Alegre beginning in 2001. As a result, international ecological organizations expanded their activities in the Amazon, focusing not only on the hazards of "slash and burn" agriculture and the pollution of rivers as a result of illegal mining, but the protection of species and the preservation of rare resources such as mahogany trees (Rodrigues 2000). Even official sources abroad now support these activist networks. For example, the G-7 group of wealthy countries supports the Pilot Program for the Amazon, which enables environmental activists in the northern states to keep the pressure on the federal environmental ministry.

Environmental management is threatened by the absence as well as the presence of the state. As more demands are placed on federal and subnational bureaucracies to create and enforce regulations, they are opposed and subverted by local groups of landowners, agribusinesses, and logging and mining interests, which gain the most from exploiting natural resources unencumbered by legal strictures. In the Amazon especially, illegal exploitation of natural resources, combined with rampant criminality in the drug war, which has largely shifted to the Amazon basin, has complicated enforcement of environmental regulations (Hochstetler and Keck 2007: 151–4). The presence of the government, particularly when it backs ecologically destructive energy development projects, can also prove problematic. One prominent example is the Belo Monte Dam in the state of Pará in the Amazon, which threatens habitats and will displace thousands of indigenous groups by the time it is completed. Due to the absence or the presence of the state, environmental activists have had to mobilize domestically and transnationally to block harmful practices (Hochstetler 2011; Carvalho 2006).

The attention that Brazil commands on environmental issues in international relations has sustained a vibrant and increasingly more professional domestic environmental movement capable of pressuring the government to make more substantive commitments to ecological protection. Domestic environmentalists have augmented their reach through international partners to lobby foreign governments, including the US, to use their influence in international financial institutions such as the World Bank to demand environmental protection for development projects funded by multilateral agencies (Keck and Sikkink 1998). Judging by the Brazilian government's reaction to these pressures, such groups have been successful. Brazil and its Mercosul signatories have ratified all of the major multilateral conventions on species depletion, climate change, and toxic waste, as well as the environmental framework agreement for Mercosul, making the customs union a notable presence in international environmental legislation (Hochstetler 2003). On climate change, domestic environmental activists have proven essential in causing Brazil to agree unilaterally to reduce its carbon dioxide emissions by 36.1 to 38.9 percent below what they would otherwise be in 2020 (Hochstetler and Viola 2012). Increasing attention to the causes of deforestation and species depletion, along with transnational networks to step up pressure on the Brazilian state to act, have worked to counteract localized resistance and, as the data on deforestation attests, to slow down the rate of environmental destruction. Conservation efforts have increased, with a total of over 60 million hectares under legal protection from exploitation. But the embrace of developmentalism challenges this record, as the pressures to find sources of growth by exploiting the Amazon will encourage the Dilma Rousseff government, already inclined as it is to exploit natural resources, to move forward with ecologically destructive projects such as the Belo Monte Dam (Hall and Branford 2012).

Perhaps the most consistent frame for understanding Brazil's foreign policy is that the country has emerged as a "middle power" (Lima and Hirst 2006; Malamud 2011). That is, it has the capacity for leading a continent (South America) but not the economic or military resources to be a global power. More important is how its leaders see Brazil's influence in the world and how particularly its neighbors view the country. On both counts, the prospects for Brazil's foreign policy are ambiguous. The foreign policy elite of Itamaraty insists that Brazil is a country of "continental size" with commensurate ambitions, but the Foreign Ministry articulates a subdued and nuanced view of Brazil's leadership within South America. By embracing reciprocal multilateralism on trade and security, Brazil shifts the burdens of leadership to others and makes its own responsibilities conditional on what neighbors are willing to do. Then, by periodically defecting from its support for cooperation, as it has with Mercosul and transborder security problems requiring greater col-laboration with neighbors and the US, Brazil underscores the importance of its own interests rather than those of a collective it leads. It is regarded by its neighbors as a critical market and diplomatic force in South America, but ties with Argentina, Peru, and Colombia, not to mention the problematic relationships with Bolivia and Venezuela, do not make Brazil the undisputed leader or representative of the continent. Its "middle power" status is based on its ability to influence neighbors and win on issues of transnational impor-tance to itself, but Brazil's standing in the region and the world does not garner the kind of suasion based on trust that causes partners of greater powers to recognize it as a leader. The fact that other South American coun-tries do not bend to Brazil's will on issues of trade and security, and openly oppose its bid to gain a permanent seat on the UN Security Council, is testa-ment enough to the limitations of the country's middle power status.

Apart from having recalcitrant neighbors, the limitations of Brazil's foreign policy are very much the result of policy-makers' own lack of vision even as the turnaround has progressed. The country has reaped few rewards from its foreign policy even as it has orchestrated important turnarounds in its eco-nomic and social policy, its governability, and the quality of its democracy. The turnaround might have been the basis for a renewed effort to redefine Brazil's interests in the world in a more robust and clear manner, but the last decade and a half of foreign policy-making has produced neither clarity nor much in the way of concrete results. Part of the problem is that foreign policy elites and the presidents they serve have been too content with Janus-faced positions. Multilateral reciprocity and nationalism do not mix any more than does recognition of the need to tackle transborder problems in areas such as security and the environment but an unwillingness to collabo-rate with neighbors and the United States in all areas. Mercosul is a reflection of the contradictions of high expectations limited at the end of the day by short-term national interests. The result is a middle power dilemma: Brazil is unable to exert its interests globally, as it is unwilling to embrace its responsibilities regionally, so it remains a middling influence in the world.

CHAPTER EIGHT

Prospects for the New Brazil

Whether the focus is macro-economic stability or social development, political governability or economic investment flows, Brazil has experienced a turnaround that has been demonstrated in each of the preceding chapters. Using an array of different indicators, it is clear that the beginning of the turnaround was the advent of the Real Plan in 1994 and the start of Fernando Henrique Cardoso's first term in 1995. This is true for major aspects of the turnaround such as governability, macro-economic stability, and some policy innovations in education and healthcare. The post-2003 period experienced another series of notable changes, with improvements in social indicators, growth, investment flows, and expansive turns in industrial policy and poverty alleviation. What separates these two sequences is a period punctuated by international financial crises in Asia in 1997 and 1998, the *real* crisis in 1999, and the Argentine financial crisis in 2001. So the turnaround has not been a single, linear process. It has been affected by Brazil's insertion into global markets, a process that has produced challenges and contradictions. The changes have greatly improved the lives of the poorest Brazilians on account of the rise in household incomes, improved health, and better access to higher quality education. But what has been accomplished thus far is not enough to meet the expectations in particular of the young urbanites who have always seen themselves as middle class. This social stratum was well represented during the mass demonstrations surrounding preparations for the World Cup. Although their demands were diffuse and they had no organization or leadership, the call of the demonstrators for a higher quality of democracy devoid of corruption and based on greater levels of elite accountability chimes with what has been set forth in this book.

Over the long arc since 1994, Brazil has experienced positive changes on the three dimensions of greatest interest to the current study: governability, policy governance, and the quality of democracy. While the performance of the political economy on these three dimensions is not perfect, Brazil is much better off on all three in comparison to democracy's first decade. This is manifest if one considers the remarkable improvements in social indicators, the record of growth with stable prices supported by a renewed developmentalist state, declining debt-to-GDP ratios, and the advent of more innovative social policies. Brazilian policy-making and democracy have also undergone improvement in the workings of institutions. There is greater predictability of presidential–legislative relations, the state enjoys stronger oversight and prosecutorial functions, citizens judge recent governments to have been generally responsive to their socio-economic concerns, and new spaces such as participatory budgeting and national conferences have tapped the networking of civil society organizations and regular citizens. In chapter 1, I asked if these changes are ephemeral and only skin-deep. Given the number of institutional changes and the intensity of the socio-economic shifts that Brazil has experienced, especially in the last decade, it would be difficult to see these trends being reversed in dramatic fashion in the years to come.

Turnarounds tend to be positive overall, but they do not ameliorate all erstwhile problems and may even hide them. The main thrust of this book has been to analyze the aspects of the Brazilian turnaround that have proven substantive and sustainable, while noting their limitations and what still needs to be done to keep the country pointed in the right direction. Social policy is a notable example. Although the Cardoso and PT governments generated significant improvements in social indicators by implementing innovative public policies in income support, healthcare, and education, they played safe by eschewing transformative policies that might have addressed the structures causing inequality. The unevenness of the pension, healthcare, and education systems piles onto historic causes of inequality such as the unequal ownership of land. Another example is the practice of coalitional presidentialism, which improved the governability of presidential–legislative relations, but only due to a highly contingent set of factors that built alliances based on discretionary budget outlays, the distribution of cabinet portfolios, and the strategic use of presidential decree powers. All of this took place mostly during a period of improving economic performance and fiscal capacity under the Cardoso and PT presidencies. But such conditions are only partially institutionalized at best. Coalitional presidentialism relies on some of the persisting tendencies of *troca de favores* that convert material rewards into votes. These are practices that undermine elite accountability, as is evident in that parliamentary oversight is vacuous in a system that depends so heavily on the dispensation of patronage to buy votes. Given the scope of public outcry against such "politics as usual," it is unclear if this system is stable or sustainable over the long term. More broadly, the oligarchical tendencies of Brazilian politics, the weakness of partisanship and ideology in voters' choices, the insufficiencies of political participation and media oversight, and the unwillingness of governments to integrate civil society into policy-making all point to the limitations on the quality of democracy that have persisted during the turnaround. Some of these problems come back to governability. The most serious example is the judiciary's general incapacity to deal with its backlog of cases and to follow through on the prosecution of corrupt officials. Continued inaction in the face of official malfeasance only reinforces the tendency of Brazilians to take to the streets and denounce the entire political system. As Peru, Ecuador, and Venezuela have demonstrated, the deepening of such "anti-politics" can turn the electorate against the system as a whole and make it much less governable.

One of the core contradictions of the turnaround has been that, as economic and social policy have registered impressive gains, allowing presidents such as Lula and Dilma to enjoy record high approval ratings, Brazilians do not feel much better about their democracy than they did twenty years ago. Citizens still regard government's ineffectiveness in dealing with corruption as a frustrating aspect of the polity. It should be remembered that both Cardoso and Lula were re-elected *despite* the fact that voters felt that neither had been sufficiently responsive to the need for political reform. Popular distrust of public officials is still as high as 70 percent in some polls, and regard for democracy falls somewhere between 50 and 60 percent, significantly below most of the other democracies of Latin America (Power 2010b). Recent governments have been judged by the material benefits that they can impart to society through economic and social policy and not their ability actually to make Brazilian democracy work better. But the mass demonstrations of 2013 suggest that good policy will no longer be sufficient to satisfy the demands of Brazil's citizens, especially those in the middle class. Despite enjoying the same high public approval as her predecessor, Dilma found that her popularity took a nosedive in the wake of the demonstrations, suggesting that the tide can turn very quickly if problems of democratic quality are not addressed sufficiently.

A secondary concern of this study is to shed light on the nature of change during the turnaround. In virtually all dimensions of Brazil's reversal of fortunes, change has come gradually, sometimes through exogenous events such as financial crises in neighboring countries, sometimes as a consequence of endogenous events such as corruption scandals. Incremental institutional changes, often layered on top of previous changes, have set down pathways for Brazilian leaders who have been interested in enhancing progress with more resources and new ideas to make policy-making and policy more efficient and effective. Brazil's leadership since 1994 has been reluctant to enact fundamental changes. Although the PT represented a change of course while it was in opposition during the 1990s, Lula adopted his predecessor's economic policies and expanded his social policies. Dilma has appeared reluctant to pursue all of her predecessor's foreign policies, though that is the exception. Otherwise, she has deepened the state's commitment to promote growth through project-based spending while strengthening social programs in poverty alleviation, health, and education. Her commitments to macroeconomic stability and her willingness to use Keynesian reflationary policies in the face of the global slowdown are actions that Cardoso or Lula would have easily taken given similar circumstances.

The remarkable level of progressive policy continuity across governments, despite their ideological differences and electoral rivalries, has sustained the turnaround. Governments of the PSDB (Cardoso) or the PT (Lula and Dilma) have now governed Brazil during two-thirds of the democratic period. This has socialized Brazilian voters, journalists, and most other observers to think that there are two major currents in the country's politics – two options, at least, for the presidency. That may change with the emergence of a candidate backed by another party, but, even then, it is difficult to imagine an alternative to the policy consensus that has been cultivated by almost two decades of PSDB and PT governments. Five points of consensus emerged between the Cardoso and Lula governments:

1 a macro-economic policy dedicated to inflation targeting;
2 the maintenance of a generally market-oriented set of economic policies with strong developmentalist inflections in industrial and strategic trade policy;
3 innovative poverty-alleviation and other welfare-enhancing policies;
4 a dedication to the logic of coalitional presidentialism in the management of the legislative process; and
5 an increasing internationalization of Brazilian interests, both entrepreneurial and governmental.[1]

On each of these points, the political class has engineered positive changes, but the work is incomplete. The following sections assess each of these consensus points in terms of what has been achieved and where there remains more to do.

Finally, it should be noted that the study of the turnaround provides scholars with an opportunity to evaluate the situation. Based on assessments of the first decade of democracy, many observers of Brazilian politics were ready to see the polity as too dangerously sclerotic in its persisting tendencies of clientelism, personalism, and weak party governance to consider that a corrective was possible. The Brazilian economy was, as Rudiger Dornbusch once quipped, "drunk" – presumably on hyperinflation and speculative bubbles. Yet the passage of time has shown Brazil's democracy to be, as Timothy Power (2010b) puts it, "a late bloomer." In reviewing the points of consensus below, it is clear that some early pessimistic assessments became obsolete, though several of the insights remain useful. Proponents of more optimistic approaches might have initially reveled in the turnaround, but, as contradictions have emerged (as they inevitably do in the complex world of politics and economic development), their explanations have had to undergo adjustments. The turnaround is ongoing and incomplete.

The Macro-Economic Policy Consensus

During the first decade of Brazilian democracy, no issue created more concern than inflation. At times, *monthly* rates of inflation from 1986 through 1994 climbed beyond 30 percent, and periodically exceeded 50 percent, the level for declaring an economy "hyperinflationary." The failure of multiple stabilization plans, and especially the highly traumatizing Collor I and II experiences, dashed popular hopes that either democracy or the state was capable of dealing with the ripping apart of the economic and social fabric of the country. As memories of this time fade, the remarkable turnaround represented by the success of the Real Plan is taken for granted. Brazil has enjoyed an average of 6 percent annual inflation since 1997. Expectations around the stability of prices have become so common that hardly any investor today thinks about the potential for a sudden return to the hyperinflationary past. Price stability has made public accounts and private contracts more transparent, underwriting efforts to improve the probity of both. Moreover, economic growth with relative price stability has been a boon to the least well-off Brazilians, who enjoy the benefits of increasing employment opportunities in the formal sector and the preservation of their buying power.

The culture of stable prices became so ingrained after 1995 that it was difficult to see how Fernando Henrique Cardoso's successor could alter it without suffering grave political costs. The pathway had also been well established by structural reforms such as liberalization and privatization. These conditions compelled Lula to embrace the principles he outlined in his "Letter to the Brazilian People." A significant turn, whether socialist or not, away from the commitment to market-oriented reforms with price stability would have dealt a fatal blow to the economy, as foreign investors would have seen such action as confirmation of their worst fears about Lula. It is also the case that Lula's commitment to carry on Cardoso's macro-economic policy presented opportunities. Economic growth allowed for an expansion of developmentalist industrial policies that had already been designed during the Cardoso administration to respect the parameters of price stability. Lula committed to two moderate pro-market reform elements of the PT, signaling his signing up to the macro-economic policy consensus: he adopted the IMF targets for the primary surplus and he vowed to continue inflation-targeting in the management of the money supply. Within two years of taking office, the debt-to-GDP ratio was on the decline and foreign currency reserves were riding a wave of stronger export earnings and growth in the domestic market.

The long-term success of macro-economic reform also relied on the strengthening of the state. Whether one considers the explosion of debt by states and municipalities based on profligacy against soft budget constraints or the tendency to roll arrears over with federal money, the fiscal decentralization of the state, codified in the 1988 Constitution, presented a fundamental challenge to inflation control and the balancing of the federal budget. Even before the Real Plan, the Collor government ordered limits on rollovers of debt to the *Banco do Brasil*. Both Collor and Itamar had the Central Bank intervene in several state banks that were unable to maintain their current obligations, thereby removing them as conduits of finance for subnational spending. Once the Real Plan squeezed the profits of the remaining state banks and the Cardoso administration used the Social Emergency Fund to keep 20 percent of constitutionally mandated transfers, the state governments had little choice but to end the spending spree and negotiate debt workouts with the federal government. The privatization or liquidation of virtually all of the state banks by 1999, and the advent the following year of the Fiscal Responsibility Law, represented the end to a stop-and-go process of re-equilibration of fiscal authority by the federal government. To be sure, reforming the fiscal structure remains a complicated and necessary task, but the rebalancing of fiscal federalism prevented the worst aspects of "robust federalism" from spiraling out of control and undermining macro-economic stabilization.

A growth model based on the preservation of stable prices, strategic commercial openness, and strong public and private investments in infrastructure, energy, and industry took hold during the PT presidencies. The Growth Acceleration programs and the industrial policies of these governments have taken advantage of favorable international conditions and have also been adjusted during the post-2008 global financial crisis to sustain more modest levels of growth. These moves have operated within the parameters of the macro-economic policy consensus that emerged during the Cardoso era. This is the most impressive example of progressive policy consistency during the turnaround.

Developmentalism and Industrial Policy

Brazil was less a latecomer to adopting neoliberal reform than it was a partial practitioner of these policies. Despite the initiation of trade liberalization during the Sarney government and the expansion of Collor's national privatization program under the Cardoso administration, Brazil gradually eschewed the Washington Consensus structural adjustment agenda. In its place, policy-makers preserved much of the developmentalist economic bureaucracy and institutions of the ISI era to refashion an industrial policy that would retain a concern for macro-economic stability and pursue more market-oriented policies of internationalization.

The pillars of Brazil's renewed commitment to developmentalism emerged over time but were clearly based on several core principles. First, the renewal of developmentalism replaced the ISI-era concern with growing the *size* of the industrial sector with a focus on the competitiveness of leading firms in domestic as well as foreign markets. This focus appeared in the BNDES's management of the national privatization program in sectors such as steel and mining and in the bank's efforts to overcome the overvaluation of the *real* by providing export support after 1995. Under the PT presidencies, BNDES lines of credit in energy and infrastructure dominated the bank's disbursements. Meanwhile, Finep's increased activity concentrated on firms seeking to integrate new technologies into production. Second, *partial* as opposed to full ownership of formerly public firms became a tool for controlling investment strategies by some of the largest firms. Sustained by the expanding role of public pension funds and BNDES disbursements, the state retained a capacity for directing private-sector resources in strategic areas such as energy and heavy industry. Third, technological innovation became a centerpiece of the industrial policies of the PT presidents, building on a decade of policy goals and actions by the BNDES and Finep that had been frustrated by underfunding. Lula's industrial policy was especially ambitious in linking the internationalization of production to technology transfer and development. BNDES and Finep funds intended to foster business-to-business linkages using new technologies became a much larger part of the portfolio of industrial policy. Finally, industrial policy-making expanded within parameters defined by the priority of macro-economic stability with inflation targeting and gradual and strategic opening of the domestic market to foreign competition. Unlike the story of ISI during the developmentalist period, the new industrial policy would not generate inflation or produce unsustainable balance-of-payments deficits.

The Lula government's Industrial, Technology, and Trade Policy (*Política Industrial, Tecnológica e de Comércio Exterior*, PITCE) set forth in March 2004 the most ambitious industrial policy Brazil had seen since the military's National Development Plan II during the 1970s. Together with its follow-up plans during Lula's second term, the PAC-1 and PAC-2, and Dilma's industrial policy, the BNDES and its partnership with Finep became the primary source of all long-term finance to industrial and infrastructure companies. The analysis I conducted with Kathryn Hochstetler of BNDES loan activity demonstrates that the PITCE's sectoral priorities differed little from the old ISI areas. The bank diversified its financial mechanisms to promote internationalization through trade (using a greatly expanded export–import facility) and outward foreign direct investment, which was unprecedented, and Finep's funds were doubled and made to operate in new areas such as venture capital. All of these aspects verified the developmentalist parameters of the new industrial policy.

The chief result of these efforts was to promote higher growth through a marked improvement in gross fixed capital formation. By financing infrastructure investments in utilities, energy, shipbuilding, terrestrial transport, electronics, and heavy industry, the BNDES provided a crucial source of long-term working and investment capital to the leading sectors in the economy. Beyond the aggregate statistics, BNDES and Finep funds financed hundreds of productivity-enhancing investments in medium-sized and smaller firms that do not register at the top of the list of big projects but have made sizable contributions to the growth trajectory of the domestic market (see Suzigan, Negri, and Silva 2007; BNDES 2011). At the very least, these efforts suggest that there was more to Brazil's economic growth during the 2000s than can be explained by commodity prices or even the performance of the large *multilatinas*.

One of the most important implications of developmentalism is what it means for state capacity. Contrary to pessimistic views that saw the Brazilian state shortly after the transition to democracy as fragmented and lacking coordination, captured by private interests, and incapable of forging its own collective national purpose, the renewed developmentalist model came together during the 1990s and was powerfully implemented by the PT presidencies. This required not only the preservation and reimagining of the mission of public agents such as the National Development Bank (BNDES), public firms, and Finep, but also the improved capacity of the presidency and the congress to address the fiscal crisis of the state. As chapter 2 notes, this necessitated the recentralization of fiscal control and oversight, a process that coincided with the expansion and reconfiguration of the mission of the BNDES. To be sure, this would not have been possible without macroeconomic stabilization under the Real Plan, but, as chapter 5 shows, even before inflation control became a reality, state managers were working on the main ideas of a new industrial policy and implementing some of them as part of the national privatization program.

Social Policy Innovation

Brazil's turnaround in social welfare indicators is real, and both quantitative and qualitative improvements to social policy are a key cause of these results. Since 2003, the combined effects of non-contributory cash transfers to the poor, the increase in the minimum wage, and the expansion of private consumption and formal-sector employment have produced a social impact comparable to the sudden effects of the Real Plan (Singer 2009: 93–4). Although Brazil remains one of the top seven most unequal countries in the world, inequality as measured by the Gini coefficient fell strongly after peaking at 0.60 in 2000. This was due not to income distribution from the top two deciles but to a notable improvement in household income among the poorest.

Poverty alleviation targeted to the poorest explains much of this, as well as its effects on improved access to education and healthcare. Conditional cash transfers represent the most important innovation in social welfare policy in Brazil. The *Programa Bolsa Família* (PBF) currently serves 13 million families, making it the largest transfer program in the world. By targeting funds to the lowest income deciles, the PBF has reduced poverty rates by 12 percent since 2003 and has represented almost a quarter of the reduction in inequality since that time. A study commissioned by the Ministry of Social Development in 2010 found that the secondary effects of the PBF in increasing school attendance and follow-up medical visits were significant (MDS 2010). It is also notable for its design. It made the distribution of social protection more universal and professionalized through the *Cadastro Único*, and it systematized mechanisms of benefit delivery that overturned erstwhile pessimistic views that welfare policy would remain a venue for clientelism and particularism. That over three-quarters of the money goes to the poorest income quintile, and more than half goes to the poorest states of the North and Northeast, suggests that the program is not subjected to these political influences. Studies of the targeting effects verify these intuitions (cf. Fried 2011; Haddad 2009; Soares, Ribas, and Osório 2010; Soares, Soares, Medeiros, and Osório 2006).

As much as the PBF has been successful, the distribution of social policy benefits is still uneven in other areas, such as pensions, healthcare, and education. The most problematic is the pension system, which favors those who can afford to pay in, leaving as many as 30 percent of all workers without retirement protection. The non-contributory pensions for public-sector workers also burden federal accounts, with the total budget going to pensions consuming more than half of all social spending. Although Cardoso and Lula alleviated some of this burden through reforms, the changes did little to address the structural unevenness of the system. Removing a similar unevenness in the healthcare area was the purpose of the Unified Health System. But the continuation of for-profit providers and favorable tax laws allowed those in the top income brackets to make more use of both the private and the public system of healthcare than what is available to the poor. The result is the incongruous finding that Brazil is the only country in the world with a universal healthcare system that spends more on private than on public healthcare. Regarding education, access and retention at the primary and secondary levels have improved, but quality of instruction remains a problem for the children of poor households, given that richer families tend to send their children to private schools where instructional quality is superior. Better preparation allows the children of the well-off to pass the *vestibular* entrance exam for the most prestigious of the federal universities, thereby adding to structures of inequality.

The inequalities inherent in the social welfare system should not cause observers to ignore its strong points. Non-contributory pension payments remain one of the top sources of income for households in the poorest quintile. Such payments to rural workers keep a sizable percentage of the population from sinking into absolute poverty. The expansion of healthcare clinics and the work of core family health teams during the 1990s and 2000s are among the main explanations for falling infant mortality rates and lower incidences of infectious diseases. Improvements to housing and sanitation services have reinforced these trends throughout Brazil. Regarding education, Cardoso's FUNDEF represented the most wide-ranging reform of education spending in Brazil's history. Lula followed suit with the expanded FUNDEB, but he also took steps to move beyond funding inequalities across schools to address differences in quality. The standardized testing regime of the Census of Basic Education and the Ideb allow the government to track the quality of instruction and identify schools as well as teachers that require more support. The historic exclusion of Afro-Brazilians from the education system, especially at the level of higher education, extends from the correlation between wealth and access, given that the poorest income deciles tend to be overwhelmingly non-white. In response, Lula's *Programa Universidade para Todos* created the largest affirmative action policy in the Americas. Dilma's effort to expand opportunities for university students to study abroad through the "Science without Borders" program promises to generate substantial improvements to the availability of highly skilled workers in a few years' time.

By operating within rather moderate parameters for social policy reform, the Cardoso and PT governments could innovate at the margins of existing welfare policy but eschewed more transformative options such as land and income distribution. After all, the PBF did not transfer income from the rich to the poor. Nor did it inspire civil society organizations to champion broader income distribution. Lobbies of beneficiaries, some CSOs, and unions opposed more broad-based reforms in pensions just as healthcare companies limited the ability of the *sanitaristas* from implementing their most ambitious plans for a truly universal healthcare system. That Cardoso and Lula had limited choices is clear, but they also played to those limits rather than attempting to go beyond them.

Coalitional Presidentialism

The bias of scholarly focus on presidential–legislative relations has produced useful insights into an understanding of governability in Brazil and how it has evolved since the democratic transition. It also generated high opportunity costs by soaking up a great deal of the time and enterprise of political scientists focused on Brazil. The findings of this study suggest that the analytical payoffs have not justified such opportunity costs. The emerging metaframe of "coalitional presidentialism" created almost as many problems as it solved, by relying on presidential styles and legislative strategies that, at best, are indeterminate predictors of governability and, at worst, require dispensations of patronage and campaign finance that have been associated with the largest corruption scandals of the democratic period. Analytically, the coalitional presidential framework largely missed the changing orientations of political parties and the ideological convergence of the political class, without which much of the governability experienced during the turnaround would not have been possible. The implications of this work for understanding political reform options have also been disappointing. On no other issue facing Brazil has so much ink been spilled diagnosing the problems and imagining solutions with little to show for it in the form of concrete action (Cheibub 2009). Coalitional presidentialism helped produce levels of governability that avoided the crisis-ridden conditions of democracy's first decade, but it has failed to create formulas that enhance the quality of democracy. The situation underscores the wisdom of Kurt Weyland's (2005) argument that Brazilian democracy is more governable because it is of low quality. This is true to a degree.

The work on coalitional presidentialism has evolved according to three mechanisms of presidential influence on the legislature:

1 the centralization of agenda-setting through the powers of the president, especially with regard to the use of provisional measures, and through the party hierarchy as it is represented in the *Colégio de Líderes*;
2 the allocation of cabinet portfolios; and
3 the budgetary discretion of the presidency vis-à-vis deputies.

All three of these mechanisms provide the presidency with the *de jure* and *de facto* powers it needs to employ an array of inducements and constraints on legislators and their parties. But legislators also have chips in this game provided that they can speak through parties, as authors such as Figueiredo and Limongi (1999) insist they do. The genius of this system is that it allows for enhanced governability via coalition politics *despite* the continuation of a fragmented multi-party system with ideologically incoherent parties.

That coalitional presidentialism provided a set of workable understandings of how Brazil avoided a continued crisis of governability during the 1990s is clear. But the weakness of the approach is that it settled upon a number of contingencies, few of which were institutionalized. The fluidity of presidential styles and strategic understandings with the congress makes the governability-enhancing effects of coalitional presidentialism depend on other factors. It is precisely the lack of programmatic governance via disciplined and ideologically coherent parties that relegates presidential–legislative relations to this unstable matrix of contingencies. For example, critics were quick to point to the origins of the *mensalão* in Lula's failure to use cabinet appointments as strategically as Cardoso did. Given, too, an electorate with only weak partisan and ideological linkages to parties, pro-government coalitions could not be made through elections. Such coalitions would have to be created at the top via the dispensation of pork. Any major failure to manage these elite pacts could produce disaster. Coalitional presidential scholars saw the routinization of governability, while the pessimists continued to see weak contingencies based on weaker institutional and mass electoral foundations. Proponents of coalitional presidentialism as a "unifying framework" inadvertently underscored the dangers of such contingency by not agreeing or arguing convincingly which components of coalitional presidentialism were permanent, necessary, and sufficient. My review of the scholarship shows a proliferation of metrics for what constitutes a "strong coalition," the inability to agree on which branch of government – presidency or congress – is the main driver of legislation, uncertainty over the level of cabinet coalescence or budgetary outlays that are required to fashion a pro-government coalition, a recognition of the obsolescence of elite pacts over time, and sensitivity to the larger context of political-economic conditions. Coalitional presidentialism scholars have successfully created new terms and variables for understanding the evolution of governability in Brazil, but they have not solved the puzzle of how the political class may avoid governability crises in the future.

Even as coalitional presidentialism was elucidating lurking variables in inter-branch politics that were contributing to the unprecedented governability of the post-1994 period, the approach was also eliding political parties and the growing ideological convergence of the political class. Like the pessimists, coalitional presidential scholars crowded out consideration of the internal workings of parties by focusing instead on the emergence of pro-government and opposition orientations in the congress. Outside of the congress, political parties continued to matter little in the OL-PR electoral system. But new work that sought to explain the PT's increasing moderation and the discipline of even catchall parties such as the PFL revived attention to political organizations and their internal distinctiveness. Specifically, as democracy became more mature, parties of the left and the right were no longer playing to type. Not only the PT but also right-wing parties such as the PL and once center-left parties such as the PSDB shifted their orientation. New research building on the Brazilian Legislative Survey tracked these movements to provide a systematic understanding from 1990 to the present of how the major parties have changed (Power and Zucco 2012). The overall effect is towards a convergent middle of the ideological spectrum, suggesting a decline of ideological polarization in the Brazilian political system. That this process began shortly after the highly charged 1989 presidential election, and well before coalitional presidentialism came to fruition during the Cardoso administration, underscores that there were causes other than those proffered by coalitional presidentialism for the improved governability Brazil had experienced since the mid-1990s.

Another area that requires more work is political reform. Given its implicit critiques of Mayhewian arguments favoring electoral system explanations, the work on coalitional presidentialism offers few clues as to the kind of political reform that would improve the prospects for governability in Brazil. The terms of the political reform debate remain surprisingly shallow after almost thirty years of democracy. Most prescriptions focus on four areas: the reduction of the number of parties, the strengthening of party control over incumbents and candidates, the proportionality of seats to votes, and malapportionment. What has been done to follow these prescriptions since 1995 has been largely insignificant. In 1995, a new law required that parties gain at least 5 percent of the national vote and 2 percent in one-third of the states to claim the right to hold seats in the Chamber of Deputies. Subsequent reforms required parallel configurations for national and subnational multiparty alliances. In 2007, a decision by the STF ended the common practice of party switching. Much more fundamental reforms have been discussed but not acted upon in any sustained way. Part of the problem is that the political class is divided on whether the way forward should be via a majoritarian formula for the lower house or a restructured form of proportional representation, with either closed lists or a mixed-member system that integrates single-member and PR characteristics. The logic of coalitional presidentialism has not helped to resolve this debate. The approach might even be used to suggest that no change is necessary, given that improved governability has been possible without a major change in the rules. But this would elide continuing problems with the incentives of politicians to cultivate personal votes and gather campaign finance (both on and off the books), and for voters to ignore programs and orient their allegiances to personalities.

Even when rule changes can clearly improve matters, erstwhile problems continue. A case in point is the malapportionment of representation. Since independence, Brazil has struggled to create formulas to prevent the Chamber of Deputies, which is based on a representative principle of population, to be dominated by the three most populous states – São Paulo, Rio de Janeiro, and Minas Gerais. During the bureaucratic-authoritarian governments, a limit was placed on how many deputies could be elected in these more urban states, since the opposition to military rule was most organized there. At the same time, the generals wished to increase the proportion of deputies from the nine northeastern states, where pro-military conservatives tended to dominate. The less populated but more conservative states of the North and Northeast enjoyed a floor of eight deputies, while the more populous states of the Southeast and South were limited to a ceiling of sixty deputies. Following the democratic transition, the overrepresentation of the less populous states increased, as six new states were created in the North and Center-West, with an additional forty-eight deputies added to the Chamber (Snyder and Samuels 2004: 148). Even as the 1988 Constitution increased the ceiling for all states to seventy, the malapportionment of representation undermined urban and anti-conservative interests in the congress. One relatively easy reform would be to reduce the problem of malapportionment by removing the ceilings and floors on the number of seats per state in the elections for the Chamber and replacing them with equal-sized districts proportional to population. While this would increase the representation of the large divided states of the South and Southeast, there is no basis for the fears of some observers that these interests would collude against the minority (Cheibub 2009). These subnational political systems are sufficiently diverse to make it difficult to imagine how they would form a coherent and sustainable regional alliance. As scholarly and public attention turns away from issues of governability and towards the quality of democracy and improved policy governance, such changes may receive the attention that they deserve.

Perhaps the most troubling aspect of coalitional presidentialism is its reliance on the distribution of material rewards to create and manage coalitions.

In this regard, coalitional presidentialism is not new. It is, in fact, the apotheosis of an erstwhile set of practices that tap into the persisting tendencies of clientelism and *troca de favores* in Brazilian politics. Although this has proven useful for propping up governability, it has presented continuing problems for improving elite accountability, government responsiveness, and other aspects of the quality of democracy. The manipulation of parliamentary investigative committees through inducements and constraints, including the use of budgetary discretion to undercut congressional support for them, damages the function of congressional oversight. The logic of politicization has a way of expanding, as chapter 4 showed, to institutions such as the media. Thus far, highly professional state agencies such as the *Ministério Público* have remained largely above reproach, but investigatory and prosecutorial bodies of this nature require a professional judiciary to follow through on the process. Observers of the judiciary believe that the corruption that has been detected in the ranks of judges and other court officials is only the tip of a very large iceberg. Without more systematic data, it is hard to tell if one should be an optimist or a pessimist on the matter. But one cost deriving from the concentration of scholars on the dynamics of coalitional presidentialism is that much less attention has come to focus on the judiciary. Matthew Taylor (2008) bemoans the paucity of study of the third branch, contrasting it with the immense amount of scholarship that has focused on macro-political institutions governing presidential–legislative relations. Given the crucial role of the courts in Brazil's "web of accountability," this unevenness favors the study of governability and policy-making and less the quality of democracy. But if Weyland's (2005) insight that governability and quality are inversely related is true, then nothing less than a shift in the focus on dependent variables is needed to lead the research program on institutions in the direction that they should now take in tackling the multidimensional aspects of democratic quality (Levine and Molina 2011).

Internationalization

As a middle power, Brazil has the capacity for leading South America but not the economic or military resources to be a global power. It faces a typical middle power dilemma of embracing strong ambitions to gain international prominence, such as a permanent seat on the UN Security Council, but it has demonstrated limited leadership in foreign economic, security, and environmental policy. Brazil has shown that it can defend its interests in multiple international arenas, but it has not evinced the kind of leadership through suasion of other countries, let alone its neighbors in South America, that would give it more influence in the world. Yet, at the same time, its economy has become more integrated into global markets. Internationalization remains a major component of the renewed developmentalist approach to industrial growth and strategic trade.

A major cause of Brazil's middle power dilemma is the tendency of its foreign policy elites to mix grand ambition in rhetoric with small-bore moves in foreign economic and security policy, often in ways that satisfy immediate interests. Its relations with the United States are a good example. Brazil has pursued different approaches at the same time across policy issues, including close collaboration, independent foreign policy, and benign restraint. It has collaborated with the US closely on the war against terror, but it has gone its own way in its relations with Iran and in its approach to nuclear proliferation. And, even as it renounced its Iranian policy under Dilma's presidency, it retains its nuclear policy. It has gathered support among developing countries in an effort of benign restraint on discriminatory trade practices in the advanced capitalist countries, but it has depended upon US leadership to protect the non-discriminatory apparatus of the World Trade Organization so that it might avail itself of this structure to protect the market access of Brazilian exporters. Brazil has at times been willing to invest heavily in regionalism, particularly in Mercosul, as a means of counteracting American power, but it has been all too willing to soften or abandon these commitments once its own short-term economic interests were threatened. It has cooperated more with the US on the interdiction of narcotrafficking, yet the specter of inviting Washington's influence further into South America is anathema to the foreign policy establishment in Brasília. Benign restraint of the US has backfired by weakening the international response to suspensions of democratic procedures in Peru, Ecuador, and Paraguay, where Brasília has frowned upon American involvement on behalf of democracy.

Whether Brasília eventually develops a foreign policy that more effectively balances national interests and international responsibilities, the weight of leadership may still burden Brazil sooner or later. Environmental degradation and climate change are perhaps the most alarming issues facing the world, and, regardless of what China, India, and the developed economies do, Brazil will find itself at the center of global processes to deal with the threat. In this regard, the country is more prepared today than it was in 1992 when domestic and transnational NGOs were still becoming acquainted. Today, environmental activists and conservationists are well positioned domestically and through transnational networks to exert pressure on the state. But, as with foreign economic and security policy, Brazil's environmental policy remains an area in which political elites wish to have it both ways. On the one hand, the government, especially under the PT presidents, has been a good environmental citizen by signing international and regional agreements protecting the environment and pledging to reduce carbon dioxide emissions. On the other hand, the PT governments, and now especially Dilma, have been intent on exploiting natural resources to maximize Brazil's growth potential. In this regard, there is considerable tension between developmentalism and environmentalism.

Despite the movement of many of the PT's more extreme leftist minds into the management of foreign policy during the Lula years, the practice of Brazil's international relations did not change fundamentally from the situation under Cardoso. Both administrations, and now Dilma's, employed methods of composing foreign policy that did not change much. All of the post-1994 administrations expanded the influence of the presidency over international relations, maintained a commitment to multilateralism and peace in security policy, and defended the country's national interests in matters of foreign economic policy. Where there were differences, these were inflections rather than fundamental shifts, and not altogether consistent from administration to adminstration. Lula's commitment to South–South ties, while not very different from Cardoso's focus on South American leadership, was expansive, but not entirely as heartfelt under Dilma as it was under her predecessor. Lula's international reputation and magnetic personality made him a global icon, but Dilma's less personal foreign policy is more in line with Cardoso's style than with that of her predecessor.

The Significance of the Brazilian Turnaround for Democratic Development in Comparative Perspective

The Brazilian turnaround offers multiple lessons for the way that scholars study change in political-economic institutions. Some of these lessons have to do with the analytical assumptions and approaches that scholars take, while others deal with the substantive implications of the Brazilian example for understanding larger phenomena of economic and democratic development. Regarding the methodological lessons, this study has emphasized the need to be mindful of multiple dimensions of the polity over time. The analysis has underscored the linkages across the chapters on several recurring propositions concerning the progressive continuity of policy and its implications, the non-linear as well as the linear connections among institutions and arenas of the polity, distal and proximal causes, and the limitations of available scholarly lenses. Concerning the substantive lessons, the periodization of Brazil's turnaround reveals a sequencing that challenges conventional approaches to the affinities between economic and political development in democratizing societies.

If we step back from the five consensus points that characterized the turnaround and consider their implications for how we study Brazil, a couple of conclusions are possible. It is clear that the passage of time has changed our observations and expectations about Brazil's democracy. During the first decade following the regime transition, scholars of the country engaged in sustained handwringing about macro-political institutions, the developmental capacity of the state, the weaknesses of the web of accountability, and the problematic aspects of "robust federalism." Although these analyses were insightful at the time and remain valuable in specific ways, their understanding was limited by their proximity to events. With the passage of time, observers could entertain more optimistic perspectives, as Brazilian democracy failed to erode into multiple crises of governability and policy decay. As frustrating as it was in the mid-1990s to try and figure out where Brazil was, adopting a holistic approach that allowed for the possibility of adjustment and change would have produced more balanced and fruitful analyses.

The holistic approach is also useful in emphasizing the interactions between institutions and how change in one can elicit change in others. What Pierson (2004) calls the "meso-institutional" level of analysis has proven crucial to understanding how improved governability in presidential–legislative relations helped recentralize fiscal resources, how the growth fostered by developmentalism enhanced the effects of innovative social policy by promoting the growth of the formal sector, and how foreign policy could project the internationalization of the Brazilian economy. The ability of presidents and congressional allies to regain programmatic control over areas of fiscal, social, and economic policy was a process with multiple dimensions, not always occurring simultaneously, but generally moving in the same direction towards stronger state capacity. And these processes could be perceived not by looking exclusively for proximate determinants but by appreciating the changes in context and approach that attention to distal and structural factors allows. Likewise, attention to non-linear relationships is as important as minding the linear ones. The pathway of economic and social reform has been non-linear on several dimensions: industrial policy, structural reform, and changes to the welfare state. Each of these areas has experienced periods of sustained innovation followed by equilibrium or stagnation and then another period of innovation. To be sure, policy in each of these areas has been insufficient for dealing with all of the challenges.

These methodological points have sometimes revealed the shortcomings of earlier scholarly approaches and analytical assumptions. All too often, studies of Brazil have unpacked institutional logics that work well within the analytical frame of the study (e.g., presidential–legislative relations, the political party system, participatory publics, etc.) but are less coherent or significant when viewed through the lens of a multilevel polity with many cross-cutting institutional logics. The scholarship on Brazil's "web of accountability" and the quality of democracy has been most sensitive to this multidimensionality. Yet it is also true that approaches that fail to envision how improved governability and elite accountability are possible in the continuing context of norms of clientelism, informal politics, and incumbency bias, among others, fall into the trap of adapting misplaced ideas to Brazil. One of the meta-lessons of the turnaround is that scholarship must understand how these persisting elements of Brazilian politics and society have coexisted and evolved with the improvements of governability, policy governance, and democratic quality.

The attempt in this book has not been to use a holistic approach to create a holistic theory, but to map out the most relevant connections, analyze their implications for the turnaround, and suggest pathways forward for integrating research in these multiple areas. Given the exclusive focus on Brazil, there is less space dedicated to substantive lessons for other countries, particularly those in Latin America. Still, the Brazilian turnaround proffers several implications for the study of political and economic development in democratizing countries.

Of the Latin American countries, Brazil has experienced less policy volatility than Bolivia, Ecuador, and Venezuela, with their more aggressively nationalistic versions of "new left" governments. After the regime transition, Brazil had few transformative moments to rival the first loss of the presidency by the Institutional Revolutionary Party (*Partido Revolucionário Institucional*) in Mexico in 2000 or the rise of anti-establishment leaders such as Hugo Chávez in Venezuela in 1998. Nor has it experienced the frenetic pace of change and bouts of intense institutional crisis felt by Peru or Argentina during the 1990s. But neither has it had the steady leadership of government parties and coalitions to the extent seen in Chile and Uruguay. That is not to say that the history of post-1985 Brazilian democracy is free of moments of institutional crisis, ambitious leaders who overreach, and periodic changes that seem at the time to be too fast and too soon. But, in the larger frame of the history of Latin America, Brazil's progress has convinced many of its own citizens that it has become a "normal country" in ways that most of its neighbors in the region have not. Taken a step further, talk of Brazil as one of the BRICs suggests that the country is not "normal" but extraordinary. In the current focus on the so-called pink tide of leftist governments elected throughout Latin America, the PT presidencies appear to be a combination of everything that was once most appealing and promising in center-right or center-left governments that embraced the Washington Consensus reform agenda – namely, that they would create sustainable patterns of economic and social development. The PT presidencies did that, working with the institutional legacies of the Cardoso administration, but they also upgraded the state's concern for social justice by significantly expanding commitments to the poor. The results are generally reassuring: Brazil today has a more mature social democracy than it has ever had.

One of the recurring themes of this book has been that "not all good things go together," and, indeed, limitations and contradictions are evident on each of the consensus points that undergird the country's turnaround. This emphasis on discontinuity of sequence and the multidimensionality of institutional layering belies conventional wisdom concerning the relationship between economic and social development, reform, and democratization. The Brazilian turnaround challenges the well-worn proposition of Seymour Martin Lipset (1959: 75) that, "the more well-to-do a nation, the greater the chances that it will sustain democracy." This pillar of "modernization theory" has withstood extensive testing and generally proven correct in large-N analyses (cf. Przeworski, Alvarez, Cheibub, and Limongi 2000). More recent "endogenous" theories of modernization offer a more direct and robust approach, holding that economic development promotes democratization rather than simply sustaining it once it already exists for other reasons (Boix 2003; Boix and Stokes 2003; Acemoglu and Robinson 2006).[2]

Yet, in the Brazilian case, the economic growth and social development components of the turnaround occurred many years after the transition to democracy. And, despite this gap, democracy survived and even improved in areas such as governability and policy governance. Overall, the periodization of stronger governability, policy governance, and democratic quality belies the expected sequence of an economic growth tide lifting all boats. Rather, the hard work of coming to terms with inflation and poor relations between the presidency and the congress preceded by many years the economic boom that would return appreciable growth levels as well as socio-economic development to Brazil. The careful task of preserving the developmentalist institutions of the state laid the groundwork for the more significant involvement of the state in the market after 2003, but no previous example of developmentalist success guided policy-makers as they continued to reform state institutions. Nor was it the case that democracy evolved in a linear fashion. Even as democratic governability has improved, democratic *quality* has remained a work in progress during a period of sustained economic development. Some aspects of the web of accountability, government responsiveness, and participation became stronger while other dimensions stagnated or even got worse. The narrative of corruption scandals afflicting the PT governments is testament to the non-linear character of political and economic change in Brazil. This suggests that some weak points of democratic quality are likely to continue even as socio-economic development and some political institutions improve.

These elements are all aspects of Brazil's reversal of fortunes, which will continue to generate additional puzzles for scholars intent on understanding its lessons for political, economic, and social development. And their struggles with this large, complicated country will confirm the wisdom of the cautionary maxim that Brazil is not for beginners. Brazil's promise of entering an age of international influence and economic and social prosperity with wise and strategic political leadership is as apparent as its designation as a BRIC and the attention it garners as the host for the 2014 World Cup and the 2016 Summer Olympic Games. These represent immediate realities but also aspirations for a country and a people that wish to see themselves as having arrived. Yet to be really understood requires an appreciation not only of what has improved but of what still remains to be done. In this regard, Brazil has much to be praised for and still much more to do.

Notes

Chapter 1   A Reversal of Fortune?

1 A similar trend in the concentration of ownership of assets has occurred in the industrial sector. See Amann and Baer (2009: 38–9).
2 Noted political scientist Barry Ames wished to use the term "pathological" to describe Brazilian democracy in his 2001 book *The Deadlock of Brazilian Democracy*.
3 Dornbusch's comments were extraordinarily pessimistic, if not dismissive, of Brazil: "When will Brazil stop being drunk?" And the answer is . . . maybe after Carnival! Or after the putsch or whichever comes first. You can't dismiss that Brazil, of all countries, will have a putsch. It's like Russia: large, inward-looking, with fantastic economic problems and a total unwillingness of the existing political system to do something about it." See Dornbusch (1993).
4 See Treasury Department/Federal Reserve, "Major Foreign Holders of Treasury Securities," www.treasury.gov/resource-center/data-chart-center/tic/Documents/mfh.txt (accessed April 1, 2013).
5 See "The Democratic Routine," *The Economist*, December 2, 2010.
6 Arguments for multi-arena analysis of Brazilian politics can be found in several places, including the study of political parties and the legislature (e.g., Pereira and Mueller 2003, 2004), federalism and decentralization (e.g., Montero 2004), foreign policy (e.g., Cason and Power 2009), voters' retrospective evaluations of politicians (e.g., Rennó 2011), and the quality of democracy (Weyland 2005).

Chapter 2   Democracy and Economy from Bust to Boom

1 The periodization used in this chapter coincides well with what Brazilian politicians themselves see as the phases of Brazilian democracy. See Power (2008). Power (2010b) adopts a similar periodization in his own work.
2 For a useful analysis of Collor's reforms and his political failures, see Kingstone (1999: 159–88) and Figueiredo (2010).
3 The designers of the Real Plan were not orthodox liberals, though they were sympathetic to market-oriented approaches. They were all top-shelf Brazilian economists: Edmar Bacha, André Lara Resende, Pedro Malan, Gustavo Franco, Winston Fritsch, Pérsio Arida, and Francisco Pinto.

4 The degree of overvaluation remained in dispute among domestic and international observers, with most believing it to be 15 percent, though foreign analysts such as the macro-economist Rudiger Dornbusch claimed in 1996 that the *real* was overvalued on the order of 40 percent.

5 The administration of the ICM (now, ICMS) had been decentralized by the military in the 1967 fiscal reform. During the 1980s, the states demanded that they be allowed to have more autonomy over the setting of their own rates.

6 Jefferson was expelled from the congress and both he and Dirceu had their political rights suspended for eight years.

7 During his trial before the high court in summer 2012, Valério claimed a link to the president, but he did so without convincing proof.

Chapter 3   Improving Governability

1 The effective number of parties accounts for the number of different parties with a weight given for their importance in the legislature. The conventional formula uses the Laakso and Taagepera (1979) equation. This formula is represented as $N = 1/\Sigma\ x^2i$, where x_i is the percentage of seats held by the i-th party. Following this formula, if the distribution of seats favors two parties in similar proportions, with a third minor party taking the remainder of seats, N will be some number between 2.0 and 3.0.

2 The floor of eight and the ceiling of seventy overrepresents small states and underrepresents more populous states such as São Paulo, which should have many more than seventy representatives.

3 Votes for individuals are still crucial for determining the allocation of seats due to vote pooling. The rank order of the votes for candidates is used to calculate each party's share. The number of seats a party receives is based on the ratio of the sum of all votes its candidates receive and the sum of all votes cast for all candidates. The d'Hondt method is used to translate votes into seats – though, crucially, the identity of the holder of each seat is determined by their personal number of votes.

4 This estimate is at the high end. Fleischer (1998) believes that it is closer to the still considerable level of 40,000 jobs.

5 The Supreme Court ruled in March 2007 that seats belong to parties and not to candidates, effectively ending the practice of party switching.

6 His coding of contested votes, however, was challenged by Lyne (2005: 197).

7 Senators are elected on a majority basis for eight-year terms. Elections are staggered so that two-thirds are chosen in one cycle and the remaining third are voted in four years later.

8 The Rice score is based on the simple equation $RICE_{ij} = |\%aye_{ij} - \%\ nay_{ij}|$, where i = party and j = vote. The percentage of those voting aye or nay are a proportion of those voting. The Rice score varies between 0, representing equal proportions of aye and nay votes, and 1, unanimous voting.

9 This body is composed of the president of the Chamber of Deputies, the leaders of all parties with at least 1 percent of seats in the Chamber of Deputies, and a non-voting deputy appointed by the president. The standing orders of the congress indicate that the *Colégio* should make decisions by consensus, but an

absolute majority vote is allowed if a consensus is not possible. Votes are weighted by the seat share of each party. The origins of this body date back to the Constituent Assembly, when party leaders negotiated amendments informally before each session. The *Colégio* became a permanent feature of the Chamber of Deputies in 1989.

10 To override a presidential veto, both houses of congress must gather an absolute majority in favor of the override.

11 There are two types of fast-track measures, *urgência* (simple urgency) and *urgência urgentíssima* (super urgency). The former requires that the congress vote within a five-month session on the legislation. Super urgency moves the bill to the top of the docket immediately, taking it out of committee.

12 The 1988 Constitution bestows upon the presidency the exclusive right to set out the priorities and content of federal budgets. Presidents implement this right on three levels. First, by the end of the first year of a presidential term, the congress must approve a long-term plan for the budget known as the *Plano Plurianual*, which is designed by the *Planalto* and details the overall priorities of federal programming and spending during the term. The *Lei de Diretrizes Orçamentárias*, which details budget priorities in particular areas of policy, must be approved by the first quarter of the second year. And, finally, the annual budget (*Lei Orçamentária Annual*) emerges from the president's office and can be amended only by the congress. The president retains the discretion to enact or veto amended sections.

13 For an astute analysis of the term and its application, see Power (2010a: 24–6), though the original concept comes from Abranches (1988).

14 The use of decrees in Brazil is a case in support of "delegation theory" in the literature on executive–legislative relations. This approach is inspired by principal–agent theory, which sees the legislature (the principal) delegating power to the executive (the agent). See Kiewiet and McCubbins (1991).

15 The distinction of delegation to the presidency versus individual presidents was first outlined by Carey and Shugart (1998) and applied in the Brazilian context by Pereira, Power, and Rennó (2005).

16 Upon taking office, Collor's party, the Party of National Reconstruction (PRN) had only 5.1 percent of the seats in the Chamber of Deputies. Collor distributed cabinet ministries to associates, many without a party, and some technocrats in key ministries such as economy. Only 30 percent of the members of his congressional coalition voted in favor of his initiatives.

17 A related tendency regarded the content of legislation. In the period up to 1999, Amorim Neto and Santos (2003) found a much lower incidence of bills being proposed with a local focus, which would indicate a parochial interest, as opposed to a national scope.

18 For a critique of this view and a reinforcement of party discipline as real, see Figueiredo and Limongi (2002).

19 This point is also made by Weyland (2005), though I qualify it in later chapters.

20 The PT is an internally factionalized party by design. Factions are seen as part of the diversity of the organization, though Lula's faction, Articulation (*Articulação*), has historically been the largest. For more on the PT factions, see Lacerda (2002) and Samuels (2004: 1011–12).

21 Samuels (2004: 1018) does not deny that Lula gained greater autonomy but asserts that this came only after the rank of pragmatists within the party increased significantly.
22 In this regard they conflated two distinct concepts: ideological cohesion and partisan discipline. For the critique, see Ames (2002) and Amorim Neto, Cox, and McCubbins (2003).
23 It should be recalled that Figueiredo and Limongi's (1995) early studies of roll-call voting focused on the period 1988–94, so they could not detect ideological change over time. Meneguello (1998) also argued that there was ideological consistency between 1988 and 1994, but her measurements were the same as those of Figueiredo and Limongi, focusing on discipline and unity in roll-call votes and not in ideological scoring.
24 The Sani–Sartori scores range from 0 to 1 and are calculated by taking the absolute difference between two parties of their mean locations on an ideological gamut of 1 to 10 and dividing by 9 (the theoretical maximum distance between any two parties). See Sani and Sartori (1983). Power (2008) uses non-member placement (reputational placements) rather than self-placement.

Chapter 4 Accountability, Participation, and Good Governance

1 Under current rules, no more than five CPIs may function at any one time in the Chamber. New CPIs created when the cap of five has been met may convene only when an existing CPI is closed. Yet extraordinary CPIs may be formed following a majority vote even when the Chamber is at the cap. Either house of congress may form them, and joint chamber CPIs are possible.
2 Figuratively, this means that all that one can do is to turn off the lights and go out for pizza.
3 The TCU also reserves the right to refer cases for criminal prosecution to the MP. In all cases, however, TCU sanctions can be challenged in the courts, effectively watering down the autonomous ability of the agency to punish misconduct (Speck 2011: 144–5).
4 Despite numerous challenges to the constitutionality of this law, it was upheld by the Supreme Court upheld in February 2012.
5 Declaratory Actions of Constitutionality are potentially dangerous, since the refusal of the court to declare a law constitutional voids that law immediately. Not surprisingly, they have been used only seven times (Nunes 2010: 326).
6 The structure of the MP coincides with the divisions of the judiciary, with federal and state prosecutors in common law, military justice, and labor law.
7 Since only 8 percent of municipalities have local television broadcasters, for most of the country the local media is AM/FM radio (Ferraz and Finan 2008: 709).
8 The community radio broadcasters (*rádios comunitárias*) began in the 1970s and 1980s as grassroots initiatives by poor people, shantytown (*favela*) organizations, and non-governmental organizations. Most initially engaged in social mobilization, but they increasingly ventured into politics following the regime transition. See Nunes (2004). Constitutional restrictions under article

54 on sitting federal legislators owning radio stations have been either ignored or circumvented by allowing concessions under the proviso that the emitter be an "educational" broadcaster (see Lima 2008).

9 This problem was most evident during the Sarney administration. See Motter (1994).

10 The percentage of broadcasters owned by politicians or family members is higher in the Northeast. In the Southeast and South, the figures reported by empirical studies are in the area of 15 to 20 percent. See Ferreira (2006).

11 "Políticos Controlam 2.000 Rádios Piratas," *Folha de São Paulo* (June 26, 2000, p. A6).

12 Brian Wampler, associate professor of political science, Boise State University, personal communication (April 17, 2013).

13 Even so, CSOs preferred to keep Lula in the presidency and opposed any effort to impeach him (Hochstetler 2008: 49–50).

14 Voting is obligatory, which helps to explain consistently high turnout, though there is evidence that the "compulsoriness" of voting has effects that differ across socio-economic categories of voters. See Power (2009).

15 For a contrary perspective, see Figueiredo and Limongi (2002: 310). Santos and Vilarouca (2004) find consistency between voters' attitudes towards inequality and their view of party labels. For a review, see Carreirão and Kinzo (2004: 135–41).

16 The "subproletariat" was originally defined by André Singer's father, Paul Singer (1981), as compensated labor that enjoys few or none of the conditions for engaging in class struggle but merely acquires enough remuneration to guarantee its own reproduction.

17 This is also true of other objectively defined group identities, such as race, age, gender, and religion, for partisanship in general. See Samuels (2006a).

18 The effect seems stronger for leftist parties than for those on the right wing. Mainwaring, Meneguello, and Power (2000) find that education is an inconsistent predictor of partisanship for conservative party supporters.

19 Limongi (1995) reports similar ideological consistency in samples drawn from São Paulo between 1989 and 1994.

20 On conventional five-point Likert scale tests, as many as half of all respondents answer incorrectly (cf. Ames and Smith 2010: 28; Carreirão and Kinzo 2004).

21 One crucial innovation in the study by Ames and Smith (2010) is that they control for the inherent bias in self-selection of response by employing a multi-step regression method (a variation on the Heckman selection model).

22 Notably, they find that this is a consistent aspect of political orientations in the legislature that has been nicknamed *a direita envergonhada* (the ashamed right).

23 These early experiences with participatory policy-making were associated with PT governments at both the municipal (Baiocchi 2005; Goldfrank 2007) and the state level (Goldfrank and Schneider 2006).

Chapter 5   The Renewed Developmental State

1 The term was not used widely until Alice Amsden presented a call for a "new developmentalism" at the February 2000 UNCTAD conference "High Level

Round Table on Trade and Development: Directions for the Twenty-First Century" in Bangkok.

2 The BRICSA countries are Brazil, Russia, India, China, and South Africa.

3 This is described well by Bresser-Pereira (2006).

4 For more on "simulated market" approaches, see Bhagwati (1988). For a sustained critique, see Wade (1990).

5 In 2001, Cardoso introduced a reform to empower negotiated exceptions of the labor code to invite flexibility. The legislation went down to defeat as the electoral cycle geared up. A similar fate met Lula's first labor reform in 2005, which was overshadowed by the *mensalão* scandal that summer and failed to be considered before the 2006 elections.

6 BNDES bureaucrats understood these tendencies in detail based on a series of sectoral surveys conducted by the bank's planning department beginning in 1994. See BNDES (1996).

7 This is evident in press accounts of PND managers such as BNDES presidents Eduardo Modiano (Collor) and Antônio Barros de Castro and Pérsio Arida (Itamar Franco), and vice president of the PND and former BNDES president Marcos Vianna. See *Jornal de Brasília* (October 14, 1992, p. 11); *Estado de São Paulo* (November 15, 1992, p. 5); *Gazeta Mercantil* (November 13, 1992, p. 3); *O Globo* (October 23, 1993, p. 26).

8 These ideas were not new. The BNDES's earlier study on capital goods emphasized the need to internationalize as central to a strategy for improving innovation. The bank underscored the necessity of expanding trade as a means of accelerating the adoption of new technologies and to compensate for the decline of domestic demand as the basis for sectoral growth (BNDES 1988: 103).

9 For an exhaustive listing of these measures and initiatives during the Lula administration, see Cano and Silva (2010).

10 "Long-term" is defined by the BNDES as an amortization of eight years (ninety-six months). By contrast, the average private bank in Brazil offers amortizations that average nine months.

11 A fuller accounting of these data can be found in Hochstetler and Montero (forthcoming).

12 Simon Romero, "As Growth Ebbs, Brazil Powers up its Bulldozers," *New York Times* (June 22, 2012, p. A1).

13 In this regard, I follow the example set by Kohli (2006a: 1254–5) in his study of Indian developmentalism.

14 Plattek (2001) shows that this is true even when GFCF is disaggregated into its private- and household-sector versus public-sector subcategories. It should also be noted that the government's share of GFCF fell dramatically during the 1990s due to privatization, from 18 percent in 1990 to 11 percent in 1999. The contribution of BNDES disbursements to the GFCF of the public sector fell even more acutely, from 12.7 percent in 1990 to 3.4 percent in 1999. So the aggregate GFCF figures I report reflect primarily private- and household-sector trends.

15 Variations on this argument can be found in Palma (2005), Nassif (2008), and Sharma (2012).

16 See "The New Brazil," *Financial Times* (June 29, 2010).

Chapter 6   Welfare and Class Mobility

1 The HDI is an index scaled 0 to 1 based on a composite of three indicators of well-being: life expectancy, per capita income, and educational attainment.

2 Massacres of landless peasant protestors at Corumbiara in 1995 and Eldorado de Carajás in 1996 pressured the Cardoso government to enact significant resettlements, increasing the average number of families relocated to 71,999 from the previous government's 10,881 (Ondetti 2008: 148–55). Although the rate of settlements had fallen by 2000, the Lula government increased the rate again and reversed the anti-occupation repression of land invasion practiced under his predecessor. All told, only one-third of the expropriated land for settlements has come from private holders, so even these significant resettlement trends failed to represent a notable redistribution of land tenure.

3 The Gini coefficient is the area between the arc and the line of equality in the Lorenz curve. The Lorenz curve is determined by calculating double the covariance of income and rank in the distribution of income, divided by the mean income of the population. The coefficient ranges from 0, for perfect equality, to 1, for perfect inequality.

4 Most of those who are illiterate live in rural areas and are older than fifty, suggesting that illiteracy is being phased out; almost total literacy has been achieved for those currently aged fifteen to twenty-four.

5 The minimum wage is a benchmark for income statistics in Brazil. It is presented as a monthly sum of daily wages paid at the threshold established by the federal government.

6 "Sweet Treats on the Never, Never," *The Economist* (April 27, 2011).

7 The 2001 expansion of the *Bolsa Escola* program was named after the late Magalhães Teixeira, who died during his second term in 1996.

8 For more on the diffusion of innovative social programs, see Sugiyama (2008, 2011).

9 The best study available on the effects of the program shows that it improved school attendance significantly, though it had a more nominal effect on poverty. See Bourguignon, Ferreira, and Leite (2003).

10 The food card ultimately became the electronic medium for the cash transfer of the *Bolsa Família*.

11 As of 2009, the average monthly transfer per family was R\$94.92 (\$43) (IPEA 2011: 70), though the Dilma Rousseff government increased the maximum monthly payment after taking office in January 2011. The PBF also transfers funds to extremely poor households that earn less than R\$70 (\$44) per month. If these households have no children, the transfers are made unconditionally at a flat rate of R\$70. Other conditions on the transfers include participation in nutrition programs and vocational training.

12 For the counter argument, see Bohn (2011).

13 One notable exception to the regressive effects of social security is the non-contributory rural pension, FUNRURAL, which provides a targeted benefit to a population that would otherwise be miserably poor. The benefit amounts to one minimum wage per beneficiary, costs 1 percent of GDP, and goes to approximately 6.5 million people, making it the largest poverty alleviation

program in Brazil (Lloyd-Sherlock 2006; Ramos and Querino 2003; Melo 2008: 166). Citizens aged sixty-seven or older who cannot pay into a pension and are not eligible for FUNRURAL are covered by a means-tested, non-contributory benefit, the Continuous Monthly Benefit (*Benefício de Prestação Continuada*), begun in 1998. Disabled workers are covered by another non-contributory pension.

14 The INSS manages all pension programs through an extensive information system on beneficiaries and their households (Lloyd-Sherlock 2006: 972).

15 Average ages for early retirement based on this provision were 54.9 for men and 53.3 for women, allowing for pensions to cover an average of 17.6 years of retirement income. See Madrid (2003: 141).

16 Inevitably, many of these women preferred to pursue unions without marriage so as to continue to collect their pension.

17 The main social contribution taxes are the CONFINS (Financing of Social Security) and the CSLL (Contributions on Net Enterprise Profits). These taxes consume an average of 30 percent of payroll (Lloyd-Sherlock 2006: 972). As of 1997, the tax on financial transactions (CPMF) has added another revenue stream for social spending.

18 A higher proportion of state and municipal spending goes to primary education. Secondary education represents a much smaller share of total education spending, though it is states and the federal government that pick up 75 percent of these costs (Draibe 2004: 381).

19 Additionally, the federal version of *Bolsa Escola* under Cardoso had transferred $800 million by 2002 to 5 million families (Melo 2008: 163).

20 By contrast, the private universities are tuition-dependent and therefore more available to the children of upper-middle-class and upper-class families.

21 Brazil uses three standardized tests for each of the levels of primary and secondary schooling: the SAEB (*Sistema de Avaliação da Educação Básica*), which tests children in the fifth through ninth years of school; the ENEM (*Exame Nacional do Ensino Médio*), which tests high-school students; and, since 2000, the OECD's Pisa exam (Program for International Student Assessment), which is used for cross-national comparisons of high-school students aged fifteen and sixteen.

22 The Ideb is scaled from 0 to 10, with the Brazilian baseline set at 3.8 in 2005. The Education Development Plan set a target of increasing the score on the index to 6 by 2022. In 2011, Brazil had achieved benchmark Ideb scores of 5 for early primary schools, 4.1 for final elementary school years, and 3.7 for middle school education.

Chapter 7   Brazilian Foreign Policy

1 The purpose of this chapter is to discuss this fluidity in terms of the strategic dimensions of Brazilian foreign policy, not to assess the determinants of foreign policy-making. On the crafting of foreign policy in Brazil, see Amorim Neto (2012b) and Cason and Power (2009).

2 Brazil, Argentina, Paraguay, and Uruguay are the original signatories of the Treaty of Asunción, which created Mercosul in 1991 and launched it in 1994. Venezuela was admitted in 2006, but ratification was blocked by Paraguay's

Senate. The removal of President Fernando Lugo in June 2012 allowed Brazil to call for Paraguay's suspension from the customs union, clearing the way for Venezuela to be fully admitted in July 2012.

3 For example, compare Amorim (2010, 2011) and Lampreia (2009).

4 Cardoso confronted developed country interests occasionally. It should be recalled that his health minister, José Serra, initiated the practice of challenging HIV/AIDS drug patents and forcing the pharmaceutical multinationals to reduce their prices. Lula moved further by breaking patents, such as Merck's on antiretroviral drugs, and institutionalizing a strategic partnership with South Africa and India on this issue.

5 For example, the signatories were able to exempt a list of products from the common external tariff. Brazil and Argentina had the fewest exemptions, with 324 and 394, respectively. Uruguay and Paraguay were able to exempt 960 and 439, respectively. Unlike the later evolution of the EEC, Mercosul has yet to develop into a common market with its own autonomous regional authority.

6 Cardoso's strongest post-crisis push to reanimate regional integration was the Regional Infrastructure Integration in South America initiative launched at the Brasília summit in 2000. This was an attempt to spur more intra-Mercosul integration as well as inter-bloc trade with the Andean Community (Bolivia, Columbia, Ecuador, and Peru).

7 The reported figure includes only capital contributions and intra-company loans. Because Brazilian official statistics do not report reinvested earnings, the figure understates the true total for FDI inflows.

8 For example, see "Enter the 'Multilatinas'," *Business Week* (December 28, 2010). It is estimated that there are 887 Brazilian firms that have invested outside of Brazil. About 31.2 percent of these operations involve sales offices, 23.1 percent conduct production or services, 18.9 percent export through licensing agreements with distributors and franchisees abroad, but only 23 firms own companies abroad. See Fleury and Fleury (2011: 197).

9 This position is reinforced as a constitutional principle. Article 4 of the 1988 Constitution defines the guiding principles of Brazilian international relations, among others, as non-intervention, the defense of peace, and the peaceful settlement of conflicts.

10 Brazil signed the Non-Proliferation Treaty (NPT) in July 1998, and the Cardoso government pledged to honor the Comprehensive Test Ban Treaty. But Lula and Dilma did not accept NPT protocols allowing more intrusive IAEA inspections of ongoing efforts to enrich uranium.

11 SIVAM's coverage includes areas of the national territories of Colombia, Peru, and Ecuador, thus making it useful to American drug eradication efforts in these countries. Brazil also has a shoot-down law (*lei do abate*), which authorizes its air force to shoot down any planes suspected of participating in drug trafficking.

12 This section focuses on the linkages between domestic and transnational environmental policies and processes. Space limitations prevent a more complete analysis of domestic environmental policy, though substantial treatments of the subject are available elsewhere. See, especially, Hochstetler and Keck (2007).

13 The Brazilian government's own National Institute for Space Research (*Instituto Nacional de Pesquisas Espaciais*, INPE) began tracking deforestation in real time through its satellite network in 2004 and made the images available on the internet in 2005. INPE's data show that 745,289 km² of Amazonian forest, equivalent to 20 percent of the total, has been lost since 1970.

Chapter 8　Prospects for the New Brazil

1 Timothy Power (2010b) offers a similar list of consensus points, though he does not mention developmentalism.
2 For the distinction between "exogenous" and "endogenous" theories of modernization and a comparative examination, see Przeworski and Limongi (1997) and Przeworski, Alvarez, Cheibub and Limongi (2000: 88–9).

References

Abers, Rebecca Neaera (1998) "From Clientelism to Cooperation: Local Government, Participatory Policy, and Civil Organizing in Porto Alegre, Brazil," *Politics and Society* 26/4: 511–37.

—— (2000) *Inventing Local Democracy: Grassroots Politics in Brazil*. Boulder, CO: Lynne Rienner.

Abranches, Sérgio Henrique Hudson de (1988) "Presidencialismo de coalização: o dilema institucional brasileiro," *Dados – Revista de Ciências Sociais* 31/1: 5–34.

Abrúcio, Fernando (1998) *Os barões da federação: os governadores e a redemocratização brasileira*. São Paulo: USP/Hucitec.

Acemoglu, Daron, and James Robinson (2006) *Economic Origins of Dictatorship and Democracy*. New York: Cambridge University Press.

Affonso, Rui de Britto Álvares (1997) "Decentralização e crise federativa: a especifidade do Brasil," paper presented at the Twentieth International Congress of the Latin American Studies Association, Gudalajara, Mexico, April 17–19.

Afonso, José Roberto Rodrigues (1995) "A questão tributária e o financiamento dos diferentes níveis de governo," in *A federação em perspectiva: ensaios selecionados*, ed. Rui de Britto Álvares Affonso and Pedro Luiz Barros Silva. São Paulo: FUNDAP, pp. 315–28.

Aldrich, J. H. (1995) *Why Parties? The Origin and Transformation of Political Parties in America*. Chicago: University of Chicago Press.

Além, Ana Cláudia (1997) *BNDES: papel, desempenho e desafios para o futuro*, Texto para discussão no. 62 (November). Rio de Janeiro: BNDES.

—— (1998) *O desempenho do BNDES no período recente e as metas da política econômica*, Texto para discussão no. 65 (July). Rio de Janeiro: BNDES.

—— (2011) Advisor to the president, BNDES, interviewed by Kathryn Hochstetler, Rio de Janeiro, July.

Além, Ana Cláudia, José Roberto Mendonça de Barros, and Fabio Giambiagi (2002) "Bases para uma política industrial moderna," mimeo, BNDES, 12 June.

Almeida, Alberto Carlos (2001) "Ideologia e comportamento eleitoral: evidências de que a ideologia não é importante para explicar o voto," paper presented at the 15th Annual Meeting of the National Association of Post-Graduate Research in the Social Sciences (*Associação Nacional de Pós-Graduação e Pesquisa em Ciências Sociais*), Caxambu, Minas Gerais, Brazil.

—— (2006) *Por que Lula? O contexto e as estratégias políticas que explicam a eleição e a crise*. Rio de Janeiro: Editora Record.

—— (2008) *A cabeça do eleitor*. Rio de Janeiro: Editora Record.

Almeida, Maria Hermínia Tavares de (1996) "Pragmatismo por necessidade: os rumos da reforma econômica no Brasil," *Dados – Revista de Ciências Sociais* 39/2: 213–34.

Almeida, Paulo Roberto de (2010) "Never Before Seen in Brazil: Luis Inácio Lula da Silva's Grand Diplomacy," *Revista Brasileira de Política Internacional* 53/2: 160–77.

Almeida, Rodrigo de (2011) "Entrando no clube: o BNDES e a inserção brasileira no capitalismo internacional," in *Variedades de capitalismo, política e desenvolvimento na América Latina*, ed. Renato R. Boschi. Belo Horizonte: Editora UFMG.

Alston, Lee J., and Bernardo Mueller (2005) "Pork for Policy: Executive and Legislative Exchange in Brazil," *Journal of Law, Economics, and Organization* 22/1: 87–114.

Alvarez, Sonia (1993) "'Deepening' Democracy: Popular Movement Networks, Constitutional Reform, and Radical Urban Regimes in Contemporary Brazil," in *Mobilizing the Community: Local Politics in the Era of the Global City*, ed. Robert Fisher and Joseph Kling. London: Sage.

Alves, Maria Helena Moreira (1985) *State and Opposition in Military Brazil*. Austin: University of Texas Press.

Amann, Edmund (2009) "Technology, Public Policy, and the Emergence of Brazilian Multinationals," in *Brazil as an Economic Superpower? Understanding Brazil's Changing Role in the Global Economy*, ed. Lael Brainard and Leonardo Martinez-Diaz. Washington, DC: Brookings Institution Press.

Amann, Edmund, and Werner Baer (2009) "The Macroeconomic Record of the Lula Administration, the Roots of Brazil's Inequality, and Attempts to Overcome Them," in *Brazil under Lula: Economy, Politics, and Society under the Worker-President*, ed. Joseph L. Love and Werner Baer. New York: Palgrave Macmillan, pp. 27–43.

Amaral, Aline Diniz, Peter R. Kingstone, and Jonathan Krieckhaus (2008) "The Limits of Economic Reform in Brazil," in *Democratic Brazil Revisited*, ed. Peter R. Kingstone and Timothy J. Power. Pittsburgh: University of Pittsburgh Press.

Ames, Barry (1994) "The Reverse Coattails Effect: Local Party Organization in the 1989 Brazilian Presidential Election," *American Political Science Review* 88/1: 95–111.

—— (1995a) "Electoral Rules, Constituency Pressures, and Pork Barrel: Bases of Voting in the Brazilian Congress," *Journal of Politics* 57/2: 324–43.

—— (1995b) "Electoral Strategy under Open-List Proportional Representation," *American Journal of Political Science* 39/2: 406–33.

—— (2001) *The Deadlock of Democracy in Brazil: Interests, Identities, and Institutions in Comparative Politics*. Ann Arbor: University of Michigan Press.

—— (2002) "Party Discipline in the Chamber of Deputies," in *Legislative Politics in Latin America*, ed. Scott Morgenstern and Benito Nacif. New York: Cambridge University Press.

Ames, Barry, and Amy Erica Smith (2010) "Knowing Left from Right: Ideological Identification in Brazil, 2002–2006," *Journal of Politics in Latin America* 2/3: 3–38.

Ames, Barry, Andy Baker, and Lucio Rennó (2008a) "Split-Ticket Voting as a Rule: Voters and Permanent Divided Government in Brazil," *Electoral Studies* 30: 1–13.

— (2008b) "The Quality of Elections in Brazil: Policy, Performance, Pageantry, or Pork?" in *Democratic Brazil Revisited*, ed. Peter R. Kingstone and Timothy J. Power. Pittsburgh: University of Pittsburgh Press.

Ames, Barry, Miguel García-Sánchez, and Amy Erica Smith (2012) "Keeping up with the Souzas: Social Influence and Electoral Change in a Weak Party System, Brazil, 2002–2006," *Latin American Politics and Society* 54/2: 51–78.

Amorim, Celso (2010) "Brazilian Foreign Policy under President Lula (2003–2010): An Overview," *Revista Brasileira de Política Internacional* 53: 214–40.

— (2011) *Conversas com jovens diplomatas*. São Paulo: Benvirá.

Amorim Neto, Octavio (2000) "Gabinetes presidenciais, ciclos eleitorais e disciplina legislativa no Brasil," *Dados – Revista de Ciências Sociais* 43/3: 479–519.

— (2002) "Presidential Cabinets, Electoral Cycles, and Coalition Discipline in Brazil," in *Legislative Politics in Latin America*, ed. Scott Morgenstern and Benito Nacif. Cambridge: Cambridge University Press, pp. 48–78.

— (2006) *Presidencialismo e Governabilidade nas Américas*. Rio de Janeiro: FGV.

— (2012a) "El presidencialismo moderno en Brasil," in *Presidencialismo y parlamentarismo: América Latina y Europa meridional: Argentina, Brasil, Chile, España, Italia, México, Portugal, Uruguay*, ed. Jorge Lanzaro. Madrid: Centro de Estudios Políticos y Constitucionales.

— (2012b) *De Dutra a Lula: a condução e os determinantes da política externa brasileira*. Rio de Janeiro: Elsevier.

Amorim Neto, Octavio, and Gary W. Cox (1997) "Electoral Institutions, Cleavage Structures, and the Number of Parties," *American Journal of Political Science* 41: 149–74.

Amorim Neto, Octavio, and Fabiano Santos (2001) "A conexão presidencial: facções pró e antigoverno e disciplina partidária no Brasil," *Dados – Revista de Ciências Sociais* 44/2.

— (2002) "A Produção Legislativa do Congresso: entre a paróquia e a nação," in *A Democracia e os três poderes no Brasil*, ed. Luiz Werneck Vianna. Belo Horizonte: UFMG.

— (2003) "O segredo ineficiente revisto: o que propõem e o que aprovam os deputados brasileiros," *Dados – Revista de Ciências Sociais* 46/4: 661–98.

Amorim Neto, Octavio, and Paulo Tafner (2002) "Governos de coalizão e mecanismos de alarme de incêndio no controle legislativo das medidas provisórias," *Dados – Revista de Ciências Sociais* 45/1: 5–38.

Amorim Neto, Octavio, Gary W. Cox, and Mathew D. McCubbins (2003) "Agenda Power in Brazil's Câmara dos Deputados, 1989–98," *World Politics* 55/4: 550–78.

Ansiliero, Graziela, and Luís Henrique Paiva (2008) "The Recent Evolution of Social Security Coverage in Brazil," *International Social Security Review* 61/3: 1–28.

Aramayo, Carlos, and Carlos Pereira (2011) "The Price of a Disproportional Cabinet: The *Paloccigate* in Brazil," *Brookings Opinion* (June 28).

Arantes, Rogério B. (1999) "Direito e política: o ministério público e a defesa dos direitos coletivos," *Revista Brasileira de Ciências Sociais* 14/39: 83–102.

— (2003) *The Brazilian Ministério Público and Political Corruption in Brazil*, Working Paper no. CBS-50-03. Centre for Brazilian Studies, University of Oxford.

— (2005) "Constitutionalism, the Expansion of Justice and the Judicialization of Politics in Brazil," in *The Judicialization of Politics in Latin America*, ed. Rachel Sieder, Line Schjolden, and Alan Angell. New York: Palgrave Macmillan.

—— (2011) "The Federal Police and the Ministério Público," in *Corruption and Democracy in Brazil: The Struggle for Accountability*, ed. Timothy J. Power and Matthew M. Taylor. Notre Dame, IN: University of Notre Dame Press.

Araújo, Clara, and José Eustáquio Diniz Alves (2007) "Impactos de indicadores sociais e do sistema eleitoral sobre as chances das mulheres nas eleições e suas interações com as cotas," *Dados – Revista de Ciências Sociais* 50/30: 535–77.

Arbix, Glauco (2009) Former director of IPEA, current director of Finep, author interview, Providence, Rhode Island, April.

Arretche, Marta (2004) "Toward a Unified and More Equitable System: Health Reform in Brazil," in *Crucial Needs, Weak Incentives: Social Sector Reform, Democratization, and Globalization in Latin America*, ed. Robert R. Kaufman and Joan M. Nelson. Washington, DC: Johns Hopkins University Press.

Averbug, André (1999) "Abertura e integração comercial brasileira na década de 90," in *A economia brasileira nos anos 90*, ed. Fabio Giambiagi and Maurício Mesquita Moreira. Rio de Janeiro: BNDES.

Avritzer, Leonardo (1995) "Transition to Democracy and Political Culture: An Analysis of the Conflict between Civil and Political Society in Post-Authoritarian Brazil," *Constellations* 2/2: 242–67.

—— (2002) *Democracy and the Public Space in Latin America*. Princeton, NJ: Princeton University Press.

—— (2009) *Participatory Institutions in Democratic Brazil*. Baltimore: Johns Hopkins University Press.

—— (2012) *Conferências Nacionais: ampliando e redefinindo os padrões de participação social no Brasil*, Texto para discussão no. 1739. Brasília: IPEA.

Ayllón Pino, Bruno (2012) "Contribuciones de Brasil al desarrollo internacional: coaliciones emergentes y cooperación Sur-Sur," *Revista CIDOB d'Afers Internacionals* 97-8 (April): 189–204.

Baer, Werner (2008) *The Brazilian Economy: Growth and Development*. 6th edn, Boulder, CO: Lynne Rienner.

Bailey, Stanley R. (2009) "Public Opinion on Nonwhite Underrepresentation and Racial Identity Politics in Brazil," *Latin American Politics and Society* 51/4: 69–99.

Baiocchi, Gianpaolo (2005) *Militants and Citizens: The Politics of Participatory Democracy in Porto Alegre*. Stanford, CA: Stanford University Press.

Baiocchi, Gianpaolo, Patrick Heller, and Marcelo Kunrath Silva (2008) "Making Space for Civil Society: Institutional Reforms and Local Democracy in Brazil," *Social Forces* 86/3: 911–36.

Baker, Andy (2002) "Reformas liberalizantes e aprovação presidencial: a politização dos debates da política econômica no Brasil," *Dados – Revista de Ciências Sociais* 45/1: 77–98.

Baker, Andy, Barry Ames, and Lucio R. Rennó (2006) "Social Context and Campaign Volatility in New Democracies: Networks and Neighborhoods in Brazil's 2002 Elections," *American Journal of Political Science* 50/2: 382–99.

Ban, Cornel (2013) "Brazil's Liberal Neo-Developmentalism: New Paradigm or Edited Orthodoxy?" *Review of International Political Economy* 20/2: 298–331.

Barreto, Antônio Sérgio, and Rebecca Arkader (1992) "Novos paradigmas de competitividade: implicações para a atuação do sistema BNDES," internal mimeo, BNDES, October.

Barros, Geraldo (2009) "Brazil: The Challenges in Becoming an Agricultural Superpower," in *Brazil as an Economic Superpower? Understanding Brazil's Changing Role in the Global Economy*, ed. Lael Brainard and Leonardo Martinez-Diaz. Washington, DC: Brookings Institution Press, pp. 81–112.

Barros, José Roberto Mendonça de, and Lídia Goldenstein (1997) "Avaliação do processo de reestruturação industrial brasileiro," *Revista de Economia Política* 17/2: 11–31.

Bayma, Israel Fernando de Carvalho (2001) "A concentração da propriedade de meios de comunicação e o coronelismo eletrônico no Brasil," *Revista Eletrónica Internacional de Economía de las Tecnologías de la Información y de la Comunicación* 3/3: 140–71.

Bezerra, Marcos Otávio (1999) *Em nome das "bases": política, favor e dependência pessoal.* Rio de Janeiro: Relume Dumará.

Bhagwati, Jagdish (1988) "Export-Promoting Trade Strategy: Issues and Evidence," *World Bank Research Observer* 3:1: 27–57.

Bianchi, Alvaro, and Ruy Braga (2005) "Brazil: The Lula Government and Financial Globalization," *Social Forces* 83/4: 1745–62.

BNDES (Banco de Desenvolvimento Econômico e Social) (1988) *Questões relativas à competitividade da indústria de bens de capital: bens de capital sob encomenda e máquinas-ferramenta.* Rio de Janeiro: BNDES.

— (1996) *A atuação do BNDES.* Rio de Janeiro: BNDES.

— (2002) *50 anos de desenvolvimento: BNDES.* Rio de Janeiro: BNDES.

— (2007) *Perspectivas do investimento 2007/2010.* Rio de Janeiro: BNDES.

— (2011) *Relatório anual do BNDES – 2010.* Rio de Janeiro: BNDES.

Boas, Taylor C. (2005) "Television and Neopopulism in Latin America: Media Effects in Brazil and Peru," *Latin American Research Review* 40/2: 27–49.

Boas, Taylor C., and F. Daniel Hidalgo (2011) "Controlling the Airwaves: Incumbency Advantage and Community Radio in Brazil," *American Journal of Political Science* 55/4: 868–84.

Bohn, Simone R. (2011) "Social Policy and Vote in Brazil: Bolsa Família and the Shifts in Lula's Electoral Base," *Latin American Research Review* 46/1: 54–79.

Boix, Carles (2003) *Democracy and Redistribution.* Princeton, NJ: Princeton University Press.

Boix, Carles, and Susan C. Stokes (2003) "Endogenous Democratization," *World Politics* 55/4: 517–49.

Borges, André (2008) "State Government, Political Competition and Education Reform: Comparative Lessons from Brazil," *Bulletin of Latin American Research* 27/2: 235–54.

Boschi, Renato (2011) "Instituições, trajetórias e desenvolvimento: uma discussão a partir da América Latina," in *Variedades de capitalismo, política e desenvolvimento na América Latina*, ed. Renato R. Boschi. Belo Horizonte: Editora UFMG.

Boschi, Renato, and Flavio Gaitán (2012) "Politics and Development: Lessons from Latin America," in *Development and Semi-Periphery: Post-Neoliberal Trajectories in South America and Central Eastern Europe*, ed. Renato Boschi and Carlos Henrique Santana. London: Anthem Press.

Bourguignon, François, Francisco H. G. Ferreira, and Phillippe G. Leite (2003) "Conditional Cash Transfers, Schooling, and Child Labor: Micro-Simulating Brazil's *Bolsa Escola* Program," *World Bank Economic Review* 17/2: 229–54.

Brainard, Lael, and Leonardo Martinez-Diaz (2009) "Brazil: The 'B' Belongs in the BRICS," in *Brazil as an Economic Superpower? Understanding Brazil's Changing Role in the Global Economy*, ed. Lael Brainard and Leonardo Martinez-Diaz. Washington, DC: Brookings Institution Press, pp. 1–16.

Bresser-Pereira, Luiz Carlos (2005) "Proposta de desenvolvimento para o Brasil," in *Novo-desenvolvimentismo: um projeto nacional de crescimento com eqüidade social*, ed. João Sicsú, Luiz Fernando de Paula, and Renaut Michel. Barueri: Editora Monole.

—— (2006) "O novo desenvolvimentismo e a ortodoxia convencional," *São Paulo em Perspectiva* 20/3: 5–24.

Bresser-Pereira, Luiz Carlos, and Yoshiaki Nakano (2002) "Uma estratégia de desenvolvimento com estabilidade," *Revista de Economia Política* 21/3: 146–77.

Burges, Sean W. (2009) *Brazilian Foreign Policy after the Cold War*. Gainesville: University Press of Florida.

Campello, Daniela (2013) "What is Left of the Brazilian Left?," unpublished paper, Princeton University.

Cano, Wilson, and Ana Lucia Gonçalves da Silva (2010) "Política industrial do governo Lula," in *Os anos Lula: contribuições para um balanço crítico 2003–2010*. Rio de Janeiro: Garamond, pp. 181–208.

Cardoso, Fernando Henrique, and Enzo Faletto (1979) *Dependency and Democracy in Latin America*. Berkeley: University of California Press.

Carey, John M., and Matthew S. Shugart, eds (1998) *Executive Decree Authority*. New York: Cambridge University Press.

Carranza, Mario E. (2003) "Can Mercosur Survive? Domestic and International Constraints on Mercosur," *Latin American Politics and Society* 45/2: 67–103.

Carreirão, Yan de Souza (2002a) *A decisão do voto nas eleições presidenciais brasileiras*. Florianópolis: Editora da UFSC.

—— (2002b) "Identificação ideológica e voto para presidente," *Opinião Pública* 8/8: 54–79.

—— (2007a) "Identificação ideológica, partidos e voto na eleição presidencial de 2006," *Opinião Pública* 13/2: 307–39.

—— (2007b) "Relevant Factors for the Voting Decision in the 2002 Presidential Election: An Analysis of the ESEB (Brazilian Electoral Study) Data," *Brazilian Political Science Review* 1/1: 70–101.

Carreirão, Yan de Souza, and Maria D'Alva Kinzo (2004) "Partidos políticos, preferência partidária e decisão eleitoral no Brasil (1989–2002)," *Dados – Revista de Ciências Sociais* 47/1: 131–67.

Carvalho, Georgia O. (2006) "Environmental Resistance and the Politics of Energy Development in the Brazilian Amazon," *Journal of Environment and Development* 15/3: 245–68.

Cason, Jeffrey (2000) "Democracy Looks South: Mercosul and the Politics of Brazilian Trade Strategy," in *Democratic Brazil: Actors, Institutions, and Processes*, ed. Peter R. Kingstone and Timothy J. Power. Pittsburgh: University of Pittsburgh Press, pp. 204–16.

Cason, Jeffrey W., and Timothy J. Power (2009) "Presidentialization, Pluralization, and the Rollback of Itamaraty: Explaining Change in Brazilian Foreign Policy Making in the Cardoso–Lula Era," *International Political Science Review* 30/2: 117–40.

Castro, Antônio Barros de (1990) *Política industrial: razões e restrições*, Texto para discussão no. 253. Rio de Janeiro: IEI/UFRJ.

—— (1995) Former president, BNDES, Itamar Franco administration, author interview, Rio de Janeiro, March 27.

—— (2008) "From Semi-Stagnation to Growth in a Sino-Centric Market," *Brazilian Journal of Political Economy* 28/1: 3–27.

Cavalcanti, Rosangela Batista (2006) "The Effectiveness of Law: Civil Society and the Public Prosecution in Brazil," in *Enforcing the Rule of Law: Social Accountability in the New Latin American Democracies*, ed. Enrique Peruzzotti and Catalina Smulovitz. Pittsburgh: University of Pittsburgh Press.

Cavarozzi, Marcelo (1992) "Beyond Transitions to Democracy in Latin America," *Journal of Latin American Studies* 24/3: 665–84.

Centeno, Miguel Ángel (1994) *Democracy within Reason: Technocratic Revolution in Mexico*. University Park, PA: Pennsylvania State University Press.

Cervo, Amado Luiz (2010) "Brazil's Rise on the International Scene: Brazil and the World," *Revista Brasileira de Política Internacional* 53: 7–32.

Chang, Ha-Joon (2011) "*Hamlet* without the Prince of Denmark: How Development Has Disappeared from Today's 'Development' Discourse," in *Towards New Developmentalism: Markets as Means Rather than Master*, ed. Shahrukh Rafi Khan and Jens Christiansen. New York: Routledge.

Cheibub, José Antônio (2009) "Political Reform in Brazil: Recent Proposals, Diagnosis, and a Suggestion," in *Brazil under Lula: Economy, Politics, and Society under the Worker-President*, ed. Joseph L. Love and Werner Baer. New York: Palgrave Macmillan, pp. 9–25.

Cheibub, José Antônio, Adam Przeworski, and Sebastian M. Saiegh (2004) "Government Coalitions and Legislative Success under Presidentialism and Parliamentarism," *British Journal of Political Science* 34: 565–87.

Coutinho, Luciano (2010) "A construção dos fundamentos para o crescimento sustentável da economia brasileira," in *O BNDES em um Brasil em transição*, ed. Ana Cláudia Além and Fabio Giambiagi. Rio de Janeiro: BNDES.

Coutinho, Luciano, and J. C. Ferraz (1994) *Estudo da competitividade da indústria brasileira*. Campinas: Papirus.

Cox, Gary (1988) *The Efficient Secret: The Cabinet and the Development of Political Parties in Victorian England*. New York: Cambridge University Press.

Cox, Gary W., and Scott Morgenstern (2002) "Epilogue: Latin America's Reactive Assemblies and Proactive Presidents," in *Legislative Politics in Latin America*, ed. Scott Morgenstern and Benito Nacif. New York: Cambridge University Press.

Cruz, Hélio Nogueira da, and Marcos Eugênio da Silva (1991) "A Situação do setor de bens de capital e suas perspectivas," *Estudos Econômicos* 21/3: 319–50.

Dagnino, Evelina (1998) "The Cultural Politics of Citizenship, Democracy and the State," in *Cultures of Politics/Politics of Cultures: Re-visioning Latin American Social Movements*, ed. Sonia E. Alvarez, Evelina Dagnino, and Arturo Escobar. Boulder, CO: Westview Press.

Della Cava, Ralph (1989) "The 'People's Church,' the Vatican, and *Abertura*," in *Democratic Brazil: Problems of Transition and Consolidation*, ed. Alfred Stepan. New York: Oxford University Press.

Desposato, Scott W. (2006a) "Parties for Rent? Ambition, Ideology, and Party Switching in Brazil's Chamber of Deputies," *American Journal of Political Science* 50/1: 62–80.

—— (2006b) "The Impact of Electoral Rules on Legislative Parties: Lessons from the Brazilian Senate and Chamber of Deputies," *Journal of Politics* 68/4: 1015–27.

Diamond, Larry, and Leonardo Morlino (2004) "The Quality of Democracy," *Journal of Democracy* 15/4: 20–31.

Dillinger, William, Guillermo Perry, and Steven B. Webb (1999) *Macroeconomic Management in Decentralized Democracies: The Quest for Hard Budget Constraints in Latin America*. Washington, DC: World Bank.

Diniz, Eli (2011) "Depois do neoliberalismo: rediscutindo a articulação estado e desenvolvimento no novo milênio," in *Variedades de capitalismo, política e desenvolvimento na América Latina*, ed. Renato R. Boschi. Belo Horizonte: Editora UFMG.

Donaghy, Maureen M. (2011) "Do Participatory Governance Institutions Matter? Municipal Councils and Social Housing Programs in Brazil," *Comparative Politics* 44/1: 83–102.

Dornbusch, Rudiger (1993) "World Economic Trends – Their Impact on Developing Countries," Eighteenth Sir Winston Scott Memorial Lecture, available at www.centralbank.org.bb/Publications/SWSML/SWSML-1993-Dornbusch.PDF (accessed August 11, 2012).

Draibe, Sônia (2004) "Federal Leverage in a Decentralized System: Education Reform in Brazil," in *Crucial Needs, Weak Incentives: Social Sector Reform, Democratization, and Globalization in Latin America*, ed. Robert R. Kaufman and Joan M. Nelson. Baltimore: Johns Hopkins University Press.

ECLAC (Economic Commission on Latin America and the Caribbean) (2012) *Foreign Direct Investment in Latin America and the Caribbean 2011*. New York: United Nations/ECLAC.

Engstrom, Par (2012) "Brazilian Foreign Policy and Human Rights: Change and Continuity under Dilma," *Critical Sociology* 38/6: 835–49.

Erber, Fábio Stéfano, and Roberto Vermulm (1993) *Ajuste estrutural e estratégias empresariais*. Rio de Janeiro: IPEA.

Evans, Peter B. (1979) *Dependent Development: The Alliance of Multinational, State, and Local Capital in Brazil*. Princeton, NJ: Princeton University Press.

Faoro, Raymundo (1958) *Os donos do poder: formação do patronato político brasileiro*. Pôrto Alegre: Globo.

Faria, Cláudia Feres (2009) "Participação, sociedade civil e governo Lula (2003–2006): construindo uma sinergia positiva?" In *O partido dos trabalhadores e a política brasileira (1980–2006)*. São Carlos: EdUFSCar, pp. 153–82.

Fenwick, Tracy Beck (2009) "Avoiding Governors: The Success of Bolsa Família," *Latin American Research Review* 44/1: 102–31.

Feres, João, Verônica Toste Daflon, and Luiz Augusto Campos (2011) "Lula's Approach to Affirmative Action and Race," *NACLA Report on the Americas* 44/2: 34–7, 39.

Ferraz, Claudio, and Frederico Finan (2008) "Exposing Corrupt Politicians: The Effects of Brazil's Publicly Released Audits on Electoral Outcomes," *Quarterly Journal of Economics* 123/2: 703–45.

Ferreira, Francisco H. G., Phillippe G. Leite, and Julie A. Litchfield (2007) "The Rise and Fall of Brazilian Inequality: 1981–2004," *Macroeconomic Dynamics* 12: 199–230.

Ferreira, Gisele Sayeg Nunes (2006) "Radiodifusão e governabilidade: Roosevelt, Vargas e a atuação dos políticos locais nas emissões comunitárias legalizadas da região noroeste do estado de São Paulo," *UNIrevista* 1/3: 1–13.

Ferreira Filho, J. B. S., and M. Horridge (2006) "Economic Integration, Poverty, and Regional Inequality in Brazil," _Revista Brasileira de Economia_ 60/4: 363–87.

Figueiredo, Argelina Cheibub (2004) "Fora do jogo: a experiência dos negros na classe média brasileira," _Cadernos Pagu_ 23 (July/December): 199–228.

—— (2007) "Government Coalitions in Brazilian Democracy," _Brazilian Political Science Review_ 1/2: 182–216.

—— (2010) "The Collor Impeachment and Presidential Government in Brazil," in _Presidential Breakdowns in Latin America: Causes and Outcomes of Executive Instability in Developing Democracies_, ed. Mariana Llanos and Leiv Marsteintredet. New York: Palgrave Macmillan, pp. 111–27.

Figueiredo, Argelina Cheibub, and Fernando Limongi (1995) "Partidos políticos na Câmara dos Deputados: 1989–1994," _Dados – Revista de Ciências Sociais_ 38/3: 497–524.

—— (1997) "O congresso e as medidas provisórias: abdicação ou delegação?" _Novos Estudos CEBRAP_ 47: 127–54.

—— (1999) _Executivo e legislativo na nova ordem constitucional_. Rio de Janeiro: Fundação Getúlio Vargas Editora.

—— (2000) "Presidential Power, Legislative Organization, and Party Behavior in Brazil," _Comparative Politics_ 32/2: 151–70.

—— (2002) "Incentivos eleitorais, partidos e política orçamentária," _Dados – Revista de Ciências Sociais_ 45/2: 303–44.

—— (2007) "Instituições Políticas e governabilidade: desempenho do governo e apoio legislativo na democracia brasileira," in _A democracia brasileira: balanço e perspectivas para o século 21_, ed. Carlos Ranulfo Melo and Manuel Alcántara Sáez. Belo Horizonte: Editora UFMG.

Figueiredo, Miguel de, and F. Daniel Hidalgo (2009) "Does Targeted Redistribution Create Partisans? Evidence from Brazil," Paper presented at the 2009 Annual Meeting of the Midwest Political Science Association, April 2–4.

Finep (2007) _Relatório da gestão da Finep 2003–2006_. Rio de Janeiro: Finep.

Finep (2012) _Relatório da gestão do exercício de 2011_. Rio de Janeiro: Finep.

Finep (2013) _Relatório da gestão da Finep 2012_. Rio de Janeiro: Finep.

Fleischer, David (1998) _Brazilian Politics: Structures, Process, Elections, Parties and Political Groups (1985–1995)_, Working Paper WP95-2, Institute of Brazilian Issues, Washington, DC.

Fleury, Afonso, and Maria Tereza Leme Fleury (2011) _Brazilian Multinationals: Competences for Internationalizaton_. New York: Cambridge University Press.

Fonseca, Celso (2011) Chief of staff of Finep, author interview, Rio de Janeiro, November.

Fried, Brian J. (2011) "Distributive Politics and Conditional Cash Transfers: The Case of Brazil's _Bolsa Família_," _World Development_ 40/5: 1042–53.

Frieden, Jeffry (1991) _Debt, Development, and Democracy: Modern Political Economy and Latin America, 1965–1985_. Princeton, NJ: Princeton University Press.

Friedman, Elisabeth Jay, and Kathryn Hochstetler (2002) "Assessing the Third Transition in Latin American Democratization: Representational Regimes and Civil Society in Argentina and Brazil," _Comparative Politics_ 35/1: 21–42.

Fritsch, Winston, and Gustavo H. B. Franco (1990) "Política industrial, competitividade e industrialização: aspectos da experiência brasileira recente," _Planejamento e Políticas Públicas_ 3: 75–100.

—— (1991) "Competition and Industrial Policies in a Technologically Dependent Economy: The Emerging Issues for Brazil," *Revista Brasileira de Economia* 45/1: 69–90.

—— (1993) *The Political Economy of Trade and Industrial Policy Reform in Brazil in the 1990s.* Santiago: United Nations/Economic Commission on Latin America.

Goldfrank, Benjamin (2007) "The Politics of Deepening Local Democracy: Decentralization, Party Institutionalization, and Participation," *Comparative Politics* 39/1: 147–68.

Goldfrank, Benjamin, and Aaron Schneider (2006) "Competitive Institution Building: The PT and Participatory Budgeting in Rio Grande do Sul," *Latin American Politics and Society* 48/3: 1–31.

Gómez Mera, Laura (2005) "Explaining Mercosur's Survival: Strategic Sources of Argentine–Brazilian Convergence," *Journal of Latin American Studies* 37: 109–40.

—— (2008) "How 'New' is the 'New Regionalism' in the Americas? The Case of Mercosur," *Journal of International Relations and Development* 11: 279–308.

—— (2009) "Domestic Constraints on Regional Cooperation: Explaining Trade Conflict in Mercosur," *Review of International Political Economy* 16/4: 746–77.

—— (2011) "Markets, Politics, and Learning: Explaining Monetary Policy Innovations in Brazil," *Studies in Comparative International Development* 46/1: 243–69.

Gordon, Nora, and Emiliana Vegas (2005) "Educational Finance Equalization, Spending, Teacher Quality, and Student Outcomes," in *Incentives to Improve Teaching: Lessons from Latin America*, ed. Emiliana Vegas. Washington, DC: World Bank.

Governo Federal (2008) *Política de desenvolvimento produtivo.* Brasília: Governo Luiz Inácio Lula da Silva.

—— (2011) *Política de desenvolvimento produtivo.* Brasília: Governo Dilma Rousseff.

Grupo Interministerial (1986) *Política industrial.* Brasília: SEPLAN, IPEA, MIC, MINIFAZ, MCT.

Guilhon Albuquerque, José Augusto (2003) "Brazil: From Dependency to Globalization," in *Latin American and Caribbean Foreign Policy*, ed. Frank O. Mora and Jeanne A. K. Hey. Lanham, MD: Rowman & Littlefield.

Haddad, Mônica A. (2009) "A Spatial Analysis of *Bolsa Família*: Is Allocation Targeting the Needy?," in *Brazil under Lula: Economy, Politics, and Society under the Worker-President*, ed. Joseph L. Love and Werner Baer. New York: Palgrave Macmillan, pp. 187–203.

Haggard, Stephan, and Robert R. Kaufman (1995) *The Political Economy of Democratic Transitions.* Princeton, NJ: Princeton University Press.

Haggard, Stephan, and Steven B. Webb (2004) "Political Incentives and Intergovernmental Fiscal Relations: Argentina, Brazil, and Mexico Compared," in *Decentralization and Democracy in Latin America*, ed. Alfred P. Montero and David J. Samuels. Notre Dame, IN: University of Notre Dame Press.

Hagopian, Frances (1990) "'Democracy by Undemocratic Means'? Elites, Political Pacts, and Regime Transition in Brazil," *Comparative Political Studies* 23/2: 147–70.

—— (1996) *Traditional Politics and Regime Change in Brazil.* New York: Cambridge University Press.

Hagopian, Frances, Carlos Gervasoni, and Juan Andres Morães (2009) "From Patronage to Program: The Emergence of Party-Oriented Legislators in Brazil," *Comparative Political Studies* 42/3: 360–91.

Hall, Anthony (2008) "Brazil's *Bolsa Família*: A Double-Edged Sword?" *Development and Change* 39/5: 799–822.
— (2012) "The Last Shall Be First: Political Dimensions of Conditional Cash Transfers in Brazil," *Journal of Policy Practice* 11: 25–41.
Hall, Anthony, and Sue Branford (2012) "Development, Dams and Dilma: The Saga of Belo Monte," *Critical Sociology* 38/6: 851–62.
Hall, Michael (2009) "The Labor Policies of the Lula Government," in *Brazil under Lula: Economy, Politics, and Society under the Worker-President*, ed. Joseph L. Love and Werner Baer. New York: Palgrave Macmillan, pp. 151–65.
Hanchard, Michael (1996) *Orpheus and Power: The Movimento Negro of Rio de Janeiro and São Paulo, Brazil, 1945–1988*. Princeton, NJ: Princeton University Press.
Handa, Sudhanshu, and Benjamin Davis (2006) "The Experience of Conditional Cash Transfers in Latin America and the Caribbean," *Development Policy Review* 24/5: 513–36.
Hillbrecht, Ronald (1997) "Federalismo e a união monetária brasileira," *Estudos Econômicos* 27: 53–67.
Hinton, Mercedes S. (2009) "Police and State Reform in Brazil: Bad Apple or Rotten Barrel?," in *Policing Developing Democracies*, ed. Mercedes S. Hinton and Tim Newburn. New York: Routledge.
Hochstetler, Kathryn (1997) "The Evolution of the Brazilian Environmental Movement and its Political Roles," in *The New Politics of Inequality in Latin America: Rethinking Participation and Representation*, ed. Douglas A. Chalmers, Carlos M. Vilas, Katherine Hite, Scott B. Martin, Kerianne Piester, and Monique Segarra. New York: Oxford University Press.
— (2000) "Democratizing Pressures from Below? Social Movements in the New Brazilian Democracy," in *Democratic Brazil: Actors, Institutions, and Processes*, ed. Peter R. Kingstone and Timothy J. Power. Pittsburgh: University of Pittsburgh Press, pp. 167–82.
— (2003) "Fading Green? Environmental Politics in the Mercosur Free Trade Agreement," *Latin American Politics and Society* 45/4: 1–32.
— (2008) "Organized Civil Society in Lula's Brazil," in *Democratic Brazil Revisited*, ed. Peter R. Kingstone and Timothy J. Power. Pittsburgh: University of Pittsburgh Press.
— (2011) "The Politics of Environmental Licensing: Energy Projects of the Past and Future in Brazil," *Studies in Comparative International Development* 46/4: 349–71.
Hochstetler, Kathryn, and Margaret E. Keck (2007) *Greening Brazil: Environmental Activism in State and Society*. Durham, NC: Duke University Press.
Hochstetler, Kathryn, and Alfred P. Montero (forthcoming) "The Renewed Developmentalist State: The National Development Bank and the Brazil Model," *Journal of Development Studies*.
Hochstetler, Kathryn, and Eduardo Viola (2012) "Brazil and the Politics of Climate Change: Beyond the Global Commons," *Environmental Politics* (July): 1–19.
Holzhacker, Denilde Oliveira, and Elizabeth Balbachevsky (2007) "Classe ideologia e política: uma interpretação dos resultados das eleições de 2002 e 2006," *Opinião Pública* 13/2: 283–306.
Htun, Mala, and Mark Jones (2002) "Engendering the Right to Participate in Decision-Making: Electoral Quotas and Women's Leadership in Latin America,"

in *Gender and the Politics of Rights and Democracy in Latin America*, ed. Nikki Craske and Maime Molyneux. New York: Palgrave.

Htun, Mala, and Timothy J. Power (2006) "Gender, Parties, and Support for Equal Rights in the Brazilian Congress," *Latin American Politics and Society* 48/4: 83–104.

Hunter, Wendy (2010) *The Transformation of the Workers' Party in Brazil, 1989–2009*. New York: Cambridge University Press.

Hunter, Wendy, and Timothy Power (2007) "Rewarding Lula: Executive Power, Social Policy, and the Brazilian Elections of 2006," *Latin American Politics and Society* 49/1: 1–30.

Hunter, Wendy, and Natasha Borges Sugiyama (2009) "Democracy and Social Policy in Brazil: Advancing Basic Needs, Preserving Privileged Interests," *Latin American Politics and Society* 51/2: 29–58.

IPEA (Instituto de Pesquisa Econômica Aplicada) (1990) *Política industrial e de comércio exterior: apoio à capacitação tecnólogica da indústria*. Brasília: IPEA.

—— (2010) "Desigualdade da renda no território brasileiro," *Comunicados do IPEA* no. 60 (August 12).

—— (2011) *Políticas sociais: acompanhamento e análise*. Brasília: IPEA.

Johnson, Ollie A. III (2008) "Afro-Brazilian Politics: White Supremacy, Black Struggle, and Affirmative Action," in *Democratic Brazil Revisited*, ed. Peter R. Kingstone and Timothy J. Power. Pittsburgh: University of Pittsburgh Press, pp. 209–30.

Kaufman, Robert R., and Joan M. Nelson (2004) *Crucial Needs, Weak Incentives: Social Sector Reform, Democratization and Globalization in Latin America*. Baltimore: Johns Hopkins University Press.

Keck, Margaret (1992) *The Workers' Party and Democratization in Brazil*. New Haven, CT: Yale University Press.

—— (1995) "Social Equity and Environmental Politics in Brazil: Lessons from the Rubber Tappers of Acre," *Comparative Politics* 27: 409–24.

Keck, Margaret, and Kathryn Sikkink (1998) *Activists beyond Borders: Advocacy Networks in International Politics*. Ithaca, NY: Cornell University Press.

Kerche, Fábio (2007) "Autonomia e discricionariedade do Ministério Público no Brasil," *Dados – Revista de Ciências Sociais* 50/2: 259–79.

Khan, Shahrukh Rafi (2007) "WTO, IMF and the Closing of Development Policy Space for Low-Income Countries: A Call for Neo-Developmentalism," *Third World Quarterly* 28/6: 1073–90.

Khan, Shahrukh Rafi, and Jens Christiansen, eds (2011) *Towards New Developmentalism: Markets as Means Rather than Master*. New York: Routledge.

Kiewiet, D. Roderick, and Mathew McCubbins (1991) *The Logic of Delegation: Congressional Parties and the Appropriations Process*. Chicago: University of Chicago Press.

Kingstone, Peter (1999) *Crafting Coalitions for Reform: Business Preferences, Political Institutions, and Neoliberal Reform in Brazil*. University Park: Pennsylvania State University Press.

—— (2003a) "Privatizing Telebrás: Brazilian Political Institutions and Policy Performance," *Comparative Politics* 36/1: 21–40.

—— (2003b) "Democratic Governance and the Dilemma of Social Security Reform in Brazil," in *Latin American Democracies in the New Global Economy*, ed. Ana Margheritis. Miami: North–South Center Press.

—— (2004) "Industrialists and Liberalization," in *Reforming Brazil*, ed. Mauricio A. Font and Anthony Peter Spanakos. Lanham, MD: Lexington Books.

Kinzo, Maria D'Alva (1992) "A eleição presidencial de 1989: o comportamento eleitoral em uma cidade brasileira," *Dados – Revista de Ciências Sociais* 35/1: 49–66.

—— (2005) "Parties in the Electorate: Public Perceptions and Party Attachments in Brazil," *Revista Brasileira de Ciências Sociais* 20/57: 65–81.

Kohli, Atul (2006a) "Politics of Economic Growth in India, 1980–2005: The 1980s," *Economic and Political Weekly* 41/13: 1251–9.

—— (2006b) "Politics of Economic Growth in India, 1980–2005: The 1990s and Beyond," *Economic and Political Weekly* 41/14: 1361–70.

Krugman, Paul (1995) "Dutch Tulips and Emerging Markets: Another Bubble Bursts," *Foreign Affairs* (July/August): 28–44.

Kurtz, Marcus J., and Sarah M. Brooks (2008) "Embedding Neoliberal Reform in Latin America," *World Politics* 60: 231–80.

Laakso, Marku, and Rein Taagepera (1979) "Effective Number of Parties: A Measure with Application to West Europe," *Comparative Political Studies* 12: 3–27.

Lacerda, Alan Daniel Freire de (2002) "O PT e a unidade partidária como problema," *Dados – Revista de Ciências Sociais* 45/1: 39–76.

Lamounier, Bolívar (1992) "Estrutura institucional e governabilidade na década de 1990," in *O Brasil e as reformas políticas*, ed. J. P. R. Velloso. Rio de Janeiro: Olympio.

—— (1994) "Brazil at an Impasse," *Journal of Democracy* 5/3: 72–87.

Lampreia, Luiz Felipe (2009) *O Brasil e os ventos do mundo: memórias de cinco décadas na cena internacional*. Rio de Janeiro: Objetiva.

Leal, Victor Nunes (1976) *Coronelismo, enxada e voto: o município e o regime representativo no Brasil*. São Paulo: Editora Alfa-Omega.

Lemos, Leany Barreiro de S. (2001) "O congresso brasileiro e a distribuição de benefícios sociais no período 1988–1994: uma análise distributivista," *Dados – Revista de Ciências Sociais* 44/3: 561–604.

Lemos-Nelson, Ana Tereza, and Jorge Zaverucha (2006) "Multiple Activations as a Strategy of Citizen Accountability and the Role of the Investigating Legislative Commissions," in *Enforcing the Rule of Law: Social Accountability in the New Latin American Democracies*, ed. Enrique Peruzzotti and Catalina Smulovitz. Pittsburgh: University of Pittsburgh Press.

Leoni, Eduardo (2002) "Ideologia, democracia e comportamento parlamentar: a Câmara dos Deputados (1991–1998)," *Dados – Revista de Ciências Sociais* 45/3: 361–86.

Levine, Daniel H., and José E. Molina (2011) "Evaluating the Quality of Democracy in Latin America," in *The Quality of Democracy in Latin America*, ed. Daniel H. Levine and José E. Molina. Boulder, CO: Lynne Rienner, pp. 1–19.

Lima, Maria Regina Soares de, and Mônica Hirst (2006) "Brazil as an Intermediate State and Regional Power: Action, Choice, and Responsibilities," *International Affairs* 82/1: 21–40.

Lima, Venício A. de (1993) "Brazilian Television in the 1989 Presidential Campaign: Constructing a President," in *Television, Politics, and the Transition to Democracy in Latin America*, ed. Thomas Skidmore. Baltimore: Johns Hopkins University Press.

—— (2008) "As concessões de radiodifusão como moeda de barganha política," *Revista Adusp* (January): 26–33.

Limongi, Fernando (1995) "Estabilidade eleitoral em São Paulo: 1989–1994," *Tipologia do Eleitorado Paulista*. São Paulo: Relatório Fapesp (no. 94: 1927–1928).

Lipset, Seymour Martin (1959) "Some Social Requisites of Democracy: Economic Development and Political Legitimacy," *American Political Science Review* 53 (March): 69–105.

Lipset, Seymour Martin, and Stein Rokkan (1967) "Cleavage Structures, Party Systems and Voter Alignments: An Introduction," in *Party Systems and Voter Alignments*, ed. Seymour Martin Lipset and Stein Rokkan. New York: Free Press.

Lloyd-Sherlock, Peter (2006) "Simple Transfers, Complex Outcomes: The Impacts of Pensions on Poor Households in Brazil," *Development and Change* 37/5: 969–95.

Lloyd-Sherlock, Peter, Armando Barrientos, Valerie Moller, and João Saboia (2012) "Pensions, Poverty, and Wellbeing in Later Life: Comparative Research from South Africa and Brazil," *Journal of Aging Studies* 26: 243–52.

Lucas, Kevin, and David Samuels (2010) "The Ideological 'Coherence' of the Brazilian Party System, 1990–2009," *Journal of Politics in Latin America* 2/3: 39–69.

Lyne, Mona M. (2005) "Parties as Programmatic Agents: A Test of Institutional Theory in Brazil," *Party Politics* 11/1: 193–216.

—— (2008) "Proffering Pork: How Party Leaders Build Party Reputations in Brazil," *American Journal of Political Science* 52/2: 290–303.

Machado, Aline (2005) "A lógica das coligações no Brasil," in *Partidos e coligações eleitorais no Brasil*, ed. Silvana Krause and Rogério Schmitt. São Paulo: Fundação Konrad Adenauer.

Maddison, Angus (2003) *The World Economy: Historical Statistics*. Paris: OECD.

Madrid, Raúl (2003) *Retiring the State: The Politics of Pension Privatization in Latin America and Beyond*. Stanford, CA: Stanford University Press.

Mahoney, James, and Kathleen Thelen (2010) "A Theory of Gradual Institutional Change," in *Explaining Institutional Change: Ambiguity, Agency, and Power*, ed. James Mahoney and Kathleen Thelen. New York: Cambridge University Press, pp. 1–37.

Mainwaring, Scott P. (1991) "Politicians, Parties, and Electoral Systems: Brazil in Comparative Perspective," *Comparative Politics* 24/1: 21–43.

—— (1993) "Presidentialism, Multipartism, and Democracy: The Difficult Combination," *Comparative Political Studies* 26/2: 198–228.

—— (1995) "Brazil: Weak Parties, Feckless Democracy," in *Building Democratic Institutions: Party Systems in Latin America*, ed. Scott Mainwaring and Timothy Scully. Stanford, CA: Stanford University Press.

—— (1998) "Electoral Volatility in Brazil," *Party Politics* 4/4: 523–45.

—— (1999) *Rethinking Party Systems in the Third Wave of Democratization: The Case of Brazil*. Stanford, CA: Stanford University Press.

—— (2003) "Introduction: Democratic Accountability in Latin America," in *Democratic Accountability in Latin America*, ed. Scott Mainwaring and Christopher Welna. New York: Oxford University Press.

Mainwaring, Scott, and Timothy Scully (1995) "Introduction: Party Systems in Latin America," in *Building Democratic Institutions: Party Systems in Latin America*, ed. Scott Mainwaring and Timothy Scully. Stanford, CA: Stanford University Press.

Mainwaring, Scott, Rachel Meneguello, and Timothy J. Power (2000) "Conservative Parties, Democracy, and Economic Reform in Contemporary Brazil," in *Conservative Parties, the Right, and Democracy in Latin America*, ed. Kevin J. Middlebrook. Baltimore: Johns Hopkins University Press, pp. 164–222.

Malamud, Andrés (2005) "Presidential Diplomacy and the Institutional Underpinnings of Mercosur: An Empirical Examination," *Latin American Research Review* 40/1: 138–64.

—— (2011) "A Leader without Followers? The Growing Divergence between the Regional and Global Performance of Brazilian Foreign Policy," *Latin American Politics and Society* 53/3: 1–24.

Manin, Bernard, Adam Przeworski, and Susan C. Stokes (1999) "Elections and Representation," in *Democracy, Accountability, and Representation*, ed. Adam Przeworski, Susan C. Stokes, and Bernard Manin. New York: Cambridge University Press, pp. 29–54.

Marques, Rosa Maria, Marcel Guedes Leite, Áquilas Mendes, and Mariana Ribeiro Jansen Ferreira (2009) "Discutindo o papel do programa Bolsa Família na decisão das eleições presidenciais brasileiras de 2006," *Revista de Economia Política* 29/1: 114–32.

Martínez, Juan, and Javier Santiso (1993) "Financial Markets and Politics: The Confidence Game in Latin American Emerging Economies," *International Political Science Review* 24/3: 363–95.

Martínez-Lara, Javier (1996) *Building Democracy in Brazil: The Politics of Constitutional Change, 1985–1995*. New York: St. Martin's Press.

Mayhew, David R. (1974) *Congress: The Electoral Connection*. New Haven, CT: Yale University Press.

McCowan, Tristan (2007) "Expansion without Equity: An Analysis of Current Policy on Access to Higher Education in Brazil," *Higher Education* 53: 579–98.

MDS (Ministério do Desenvolvimento Social e Combate à Fome) (2010) *Síntese do 1º relatório contendo os principais resultados da pesquisa de avaliação de impacto do Bolsa Família – 2ª rodada – AIBF II*. Nota Técnica no. 110 (August 4).

Melo, Marcus André (1997) "O jogo das regras: a política da reforma constitucional de 1993/96," *Revista Brasileira de Ciências Sociais* 33 (February): 63–85.

—— (2005) "O Sucesso inesperado das reformas de segunda geração: federalismo, reformas constitucionais e política social," *Dados – Revista de Ciências Sociais* 48/4: 845–89.

—— (2008) "Unexpected Successes, Unanticipated Failures: Social Policy from Cardoso to Lula," in *Democratic Brazil Revisited*, ed. Peter R. Kingstone and Timothy J. Power. Pittsburgh: University of Pittsburgh Press, pp. 161–84.

Melo, Marcus André, and Jonathan Rodden (2007) *Decentralization in Brazil*, report submitted to the Independent Evaluation Group, World Bank Task Force: Evaluation of World Bank Support for Decentralization. Washington, DC: World Bank.

Meneguello, Rachel (1989) *PT: a formação de um partido, 1979–1982*. São Paulo: Paz e Terra.

—— (1998) *Partidos e governos no Brasil contemporâneo (1985–1997)*. São Paulo: Paz e Terra.

Meyer, Peter J. (2013) "Brazil–U.S. Relations," *Congressional Research Service Report for Congress*, no. 7-5700. Washington, DC: CRS.

Meyer-Stamer, Jörg (1992) "The End of Brazil's Informatics Policy," *Science and Public Policy* 19/2: 99–110.

—— (1997) "New Patterns of Governance for Industrial Change: Perspectives for Brazil," *Journal of Development Studies* 33/3: 364–91.

Ministério da Defesa (2008) *Estratégia nacional da defesa militar brasileira*. Brasília: Governo Federal.

Ministério de Minas e Energia (2010) *Plano decenal de expansão de energia*. Brasília: Ministério de Minas e Energia, Empresa de Pesquisa Energética.

Mitchell, Gladys (2009) "Campaign Strategies of Afro-Brazilian Politicians: A Preliminary Analysis," *Latin American Politics and Society* 51/3: 111–42.

Moisés, José Álvaro (2011) "Political Discontent in New Democracies: The Case of Brazil and Latin America," *International Review of Sociology* 21/2: 339–66.

Montero, Alfred P. (1998) "State Interests and the New Industrial Policy in Brazil: The Privatization of Steel, 1990–1994," *Journal of Interamerican Studies and World Affairs* 40/3: 27–62.

—— (2000) "Devolving Democracy? Political Decentralization and the New Brazilian Federalism," in *Democratic Brazil: Actors, Institutions, and Processes*, ed. Peter R. Kingstone and Timothy J. Power. Pittsburgh: University of Pittsburgh Press.

—— (2004) "Competitive Federalism and Distributive Conflict," in *Reforming Brazil*, ed. Mauricio A. Font and Anthony Peter Spanakos. Lanham, MD: Lexington Books.

—— (2005) *Brazilian Politics: Reforming a Democratic State in a Changing World*. Cambridge: Polity.

—— (2011) "Brazil: The Persistence of Oligarchy," in *The Quality of Democracy in Latin America*, ed. Daniel H. Levine and José E. Molina. Boulder, CO: Lynne Rienner, pp. 111–36.

Moreira, Maurício Mesquita (1994) "Industrialization, Trade and Market Failures: The Role of Government Intervention in Brazil," *Revista Brasileira de Economia* 48/3: 295–324.

—— (1999) "A indústria brasileira nos anos 90: o que já se pode dizer?" In *A economia brasileira nos anos 90*, ed. Fabio Giambiagi and Maurício Mesquita Moreira. Rio de Janeiro: BNDES.

—— (2009) "Brazil's Trade Policy: Old and New Issues," in *Brazil as an Economic Superpower? Understanding Brazil's Changing Role in the Global Economy*, ed. Lael Brainard and Leonardo Martinez-Diaz. Washington, DC: Brookings Institution Press.

Motter, Paulino (1994) "O uso político das concessões das emissoras de rádio e televisão no governo Sarney," *Comunicação & Política* 1/1: 89–116.

Nardini, Bruno (1990) "O BNDES e o desenvolvimento industrial brasileiro: o passado e perspectivas futuras," in *Política industrial e desenvolvimento econômico*, ed. Carlos de Faro Passos. São Paulo: Planef.

Nassif, A. (2008) "Há evidencias de desindustrialização no Brasil?," *Revista de Economía Política* 28/1: 109.

Negretto, Gabriel (2004) "Government Capacities and Policy Making by Decree in Latin America," *Comparative Political Studies* 37/5: 531–62.

Negri, João Alberto de, Fernanda de Negri, and Mauro Borges Lemos (2008) "O impacto do programa FNDCT sobre o desempenho e o esforço tecnológico das empresas industriais brasileiras," in *Políticas de incentivo à inovação tecnológica no Brasil*, ed. João Alberto de Negri and Luis Claudio Kubota. Brasília: IPEA.

Neri, Marcelo (2009) "Income Policies, Income Distribution, and the Distribution of Opportunities in Brazil," in *Brazil as an Economic Superpower? Understanding Brazil's Changing Role in the Global Economy*, ed. Lael Brainard and Leonardo Martinez-Diaz. Washington, DC: Brookings Institution Press, pp. 221–69.

—— (2010) "A Decade of Falling Income Inequality and Formal Employment Generation in Brazil," in *Tackling Inequalities in Brazil, China, India, and South Africa: The Role of Labour Market and Social Policies*. Paris: OECD, pp. 57–107.

—— (2011) *A nova classe média: o lado brilhante da base da pirâmide*. São Paulo: Editora Saraiva.

Neustadt, Richard E. (1960) *Presidential Power: The Politics of Leadership*. New York: John Wiley.

Nichter, Simeon (2009) "Declared Choice: Citizen Strategies and Dual Commitment Problems in Clientelism," paper presented at the Annual Meeting of the American Political Science Association, Toronto, September 3–6.

Nicolau, Jairo Marconi (2000) "Disciplina partidária e base parlamentar na Câmara dos Deputados no primero governo de Fernando Henrique Cardoso (1995–1998)," *Dados – Revista de Ciências Sociais* 43/4: 709–34.

Nunes, Márcia Vidal (2004) "As rádios comunitárias nas campanhas eleitorais: exercício da cidadania ou instrumentalização (1998–2000)," *Revista de Sociologia e Política* 22 (June): 59–76.

Nunes, Rodrigo M. (2010) "Politics without Insurance: Democratic Competition and Judicial Reform in Brazil," *Comparative Politics* 42/3: 313–31.

Nylen, William R. (2002) "Testing the Empowerment Thesis: The Participatory Budget in Belo Horizonte and Betim, Brazil," *Comparative Politics* 34/2: 127–45.

—— (2003) *Participatory Democracy versus Elitist Democracy: Lessons from Brazil*. New York: Palgrave Macmillan.

O'Donnell, Guillermo (2003) "Horizontal Accountability: The Legal Institutionalization of Mistrust," in *Democratic Accountability in Latin America*, ed. Scott Mainwaring and Christopher Welna. New York: Oxford University Press.

Oliva, Rafael, and Patricia Zendron (2010) "Políticas governamentais pró-investimento e o papel do BNDES," in *O BNDES em um Brasil em transição*, ed. Ana Cláudia Além and Fabio Giambiagi. Rio de Janeiro: BNDES.

Oliveira, Ana Maria Hermeto Camilo de, Mônica Viegas Andrade, Anne Caroline Costa Resende, Clarissa Guimarães Rodrigues, Laeticia Rodrigues, and Rafael Perez Ribas (2007) "The First Results of the Baseline Impact Evaluation of Bolsa Família," in *Evaluation of MDS Programs and Policies – Results*, ed. Jeni Vaitsman and Rômulo Paes-Souza. Brasília: Ministerio de Desenvolvimento Social.

Ondetti, Gabriel (2008) *Land, Protest, and Politics: The Landless Movement and the Struggle for Agrarian Reform in Brazil*. College Park: Pennsylvania State University Press.

Paes de Barros, Ricardo, Mirela de Carvalho, Samuel Franco, and Rosane Mendonça (2007) *A queda recente da desigualdade de renda no Brasil*, Texto para discussão no. 1258. Rio de Janeiro: IPEA.

Palma, J. G. (2005) "Four Sources of Deindustrialization and a New Concept of the Dutch Disease," in *Beyond Reforms*, ed. J. A. Ocampo. Stanford, CA: Stanford University Press.

Partido dos Trabalhadores (1998) *Resoluções de encontros e congressos: 1979–1998*. São Paulo: Partido dos Trabalhadores.

Payne, Leigh (1994) *Brazilian Industrialists and Democratic Change*. Baltimore: Johns Hopkins University Press.

Pecequilo, Cristina Soreanu (2008) "A política externa no Brasil no século XXI: os eixos combinados de cooperação horizontal e vertical," *Revista Brasileira de Política Internacional* 51/2: 136–53.

Pereira, Anthony (2008) "Public Security, Private Interests, and Police Reform in Brazil," in *Democratic Brazil Revisited*, ed. Peter R. Kingstone and Timothy J. Power. Pittsburgh: University of Pittsburgh Press.

—— (2012) "Continuity Is Not Lack of Change," *Critical Sociology* 38/6: 777–87.

Pereira, Carlos, and Andrés Mejía Acosta (2010) "Policymaking in Multiparty Presidential Regimes: A Comparison between Brazil and Ecuador," *Governance: An International Journal of Policy, Administration, and Institutions* 23/4: 641–66.

Pereira, Carlos, and Bernardo Mueller (2000) "Uma teoria da preponderância do poder executivo: o sistema de comissões no legislativo brasileiro," *Revista Brasileira de Ciências Sociais* 15/43: 45–67.

—— (2002) "Comportamento estratégico em presidencialismo de coalizão: as relações entre executivo e legislativo na elaboração do orçamento brasileiro," *Dados – Revista de Ciências Sociais* 44/2: 265–301.

—— (2003) "Partidos fracos na arena eleitoral e partidos fortes na arena legislativa: a conexão eleitoral no Brasil," *Dados – Revista de Ciências Sociais* 46/4: 735–71.

—— (2004) "A Theory of Executive Dominance of Congressional Politics: The Committee System in the Brazilian Chamber of Deputies," *Journal of Legislative Studies* 10/1: 9–49.

Pereira, Carlos, and Lucio Rennó (2003) "Successful Re-Election Strategies in Brazil: The Electoral Impact of Distinct Institutional Incentives," *Electoral Studies* 22: 425–48.

—— (2007) "O que é que o reeleito tem? O retorno: o esboço de uma teoria da reeleição no Brasil," *Revista de Economia Política* 27/4: 664–83.

Pereira, Carlos, Timothy J. Power, and Eric D. Raile (2011) "Presidentialism, Coalitions, and Accountability," in *Corruption and Democracy in Brazil: The Struggle for Accountability*, ed. Timothy J. Power and Matthew M. Taylor. Notre Dame, IN: University of Notre Dame Press.

Pereira, Carlos, Timothy J. Power, and Lucio R. Rennó (2005) "Under What Conditions Do Presidents Resort to Decree Power? Theory and Evidence from the Brazilian Case," *Journal of Politics* 67/1: 178–200.

—— (2008) "Agenda Power, Executive Decree Authority, and the Mixed Results of Reform in the Brazilian Congress," *Legislative Studies Quarterly* 33/1: 5–33.

Pereira, Carlos, Lucio R. Rennó, and David J. Samuels (2011) "Corruption, Campaign Finance, and Reelection," in *Corruption and Democracy in Brazil: The Struggle for Accountability*, ed. Timothy J. Power and Matthew M. Taylor. Notre Dame, IN: University of Notre Dame Press.

Peruzzotti, Enrique, and Catalina Smulovitz (2006) "Social Accountability: An Introduction," in *Enforcing the Rule of Law: Social Accountability in the New Latin*

Location	Qty	Item	Description
325 – 018 – 50	1	9780745661650	BRAZIL

Type 0W2   Qty 1   Plan# 30467   Parcel# 127384702
Group# 264172

Seq# 4   **004**

American Democracies, ed. Enrique Peruzzotti and Catalina Smulovitz. Pittsburgh: University of Pittsburgh Press.

Pierson, Paul (2004) *Politics in Time: History, Institutions, and Social Analysis*. Princeton, NJ: Princeton University Press.

Pinheiro, Armando Castelar (1999) "Privatização no Brasil: por qûe? Até onde? Até quando?," in *A economia brasileira nos anos 90*, ed. Fabio Giambiagi and Maurício Mesquita Moreira. Rio de Janeiro: BNDES.

Pinheiro, Armando Castelar, Fabio Giambiagi, and Joana Gostkorzewicz (1999) "O desempenho macroeconômico do Brasil nos anos 90," in *A economia brasileira nos anos 90*, ed. Fabio Giambiagi and Maurício Mesquita Moreira. Rio de Janeiro: BNDES.

Pion-Berlin, David (2000) "Will Soldiers Follow? Economic Integration and Regional Security in the Southern Cone," *Journal of Interamerican Studies and World Affairs* 42/1: 43–69.

Plattek, Mauro (2001) "Contribuição dos desembolsos do BNDES para a formação bruta de capital fixo: uma análise para a década de 90," *Revista do BNDES* 8/15: 104–24.

Pochmann, Marcio (2012) *Nova classe média? O trabalho na base da pirâmide social brasileira*. São Paulo: Boitempo Editorial.

Poole, Keith, and Howard Rosenthal (1985) "A Spatial Model of Legislative Roll Call Analysis," *American Journal of Political Science* 29/2: 357–84.

Porto, Mauro (2003) "Mass Media and Politics in Democratic Brazil," in *Brazil Since 1985: Politics, Economy, and Society*, ed. Maria D'Alva Kinzo and James Dunkerly. London: Institute of Latin American Studies.

—— (2011) "The Media and Political Accountability," in *Corruption and Democracy in Brazil: The Struggle for Accountability*, ed. Timothy J. Power and Matthew M. Taylor. Notre Dame, IN: University of Notre Dame Press.

Powell, G. Bingham (2000) *Elections as Instruments of Democracy: Majoritarian and Proportional Visions*. New Haven, CT: Yale University Press.

Power, Timothy J. (1998) "Brazilian Politicians and Neoliberalism: Mapping Support for the Cardoso Reforms, 1995–1997," *Journal of Interamerican Studies and World Affairs* 40 (Winter): 51–72.

—— (2000) *The Political Right in Postauthoritarian Brazil*. University Park, PA: Pennsylvania State University Press.

—— (2008) "Centering Democracy? Ideological Cleavages and Convergence in the Brazilian Political Class," in *Democratic Brazil Revisited*, ed. Peter R. Kingstone and Timothy J. Power. Pittsburgh: University of Pittsburgh Press.

—— (2009) "Compulsory for Whom? Mandatory Voting and Electoral Participation in Brazil, 1986–2006," *Journal of Politics in Latin America* 1/1: 97–122.

—— (2010a) "Optimism, Pessimism, and Coalitional Presidentialism: Debating the Institutional Design of Brazilian Democracy," *Bulletin of Latin American Research* 29/1: 18–33.

—— (2010b) "Brazilian Democracy as a Late Bloomer: Reevaluating the Regime in the Cardoso–Lula Era," *Latin American Research Review* 45: 218–47.

Power, Timothy J., and Matthew M. Taylor (2011a) "Introduction: Accountability Institutions and Political Corruption in Brazil," in *Corruption and Democracy in Brazil: The Struggle for Accountability*, ed. Timothy J. Power and Matthew M. Taylor. Notre Dame, IN: University of Notre Dame Press.

—— (2011b) "Conclusion: The Web of Accountability Institutions in Brazil," in *Corruption and Democracy in Brazil: The Struggle for Accountability*, ed. Timothy J. Power and Matthew M. Taylor. Notre Dame, IN: University of Notre Dame Press.

Power, Timothy J., and César Zucco (2009) "Estimating Ideology of Brazilian Legislative Parties, 1990–2005," *Latin American Research Review* 44/1: 218–46.

—— (2012) "Elite Preferences in a Consolidating Democracy: The Brazilian Legislative Surveys, 1990–2009," *Latin American Politics and Society* 54/4: 1–27.

Presidência da República (1991) *Programa de competitividade industrial*. Brasília: Governo Fernando Collor de Mello.

—— (1995) *Política industrial, tecnológica e de comércio exterior: reestruturação e expansão competitivas do sistema industrial brasileiro*. Brasília: Governo Fernando Henrique Cardoso.

—— (1998) *Real: quatro anos que mudaram o Brasil*. Brasília: Governo Fernando Henrique Cardoso.

—— (2003) *Diretrizes de polítical industrial, tecnológico e de comércio exterior*. Brasília: Governo Luiz Inácio Lula da Silva.

Przeworksi, Adam, and Fernando Limongi (1997) "Modernization: Theories and Facts," *World Politics* 49/2: 155–83.

Przeworski, Adam, Michael E. Alvarez, José Antonio Cheibub, and Fernando Limongi (2000) *Democracy and Development: Political Institutions and Well-Being in the World, 1950–1990*. New York: Cambridge University Press.

Quadros, Waldir José de (2007) "O encolhimento da classe média brasileira," *CESIT Carta Social e do Trabalho* 5 (September): 5–12.

Quadros, Waldir José de, and David José Nardy Antunes (2001) "Classes sociais e distribuição de renda no Brasil dos anos noventa," *Cadernos do CESIT* no. 30 (October): 1–17.

Ragin, Charles (1987) *The Comparative Method: Moving beyond Qualitative and Quantitative Strategies*. Berkeley: University of California Press.

Raile, Eric D., Carlos Pereira, and Timothy J. Power (2011) "The Executive Toolbox: Building Legislative Support in a Multiparty Presidential Regime," *Political Research Quarterly* 64/2: 323–34.

Ramos, Daniela Peixoto, and Ana Carolina Querino (2003) "Impacto dos benefícios não contributivos sobre a pobreza no Brasil," in *Política social preventiva: desafio para o Brasil*, ed. Dieter W. Benecke and Renata Nascimento. Rio de Janeiro: Konrad Adenauer Stiftung.

Reich, Gary, and Pedro dos Santos (forthcoming) "The Rise (and Frequent Fall) of Evangelical Politicians: Organization, Theology, and Church Politics," *Latin American Politics and Society*.

Remmer, Karen L. (1998) "Does Democracy Promote Interstate Cooperation? Lessons from the MERCOSUR Region," *International Studies Quarterly* 42/1: 25–51.

Rennó, Lucio R. (2007) "Escândalos e voto: as eleições presidenciais brasileiras de 2006," *Opinião Pública* 13/2: 260–82.

—— (2011) "Corruption and Voting," in *Corruption and Democracy in Brazil: The Struggle for Accountability*, ed. Timothy J. Power and Matthew M. Taylor. Notre Dame, IN: University of Notre Dame Press.

Resende-Santos, João (2002) "The Origins of Security Cooperation in the Southern Cone," *Latin American Politics and Society* 44/4: 89–126.

Ribeiro, Pedro Floriano (2009) "O PT, o estado e a sociedade (1980–2005)," in *O partido dos trabalhadores e a política brasileira (1980–2006)*. São Carlos: EdUFSCar, pp. 183–217.

—— (2010) *Dos sindicatos ao governo: a organização nacional do PT de 1980 a 2005*. São Paulo: EdUFSCar/FAPESP.

Rigolon, Francisco José Zagari (1996) *A retomada do crescimento e o papel do BNDES*, Texto para discussão no. 41 (May). Rio de Janeiro: BNDES.

Roberts, Kenneth (n.d.) *Party Systems and Electoral Volatility during Latin America's Transition to Economic Liberalism*, working paper, http://sitemaker.umich.edu/comparative.speaker.series/files/ken_roberts.pdf.

Roberts, Kenneth, and Erik Wibbels (1999) "Party Systems and Electoral Volatility in Latin America: A Test of Economic, Institutional, and Structural Explanations," *American Political Science Review* 93/3: 575–90.

Rodrigues, Maria Guadalupe (2000) "Environmental Protection Issue Networks in Amazonia," *Latin American Research Review* 35/3: 125–53.

Rodriguez, Vicente (1995) "Federalismo e interesses regionais," in *A federação em perspectiva: ensaios selecionados*, ed. Rui de Britto Álvares Affonso and Pedro Luiz Barros Silva. São Paulo: FUNDAP, pp. 431–48.

Rodrik, Dani (2007) *One Economics, Many Recipes: Globalization, Institutions, and Economic Growth*. Princeton, NJ: Princeton University Press.

Rosas, Guillermo (2005) "The Ideological Organization of Latin American Legislative Parties: An Empirical Analysis of Elite Policy Preferences," *Comparative Political Studies* 38/7: 824–49.

Rua, Maria das Graças, and Alessandra T. Aguiar (1995) "A política industrial no Brasil, 1985–1992: políticos, burocratas e interesses organizados no processo de policy-making," *Planejamento e Políticas Públicas* 12: 233–75.

Sadek, Maria Tereza, and Rosângela Batista Cavalcanti (2003) "The New Brazilian Prosecution: An Agent of Accountability," in *Democratic Accountability in Latin America*, ed. Scott Mainwaring and Christopher Welna. New York: Oxford University Press.

Samuels, David (2000) "The Gubernatorial Coattails Effect: Federalism and Congressional Elections in Brazil," *Journal of Politics* 62/1: 240–53.

—— (2001a) "Money, Elections, and Democracy in Brazil," *Latin American Politics and Society* 43/2: 27–48.

—— (2001b) "Incumbents and Challengers on a Level Playing Field: Assessing the Impact of Campaign Finance in Brazil," *Journal of Politics* 63/2: 569–84.

—— (2002) "Pork Barreling Is Not Credit Claiming or Advertising: Campaign Finance and the Sources of the Personal Vote in Brazil," *Journal of Politics* 64/3: 845–63.

—— (2003a) "Fiscal Straitjacket: The Politics of Macroeconomic Reform in Brazil, 1995–2002," *Journal of Latin American Studies* 35/3: 545–69.

—— (2003b) *Ambition, Federalism, and Legislative Politics in Brazil*. New York: Cambridge University Press.

—— (2004) "From Socialism to Social Democracy: Party Organization and the Transformation of the Workers' Party in Brazil," *Comparative Political Studies* 37/9: 999–1024.

—— (2006a) "Sources of Mass Partisanship in Brazil," *Latin American Politics and Society* 48/2: 1–27.

—— (2006b) "Informal Institutions When Formal Contracting Is Prohibited: Campaign Finance in Brazil," in *Informal Institutions and Democracy: Lessons from Latin America*, ed. Gretchen Helmke and Steven Levitsky. Baltimore: Johns Hopkins University Press.

—— (2008) "A evolução do petismo," *Opinião Pública* 14/2: 302–18.

Samuels, David, and Fernando Luiz Abrúcio (2000) "Federalism and Democratic Transitions: The 'New' Politics of the Governors in Brazil," *Publius: The Journal of Federalism* 30/2: 43–61.

Samuels, David, and Scott Mainwaring (2004) "Strong Federalism, Constraints on the Central Government, and Economic Reform in Brazil," in *Federalism and Democracy in Latin America*, ed. Edward L. Gibson. Baltimore: Johns Hopkins University Press, pp. 85–130.

Samuels, David, and César Zucco (n.d.) *Crafting Mass Partisanship at the Grass Roots, from the Top Down*. Working Paper, University of Minnesota and Rutgers University.

Sani, Giacomo, and Giovanni Sartori (1983) "Polarization, Fragmentation, and Competition in Western Democracies," in *Western European Party Systems: Continuity and Change*, ed. Hans Dalder and Peter Mair. Beverly Hills, CA: Sage, pp. 307–40.

Santana, Carlos Henrique (2011) "Conjuntura crítica, legados institucionais e comunidades epistêmicas: limites e possibilidades de uma agenda de desenvolvimento no Brasil," in *Variedades de capitalismo, política e desenvolvimento na América Latina*, ed. Renato R. Boschi. Belo Horizonte: Editora UFMG.

—— (2012) "Critical Junctures, Institutional Legacies and Epistemic Communities: A Development Agenda in Brazil," in *Development and Semi-Periphery: Post-Neoliberal Trajectories in South America and Central Eastern Europe*, ed. Renato Boschi and Carlos Henrique Santana. London: Anthem Press.

Sant'Anna, A. A., F. P. Puga, and M. M. Nascimento (2009) *Exportação responde por mais da metade da queda da produção industrial*, Visão do desenvolvimento no. 66 (June). Rio de Janeiro: BNDES.

Santos, Boaventura de Sousa (1998) "Participatory Budgeting in Porto Alegre: Toward a Redistributive Democracy," *Politics and Society* 26/4: 461–510.

Santos, Fabiano (1997) "Patronagem e poder de agenda na política brasileira," *Dados – Revista de Ciências Sociais* 40/3.

—— (1999a) "Recruitment and Retention of Legislators in Brazil," *Legislative Studies Quarterly* 24/2: 209–37.

—— (1999b) "Instituições eleitorais e desempenho do presidencialismo no Brasil," *Dados – Revista de Ciências Sociais* 42/1: 111–38.

—— (2002) "Partidos e comissões no presidencialismo de coalizão," *Dados – Revista de Ciências Sociais* 45/2: 237–64.

—— (2003) *O poder legislativo no presidencialismo de coalizão*. Belo Horizonte: Editora UFMG.

Santos, Fabiano, and Lucio Rennó (2004) "The Selection of Committee Leadership in the Brazilian Chamber of Deputies," *Journal of Legislative Studies* 10/1: 50–70.

Santos, Fabiano, and Márcio Grijó Vilarouca (2004) "Desigualdades e política partidária no Brasil contemporâneo," in *Imagens da desigualdade*, ed. Celi Scalon. Belo Horizonte: Editora UFMG.

—— (2008) "Political Institutions and Governability from FHC to Lula," in *Democratic Brazil Revisited*, ed. Peter R. Kingstone and Timothy J. Power. Pittsburgh: University of Pittsburgh Press.

Santos, José Alcides Figueiredo (2001) "Mudanças na estrutura de posições e segmentos de classe no Brasil," *Dados – Revista de Ciências Sociais* 44:1.

Santos Filho, Otaviano C. dos, and Hamilton M. Ferreira Junior (1987) *Coréia do Sul e Taiwan: histórico-estruturais e política industrial*, Relatório de pesquisa FECAMP-BNDES. Campinas: Instituto de Economia.

Saraiva, Miriam Gomes (2007) "As estratégias de cooperação Sul–Sul nos marcos da política externa brasileira de 1993 a 2007," *Revista Brasileira de Política Internacional* 50/2: 42–59.

Schmitt, Rogério (2000) *Partidos políticos no Brasil (1945–2000)*. Rio de Janeiro: Jorge Zahar.

Schneider, Ben Ross (2009) "Big Business in Brazil: Leveraging Natural Endowments and State Support for International Expansion," in *Brazil as an Economic Superpower? Understanding Brazil's Changing Role in the Global Economy*, ed. Lael Brainard and Leonardo Martinez-Diaz. Washington, DC: Brookings Institution Press.

Schwarz, Roberto (1992) *Misplaced Ideas: Essays on Brazilian Culture*, trans. John Gledson. London: Verso.

Schweller, Randall (2011) "Emerging Powers in an Age of Disorder," *Global Governance* 17: 285–97.

Scott, James (1969) "Corruption, Machine Politics, and Political Change," *American Political Science Review* 63: 1142–58.

SEPLAN (1986) *Plano de metas: sustentação do crescimento e combate à pobreza*. Brasília: SEPLAN.

Sharma, Ruchir (2012) "Bearish on Brazil," *Foreign Affairs* 91/1: 80–7.

Sheriff, Robin (2001) *Dreaming Equality: Color, Race, and Racism in Urban Brazil*. New Brunswick, NJ: Rutgers University Press.

Shugart, Matthew Soberg, and John M. Carey (1992) *Presidents and Assemblies: Constitutional Design and Electoral Dynamics*. New York: Cambridge University Press.

Sikkink, Kathryn (1991) *Ideas and Institutions: Developmentalism in Argentina and Brazil*. Ithaca, NY: Cornell University Press.

Silva, Patricio (2008) *In the Name of Reason: Technocrats and Politics in Chile*. University Park: Pennsylvania State University Press.

Silveira, Flavio Eduardo (1998) *A decisão do voto no Brasil*. Porto Alegre: EDIPUCRS.

Silveira-Neto, Raul M., and Carlos R. Azzoni (2012) "Social Policy as Regional Policy: Market and Nonmarket Factors Determining Regional Inequality," *Journal of Regional Science* 52/3: 433–50.

Singer, André (1999) *Esquerda e direita no eleitorado brasileiro: a identificação ideológica nas disputas presidenciais de 1989 e 1994*. São Paulo: Editora Edusp/Fapesp.

—— (2009) "Raízes sociais e ideológicas do Lulismo," *Novos Estudos CEBRAP* 85: 83–102.

—— (2010) "A segunda alma do partido dos trabalhadores," *Novos Estudos CEBRAP* 88: 89–111.

—— (2012) *Os sentidos do Lulismo: reforma gradual e pacto conservador*. São Paulo: Editora Schwarcz.

Singer, Paul (1981) *Dominação e desigualdade: estrutura de classes e repartição de renda no Brasil*. São Paulo: Paz e Terra.

Skidmore, Thomas (1967) *Politics in Brazil 1930–1964: An Experiment in Democracy*. New York: Oxford University Press.

—— (2004) "Brazil's Persistent Income Inequality: Lessons from History," *Latin American Politics and Society* 46/2: 133–50.

Snyder, Richard, and David J. Samuels (2004) "Legislative Malapportionment in Latin America: Historical and Comparative Perspectives," in *Federalism and Democracy in Latin America*, ed. Edward L. Gibson. Baltimore: Johns Hopkins University Press, pp. 131–72.

Soares, Fábio Veras, Rafael Perez Ribas, and Rafael Guerreiro Osório (2010) "Evaluating the Impact of Brazil's *Bolsa Família*: Cash Transfer Programs in Comparative Perspective," *Latin American Research Review* 45/2: 173–90.

Soares, Fábio Veras, Sergei Soares, Marcelo Medeiros, and Rafael Guerreiro Osório (2006) *Cash Transfer Programmes in Brasil: Impacts on Inequality and Poverty*, UNDP International Poverty Centre Working Paper no. 21 (June).

Soares, Sergei (1998) *The Financing of Education in Brazil*, Human Development Paper no. 17. Washington, DC: World Bank.

Soares, Sergei Suarez Dillon, and Paulo A. Meyer M. Nascimento (2011) *Evolução do desempenho cognitivo do Brasil de 2000 a 2009 face aos demais países*, Texto para discussão no. 1641. Brasília: Instituto de Pesquisa Econômica Aplicada.

Sola, Lourdes, Christopher Garman, and Moisés Marques (1998) "Central Banking, Democratic Governance, and Political Authority: The Case of Brazil in a Comparative Perspective," *Revista de Economia Política* 18 (April/June): 106–31.

Sotomayor Velázquez, Arturo C. (2004) "Civil–Military Affairs and Security Institutions in the Southern Cone: The Sources of Argentine–Brazilian Nuclear Cooperation," *Latin American Politics and Society* 46/4: 29–60.

Souza, Amaury de (2009) *A agenda internacional do Brasil: a política externa brasileira de FHC a Lula*. Rio de Janeiro: Elsevier.

Souza, Amaury de, and Bolívar Lamounier (2010) *A classe média brasileira: ambições, valores, e projetos de sociedade*. Rio de Janeiro: Elsevier.

Souza, Celina (1997) *Constitutional Engineering in Brazil: The Politics of Federalism and Decentralization*. London: Macmillan.

Souza, José Paulo Lins da Câmara e (1994) "O BNDES e o investimento de empresas brasileiras no exterior," *Revista do BNDES* 11: 213–18.

Speck, Bruno W. (2011) "Auditing Institutions," in *Corruption and Democracy in Brazil: The Struggle for Accountability*, ed. Timothy J. Power and Matthew M. Taylor. Notre Dame, IN: University of Notre Dame Press.

Stallings, Barbara, and Rogerio Studart (2006) *Finance for Development: Latin America in Comparative Perspective*. Washington, DC: Brookings Institution Press/CEPAL.

Stokes, Susan C. (2001) *Mandates and Democracy: Neoliberalism by Surprise in Latin America*. New York: Cambridge University Press.

Sucupira, Renato J., and Mauricio Mesquita Moreira (2001) "Exports and Trade Finance: Brazil's Recent Experience," in *The Ex-Im Bank in the 21st Century: A New Approach?*, ed. G. C. Hufbauer and R. M. Rodríguez, Special Report no. 14. Washington, DC: Institute for International Economics.

Sugiyama, Natasha Borges (2008) "Ideology and Networks: The Politics of Social Policy Diffusion in Brazil," *Latin American Research Review* 43/3: 82–108.

—— (2011) "Bottom-up Policy Diffusion: National Emulation of a Conditional Cash Transfer Program in Brazil," *Publius: The Journal of Federalism* 42/1: 25–51.

Suzigan, Wilson (1978) "Política industrial no Brasil," in *Indústria: política, instituições, e desenvolvimento*, ed. Wilson Suzigan. Rio de Janeiro: IPEA/INPES.

—— (1986) "A indústria brasileira em 1985/86: desempenho e política," in *Política econômica da nova república*, ed. Ricardo Larneiro. Rio de Janeiro: Paz e Terra.

—— (1988) "Estado e industrialização no Brasil," *Revista de Economia Política* 8/4: 5–16.

—— (1991) "Situação atual da indústria brasileira e implicações para a política industrial," *Planejamento e Políticas Públicas* 6 (December): 121–43.

—— (1992) "A indústria brasileira após uma década de estagnação: questões para política industrial," *Economia e Sociedade* 1: 89–109.

Suzigan, Wilson, João Alberto de Negri, and Alexandre Messa Silva (2007) "Structural Change and Microeconomic Behavior in Brazilian Industry," in *Technological Innovation in Brazilian and Argentine Firms*, ed. João Alberto de Negri and Lenita Maria Turchi. Brasília: IPEA.

Taylor, Matthew M. (2008) *Judging Policy: Courts and Policy Reform in Democratic Brazil*. Stanford, CA: Stanford University Press.

—— (2009) "Corruption, Accountability Reforms, and Democracy in Brazil," in *Corruption and Democracy in Latin America*, ed. Charles H. Blake and Stephen D. Morris. Pittsburgh: University of Pittsburgh Press.

—— (2010) "Brazil: Corruption as Harmless *Jeitinho* or Threat to Democracy?," in *Corruption and Politics in Latin America: National and Regional Dynamics*, ed. Stephen D. Morris and Charles H. Blake. Boulder, CO: Lynne Rienner.

—— (2011) "The Federal Judiciary and Electoral Courts," in *Corruption and Democracy in Brazil: The Struggle for Accountability*, ed. Timothy J. Power and Matthew M. Taylor. Notre Dame, IN: University of Notre Dame Press, pp. 162–83.

Taylor, Matthew M., and Vinícius C. Buranelli (2007) "Ending up in Pizza: Accountability as a Problem of Institutional Arrangement in Brazil," *Latin American Politics and Society* 49/1: 59–87.

Teichman, Judith A. (2001) *The Politics of Freeing Markets in Latin America: Chile, Argentina, and Mexico*. Chapel Hill: University of North Carolina Press.

Telles, Edward E. (1993) "Urban Labor Market Segmentation and Income in Brazil," *Economic Development and Cultural Change* 41/2: 231–49.

Tourinho, Octavio A. F., and Ricardo L. L. Vianna (1993) *Avaliação e agenda do programa nacional de desestatização*, Texto para discussão no. 322. Rio de Janeiro: IPEA.

UNCTAD (United Nations Conference on Trade and Development) (2004) *Outward FDI from Brazil: Poised to Take Off?*, Occasional Note UNCTAD/WEB/ITE/IIA/2004/16.

—— (2012) *World Investment Report 2012*. New York: UNCTAD.

UNDP (United Nations Development Programme) (2006) *Human Development Report*. New York: UNDP/Palgrave Macmillan.

—— (2011) *Human Development Report*. New York: UNDP/Palgrave Macmillan.

Veiga, Pedro da Motta (2009) "Brazil Trade Policy: Moving Away from Old Paradigms?," in *Brazil as an Economic Superpower? Understanding Brazil's Changing Role in the Global Economy*, ed. Lael Brainard and Leonardo Martinez-Diaz. Washington, DC: Brookings Institution Press.

Venturi, Gustavo (2010) "PT 30 anos: crescimento e mudanças na preferência partidária – impacto nas eleições de 2010," *Perseu* 4/5: 197–214.

Vigevani, Tullo, and Gabriel Cepaluni (2007) "Lula's Foreign Policy and the Quest for Autonomy through Diversification," *Third World Quarterly* 28/7: 1309–26.

Vigevani, Tullo, and Haroldo Ramanzini Júnior (2011) "The Impact of Domestic Politics and International Changes on the Brazilian Perception of Regional Integration," *Latin American Politics and Society* 53/1: 125–55.

Vilaça, Marcos Vinicios, and Roberto Cavalcanti de Albuquerque (1988) *Coronel, coronéis*. 3rd edn, Rio de Janeiro: Tempo Brasileiro/EDUUF.

Vilela, Elaine, and Pedro Neiva (2011) "Temas e regiões nas políticas externas de Lula e Fernando Henrique: comparação do discurso dos dois presidentes," *Revista Brasileira de Política Internacional* 54/2: 70–96.

Wade, Robert (1990) *Governing the Market: Economic Theory and the Role of Government in East Asian Industrialization*. Princeton, NJ: Princeton University Press.

—— (2011) "The Market as Means Rather than Master: The Crisis of Development and the Future Role of the State," in *Towards New Developmentalism: Markets as Means Rather than Master*, ed. Shahrukh Rafi Khan and Jens Christiansen. New York: Routledge.

Wampler, Brian (2007a) *Participatory Budgeting in Brazil: Contestation, Cooperation, and Accountability*. University Park: Pennsylvania State University Press.

—— (2007b) "Can Participatory Institutions Promote Pluralism? Mobilizing Low-Income Citizens in Brazil," *Studies in Comparative International Development* 41/4: 57–78.

—— (2008) "When Does Participatory Democracy Deepen Democracy? Lessons from Brazil," *Comparative Politics* 41/1: 61–82.

—— (2012) "Entering the State: Civil Society Activism and Participatory Governance in Brazil," *Political Studies* 60/2: 341–62.

Wampler, Brian, and Leonardo Avritzer (2004) "Participatory Publics: Civil Society and New Institutions in Democratic Brazil," *Comparative Politics* 36: 291–312.

—— (2005) "The Spread of Participatory Budgeting in Brazil: From Radical Democracy to Participatory Good Government," *Journal of Latin American Urban Studies* 7: 37–52.

Werlang, Sergio R., and Armínio Fraga Neto (1995) "Os bancos estaduais e o descontrole fiscal: alguns aspectos," *Revista Brasileira de Economia* 49/2: 265–75.

Weyland, Kurt (1996) *Democracy without Equity: Failures of Reform in Brazil*. Pittsburgh: University of Pittsburgh Press.

—— (1998) "From Leviathan to Gulliver? The Decline of the Developmental State in Brazil," *Governance: An International Journal of Policy and Administration* 11/1: 51–75.

—— (2000) "The Brazilian State in the New Democracy," in *Democratic Brazil: Actors, Institutions, and Processes*, ed. Peter R. Kingstone and Timothy J. Power. Pittsburgh: University of Pittsburgh Press, pp. 36–57.

—— (2005) "The Growing Sustainability of Brazil's Low-Quality Democracy," in *The Third Wave of Democratization in Latin America: Advances and Setbacks*, ed. Frances Hagopian and Scott Mainwaring. New York: Cambridge University Press, pp. 90–120.

WHO (World Health Organization) (2010) *World Health Statistics*. New York: United Nations.

Williamson, John (1990) "The Progress of Policy Reform in Latin America," in *Latin American Adjustment: How Much Has Happened?*, ed. John Williamson. Washington, DC: Washington Institute for International Economics, pp. 353–420.

World Bank (2002) *Brazil Municipal Education: Resources, Incentives, and Results*, 2 vols. Washington, DC: World Bank.

——(2004)*Brazil: Equitable, Competitive, Sustainable: Contributions for Debate.* Washington, DC: World Bank.

Zucco, César (2008) "The President's 'New' Constituency: Lula and the Pragmatic Vote in Brazil's 2006 Presidential Elections," *Journal of Latin American Studies* 40: 29–49.

—— (2009) "Ideology or What? Legislative Behavior in Multiparty Presidential Settings," *Journal of Politics* 71/3: 1076–92.

Index

accountability of political elites, 4–8,
    16, 70, 73–4, 82–3, 177, 189
  auditing institutions, 9, 17, 74, 100
  congressional oversight and, 26,
    43–4, 60, 73–5, 177, 189
  definition, 71–2
  investigatory and prosecutorial
    institutions, 10, 78–9, 176; *see also*
    congress, oversight powers
  judiciary and, 9, 70, 72, 75–8
  social accountability, 72, 79, 100
  voter-imposed, 83–4
affirmative action, 99, 149
Africa, 157
Afro-Brazilians, 99, 149
Alagoas state, 25
Alfonsín, Raúl, 160
Almeida, Maria Hermínia Tavares de,
    128
Amaral, Roberto, 163
Amazon, 168–70, 172–3
Amazon Surveillance System (*Sistema
    de Vigilância da Amazônia*, SIVAM),
    170–1
Ames, Barry, 5, 49–50, 195n2
Amorim, Celso, 154, 157, 168, 170
Amsden, Alice, 199n1
Andean Community, 203n6
Argentina, 11, 102, 122, 127, 154–5,
    158, 160–1, 169–70, 175, 193
Arida, Pérsio, 195n3, 200n7
Asia, 157
authoritarianism, 1, 4, 21, 154, 188
  foreign policy of authoritarian
    period, 154–5
  liberalization of, 21–2
Azevedo, Roberto, 163

Bacha, Edmar, 195n3
Banco do Brasil, 32, 110–11, 117, 180
  pension fund, 111
Baron of Rio Branco, 154, 168
Barros, Adhemar de, 82
Belo Horizonte, 96
Belo Monte Dam, 173–4
Bezerra, Marcos Otávio, 13
Bolivia, 155, 158, 161, 169, 175, 193
Bovespa, 111
Brasília, 158
Brazilian Agency of Industrial
    Development (*Agência Brasileira do
    Desenvolvimento Industrial*), 107
Brazilian Agricultural Research
    Company (*Empresa Brasileira de
    Pesquisa Agropecuária*, Embrapa),
    106, 112–13, 126
Brazilian Democratic Movement
    (*Movimento Democrático Brasileiro*,
    MDB), 21–3, 48
Brazilian Institute of Geography and
    Statistics (*Instituto Brasileiro de
    Geografia e Estatística*, IBGE), 135
Brazilian Labor Party (*Partido
    Trabalhista Brasileiro*, PTB), 22, 30,
    43, 67
Brazilian Legislative Survey (BLS),
    66–8, 187
Brazilian National Election Study
    (*Estudo Eleitoral Brasileiro*), 91
Brazilian Program of Quality and
    Productivity (*Programa Brasileiro de
    Qualidade e Produtividade*, PBQP),
    112, 122
Brazilian Social Democratic Party
    (*Partido da Social Democracia*